Policing and the Power of Persuasion

The Changing Role of the Association of Chief Police Officers

This book is dedicated to:

Marjorie and the memory of George Savage
Liz and the memory of Ken Charman
Kay and Geoff Cope

Policing and the Power of Persuasion

The Changing Role of the Association of Chief Police Officers

Stephen P. Savage
Sarah Charman
and
Stephen Cope

BLACKSTONE
PRESS LIMITED

This book has been printed digitally and produced in a standard specification
in order to ensure its continuing availability

OXFORD
UNIVERSITY PRESS

Great Clarendon Street, Oxford OX2 6DP

Oxford University Press is a department of the University of Oxford.
It furthers the University's objective of excellence in research, scholarship,
and education by publishing world-wide in

Oxford New York

Auckland Bangkok Buenos Aires Cape Town Chennai
Dar es Salaam Delhi Hong Kong Istanbul Karachi Kolkata
Kuala Lumpur Madrid Melbourne Mexico City Mumbai Nairobi
São Paulo Shanghai Taipei Tokyo Toronto

Oxford is a registered trade mark of Oxford University Press
in the UK and in certain other countries

Published in the United States
by Oxford University Press Inc., New York

ISBN 1-84174-247-3

Antony Rowe Ltd., Eastbourne

Contents

Acknowledgements

The authors would like to thank Pete Starie for his contribution in the area of policy networks which has informed parts of this study. We would also like to thank Kellie Diggins for her assistance in the preparation of this book. Finally we would like to thank all of those members of ACPO, both past and present, who supported this project and who gave their time to be interviewed. However, the views represented here are very much our own.

Abbreviations

ACC	Association of County Councils
ACPO	Association of Chief Police Officers
ACPOS	Association of Chief Police Officers (Scotland)
AMA	Association of Metropolitan Authorities
APA	Association of Police Authorities
APS	Accelerated Promotion Scheme
BMA	British Medical Association
CI	Constabulary Independence
CID	Criminal Investigation Department
CoLPA	Committee of Local Police Authorities
CPOSA	Chief Police Officers Staff Association
EI	Extended Interview
GES	Graduate Entry Scheme
HMI	Her Majesty's Inspector
HMIC	Her Majesty's Inspectorate of Constabulary
LAA	Local Authority Association
LPA	Local Police Authority
MPS	Metropolitan Police Service
NCIS	National Criminal Intelligence Service
NCS	National Crime Squad
NPM	'New Public Management'
NPT	National Police Training
NRC	National Reporting Centre
NUM	National Union of Mineworkers

PITO	Police Information Technology Organisation
PMCA	Police and Magistrates' Couts Act
PSA	Police Superintendents' Association
RCCP	Royal Commission on Criminal Procedure
SCC	Strategic Command Course

Introduction

'ACPO' is a term which means a great deal to many different audiences, but it is a term which means different things to those audiences. To the critical criminologist, particularly in the form of the critical criminologist of the 1980s, 'ACPO' refers to a secretive body which can act to subvert the democratic process and press successfully for its own agenda, one which is typically at odds with the public interest. To many within the Home Office, 'ACPO' is the label of an organisation whose support is often sought in order to push through change and reform but which can, if it wishes, frustrate those ambitions. To lower and middle ranking police officers, 'ACPO' can be a body which drives them down this or that line of policy or, more negatively, can slow down or scupper their own initiatives. To those within the organisation of the Association of Chief Police Officers, 'ACPO' can mean the force behind their own collective endeavours, taking them and the police service as a whole onto greater things, or it can be 'that body down there in London' which threatens to impinge on their own operational independence and inhibit their own localised approach to policing. More generally, 'ACPO' seems to be a somewhat enigmatic organisation which seems to be an extremely important part of the British policing scene, or more accurately the policing scene of England and Wales, but in a way and to an extent that is not clear. This latter sentiment was very much our own starting point.

This research was based on a general interest in the working of the Association of Chief Police Officers — 'ACPO' to both its friends and adversaries and 'ACPO' as far as this study is concerned — but stimulated by the peculiar circumstances facing British policing in the early- to mid-1990s in general and the activities of ACPO in particular. On the one hand the police service was confronted by the most radical agenda for change and reform than at any time since the early 1960s, and arguably well beyond that into the nineteenth century. The Police and Magistrates' Courts Act 1994 created new forms of police governance, including new powers for the Home Secretary to steer policing and newly configured local police authorities. The Sheehy Inquiry (Home Office, 1993a) into rewards and responsibilities challenged in fundamental ways the conditions of employment of police officers and the way in which police officers were to be managed. The Posen Inquiry (Home Office, 1995) was a Government led review of the roles and functions of police officers which asked bold questions about what roles the police *should*, and more significantly what they *should not*, be undertaking. Taken together, the whole foundation of the 'British way' of policing was up for debate. On the other hand, in response to this agenda for reform, ACPO appeared to be notably active in ways far more explicit — and arguably far more effective — than it had been in the recent or not so recent past. ACPO seemed at the very least to have 'gone up a gear' in its approach to campaigning and the art of politics. Was this a 'new era' in the role of ACPO and its approach to lobbying and exercising its influence? This sort of question coincided with internal changes within ACPO, including, as we make clear in chapter 3, the 'splitting' of ACPO into two bodies, one concerned centrally with the pay and conditions of employment of ACPO members, now effectively the senior officers' 'staff association', the other concerned with 'professional' and policy affairs which could more clearly represent the police service as a whole. The combination of a highly charged environment of police reform and the internal transformations taking place within the organisation representing Britain's most senior police officers conspired to make ACPO a distinctly suitable case for research.

Of course ACPO was not to be the most easily accessible area for research. Indeed, ACPO itself holds great sway over police research *in general* and often insists on the right to condone or not a particular research proposal. 'ACPO approval' is a highly sought after accolade because in many cases it is the basis on which certain police research projects can proceed. If this is the case then gaining approval and access to research ACPO *itself* was to be no straightforward task. Nevertheless, an initial research proposal was submitted to the President of ACPO outlining plans to examine the 'changing role of the Association of Chief Police Officers' and requesting ACPO permission to grant access to undertake the research, the basis of which was to be interviews with a large number of ACPO members — officers of the rank of assistant chief constable and above and their counterparts in the Metropolitan Police Service. The proposal was given initial approval by the 'Presidential Team' of ACPO and then proceeded to gain formal approval by ACPO's Chief Constables' Council which, as we shall see at various points in this study, is the 'final court' in ACPO's decision-making process. The reasons behind the decision to grant full approval to the project — undoubtedly a bold decision because there are risks for any organisation which 'opens its doors' to outside researchers — are a matter of some conjecture. Of course the authors of this study might lay claim to having devised a proposal the logic of which was beyond dispute! It would seem, however, that a combination of factors may have proved decisive to the outcome. First, there was clearly an element of 'sponsorship' of the proposal by influential key role-holders, who placed their personal authority and influence behind the project and its aims. Some individuals within ACPO carry a great degree of 'clout' and this is not solely down to their formal position within ACPO. The very fact that such individuals support a case can carry the day in many areas of ACPO business. Secondly, given that ACPO was itself in the process of organisational change, internally and externally, it meant that some sort of 'taking stock' and review by outsiders may have been welcomed, by some at least, as a useful and (potentially) informative exercise. This is another way of restating the rule that *timing* can be important to the destiny of a research proposal, particularly where access to sensitive issues and high profile individuals is concerned. Linked to the question of timing is a third possible factor. A number of commentators, ourselves included (see chapter 6 of this study), have argued that an important factor in ACPO's (partially successful) campaigns around the police reform programme of the early- to mid-1990s was the strategy for ACPO to form *'strategic alliances'* with other bodies, such as the local authority associations, in pursuit of their case. In this context little has been said about the 'alliances' between the police associations and parts of the *academic* world, as those associations marshalled their arguments against key elements of the Conservative Government's police reform agenda during that period. Key academic commentators on policing were invited to speak at police conferences (not something that had happened much in the past!)

during the debate over police reform and their message was often consistent with that of the police associations, including ACPO — such as the opposition to the 'centralisation' of policing and the apparent loss of 'localism' in police accountability which the new agenda was thought to bring about. As a result, in terms of 'timing', our research proposal coincided with a sense of a more positive and constructive relationship between ACPO and the world of 'academia' than had been the case before. A significant degree of *trust* had permeated that relationship, in some quarters at least. Whatever the balance of factors behind the decision to approve, full access to conduct the research was granted.

QUESTIONS FOR RESEARCH

The research project which forms the bulk of this study set out with the central hypothesis that ACPO had become a more corporate, strategic and effective body in recent years and, furthermore, that this process had been reflected in two areas of policy-making. On the one hand that ACPO had become a more influential body in influencing and shaping *force* or *service* level policing policy, i.e., had become more influential over the 43 individual police forces which make up the police service of England and Wales. The traditions of British policing have it that policing is, or should be, essentially a *local* and *localised* affair and that as a consequence policing policies can and do differ from force to force. We hypothesised that within this framework ACPO had managed over time to bring individual forces more and more into line with a common policy for most areas of policing. On the other hand, ACPO had become a more effective body campaigning on the *national* scene to influence policing and wider criminal justice policy, including legislation in these areas. In this case it was hypothesised that ACPO had become more effective in the *external* politics of representation. With this framework of general research questions we set out to formulate the detail of more specific lines of investigation. In the final analysis the project was differentiated into three sections, the basis of each of which we can now outline.

The Presidential Team and Past President Study

In order to trace the development of ACPO over time and to capture the views of key role holders within ACPO, we set out to interview those that had been, were or were shortly to become the President of ACPO. First, this involved a number of senior ACPO members who constituted the 'Presidential Team'. The Team comprised the (then) current President, the immediate past President and the First and Second Vice-Presidents. ACPO Presidents serve for a term of one year; the retiring President continues to serve as part of the Presidential Team for one year after his or her term of office (to maintain continuity). The First Vice-President is the member elected to serve as President in the following year, the Second Vice-President the year after that (see chapter 3). All members of the Presidential Team agreed to be interviewed. In relation to this we also interviewed members of the ACPO Secretariat who provide support to the Presidential Team and the administration of the organisation, in order to gain detailed background information. We then set out to trace as many past Presidents of ACPO as possible. Of those we contacted and approached, all but one (who was in fact very ill at the time), agreed to be interviewed, generating a further ten interviews, including one past President who was President in the late 1970s. Fourteen current and past members were interviewed therefore as part of this area of the research. Interviews were conducted through the 'semi-structured' interview format. The interviews were framed around the following major themes:

(a)   Career background, prior to and within ACPO.

(b)   The extent of ACPO's influence over force-level policy making and how that had changed over the time of the respondents' period within ACPO.

(c)   'Watersheds' or key factors in ACPO's development or change over time.

(d)   Views on how ACPO functions and/or how it did function, including sources of power within the organisation.

(e)   The nature of ACPO's relationships with other bodies associated with policing, including the Home Office, Her Majesty's Inspectorate of Constabulary, local police authorities and the Police Federation.

The 'Presidential Team and Past President Study' enabled us to gather experiences of and views on ACPO over a considerable period of time. Even the (then) current Presidential Team could offer observations on the organisation stretching back some considerable way into the past.

Not only did these members have considerable experience within ACPO as active members, they had in most cases served as 'staff officer' to chief officers when they were more junior and had gained experience of the workings of ACPO as a result. Taken together, this part of the study provided information and comment on the role and development of ACPO going back over twenty years. The interviews also provided rich opportunities to question some of the most famous (if not notorious) former chief constables whose actions and reputations had much to do with the heated debates over police accountability, including the accountability of ACPO itself, during the 1980s.

The ACPO Members' Study

The primary basis on which we investigated the relationship between ACPO the organisation and policing and police policy at force- or service-level was an interview programme with a sample of the ACPO membership. However, this part of the study also allowed the investigation of a range of related issues and areas to do with the way ACPO operates. ACPO's total membership was, at the time of our research (the mid- to late-1990s) approximately 240. From this we selected a stratified sample of 42 members, chosen on the basis of *rank, age* and *gender*. An attempt was also made to include members from as many forces as possible, so that in effect *force size* and *geographical area* were also represented in our sample. Given that some of the individuals who could have been part of the sample were well known and had high profiles within the policing world, we were assisted in the drafting of the sample by a statistician with little direct knowledge of the police service, to help counteract any tendency to 'cherry pick' the sample. Of the original 42, one member declined to be interviewed (the *only* one to do so) and there were three substitutions from the scheduled sample due to retirement or illness. The final sample size was 41. For the purposes both of equivalence and to protect those whose specific designation would reveal their identity, ACPO members from the Metropolitan Police Service and the City of London Police were aggregated under equivalent 'provincial' force titles. Thus, for example, 'assistant commissioner' in the Metropolitan Police Service was equated with 'chief constable' in the other forces and 'commander' in the Metropolitan Police Service with 'assistant chief constable' in the other forces. The final sample was as follows:

(a)   23 assistant chief constables.
(b)   8 deputy/deputy assistant chief constables.
(c)   10 chief constables.

Interviews with the sample of members were undertaken using the 'semi-structured' interview format, although for one area a closed questionnaire asking members to rank other police-related organisations, in terms of their influence over force-level policy-making was utilised. In this respect some statistical analysis was made possible. The following themes guided the interview:

(a)   Social and career profile, including educational background.
(b)   Experiences of and views on the recruitment, training and selection process of 'becoming an ACPO member', including the role of the Bramshill Police College and the nature of the 'Extended Interview' used for selection as a candidate for ACPO rank.
(c)   Perceptions of ACPO prior to and since becoming an ACPO member.
(d)   Views on relevance of ACPO as an organisation to members' own roles; functions and working of ACPO overall.
(e)   Views on nature of sources of 'power' within ACPO; role of the Metropolitan Police Service within ACPO.
(f)   Resourcing of ACPO work undertaken by ACPO members and proportion of time spent on ACPO 'business'.
(g)   Influence of the following bodies in terms of force-level policy-making, including ranking of influence and changing nature of those bodies over time: the Home Office, Her Majesty's Inspectorate of Constabulary, the Audit Commission, the local police authorities and ACPO.
(h)   Views on the role of ACPO in relation to constabulary independence and police accountability.
(i)   Influence of ACPO over national policy for policing and criminal justice; relationship between ACPO and the Police Federation.
(j)   Views on the future of ACPO in relation to views on the future of policing.

In addition to the sample of members as outlined above we also undertook a 'force-level case study', interviewing the whole 'ACPO team', four officers in all, of one particular police force, together with members of the local police authority. In the case study we pursued the same lines of questioning as with the members' sample, but also probed deeper into the ACPO's role in force-level policy-making and the importance of ACPO as a national body for the day-to-day workings of a police force.

Interviews with the ACPO members' sample took on average 90 minutes and, it must be noted, members were typically forthcoming and outspoken in their responses, giving little evidence that they were representing any form of 'party line' on the ACPO and its workings. Indeed, much of what members had to say was of an extremely sensitive nature, not least in relation to their own personal position if not future prospects.

The 'Other Parties' Study

In order to gather views from 'outside' as well from 'inside' ACPO about the organisation, its role and activities, we set out a framework to investigate the experiences and views of a wide range of individuals connected with the police service and thus with ACPO in some way or another. The focus in this respect was on key role holders and most senior representatives in the following organisations:

(a) Home Office.
(b) Her Majesty's Inspectorate of Constabulary.
(c) Local government associations.
(d) Audit Commission.
(e) National Audit Office.
(f) Central Police Services (including Bramshill).
(g) Chairs of two major ACPO Committees.
(h) Police Federation.
(i) Police Superintendents' Association.

We also interviewed two former Home Secretaries and a number of crime/home affairs correspondents from the national press. In total this generated more than 30 additional interviews all of which, again, followed the 'semi-structured' interview format. The themes which this area of the research pursued included the following:

(a)   Nature of the respondent's organisation and its relationship with ACPO.

(b)   Experiences of working with ACPO and/or role of ACPO within respondent's area of work.

(c)   Views on changes in ACPO's role and activities over time.

(d)   Comparisons of ACPO's work with other bodies with which respondent's organisation have a relationship.

(e)   General views on role and future of ACPO.

Not only would the 'other parties' study expose the views of those with whom ACPO most comes into contact as 'recipients' in part of ACPO's activities, it would also allow us to assess more fully the claims made by ACPO members themselves about the way ACPO goes about its business and what ACPO is essentially 'about'.

These three dimensions to our study outlined above were supplemented by documentary analysis of papers and proceedings relating to ACPO's work and observation of a range of ACPO conferences, seminars, functions and meetings. Taken together with our interview programmes, we would argue that we have been able to get sufficiently close to the inner workings of ACPO to offer at least a 'plausible account' of the changing role of the Association of Chief Police Officers.

The reader should note the following:

(a)   In the citations which follow in this text from the interviews conducted in these three study areas, we designate respondents as follows: interviewees from the 'Presidential Team and Past Presidents Study' are designated as 'P' (plus interview number); interviewees from the 'ACPO Members Study' are designated as 'M' (plus interview number); interviewees from the 'Other Parties Study' are designated as 'E' (plus interview number).

(b)   Reference to 'British' policing in this text means specifically policing in England and Wales (and for the purposes of ACPO this includes Northern Ireland). Scotland has a somewhat distinct police service and a separate organisation for senior officers, the Association of Chief Police Officers (Scotland) (ACPOS). Scotland has remained outside the scope of this study.

Chapter 1
Police Governance and Policing
Policy-making

INTRODUCTION: THE CONSTITUTIONAL ARCHITECTURE
OF THE POLICE

This chapter provides a wider theoretical and empirical picture within which the role of ACPO can be cited: ACPO cannot be fully understood without reference to police governance and policing policy-making. Furthermore, the governance of the police and the making of policing policy cannot be understood without reference to wider theoretical and empirical perspectives of governance and policy-making. The chapter largely rejects the formal constitutional–legal accounts as a way of understanding police governance and policing policy-making. A widely agreed definition of the constitution is that it embodies 'the system of laws, customs and conventions which define the composition and powers of organs of the State, and regulate the relations of the various State organs to one another and to the private citizen' (Hood Phillips and Jackson, 1987:5). From this perspective, the following constitu-tional-legal narrative can be told about the police service.

Outside London and Northern Ireland, the Police Act 1964 estab-lished a tripartite system of police governance, involving local police authorities (comprising a majority of elected councillors, plus magistrates), chief constables and the Home Secretary (Lustgarten, 1986; Marshall, 1965:84–104). Police authorities were obliged to maintain 'adequate and efficient' police forces; chief constables were to provide 'direction and control' of their police forces; and the Home Secretary was to 'promote' the efficiency of police forces. In London and Northern Ireland, central government, not local government, was the police authority overseeing the Metropolitan Police and Royal Ulster Constabulary, with the exception of the City of London Police which had its own local police authority. However, the Police and Magistrates' Courts Act 1994 (and the Police Act 1996) altered substantially this tripartite structure (Cope *et al.*, 1996; Loveday, 1994; Loveday, 1996b). Essentially this Act upgraded the status of both chief constables and the Home Secretary at the expense of police authorities, which have become free-standing corporate bodies independent of local government (again with the exception of the City of London). Chief constables have been given greater powers to manage their police services and must be consulted by police authorities in formulating local policing plans. The Home Secretary has been given powers to nominate a significant number of members of police authorities and to set the strategic policing framework (including key national policing objectives) within which chief constables and police authorities must operate (Home Office, 1993b). Though the Police and Magistrates' Courts Act 1994 nominally retained the tripartite system of police governance, it fundamentally altered the balance of power between the three constituent parts of the system. More recently the present Labour Government have introduced legislative plans to provide local police authorities for the Metropolitan Police and the to-be-renamed Royal Ulster Constabulary.

However, this constitutional–legal narrative, though condensed, largely treats laws, customs and conventions as given entities, rarely recognising that constitutions are shaped by wider economic, political and social pressures. Constitutional–legal accounts largely ignore, or at least downplay, these wider pressures shaping the constitutional architecture of the police. For example, Norton stated that the police service has been 'a nonpolitical force in that it has been kept largely at one remove from direct governmental control' (1991:356), arguing that the police service is essentially locally, not nationally, organised. This constitutional–legal account has been widely challenged and rejected over the last three decades, and following Griffith's observation that a constitution 'is what happens' (taken from Hennessy, 1989:306), many writers have argued that the police service has become increasingly centralised, if not fully centralised. For example, Jenkins argued the police are 'yet another nationalized service' (1995:109), and observed:

> Ever since the establishment of a statutory constabulary in the reign of Queen Victoria, responsibility for police had been a tug-of-war between local and central government. Slowly central government edged ahead. In 1994 it justifiably declared itself the winner (1995:89).

The Police and Magistrates' Courts Act 1994, according to Loveday, effectively made the police authority 'an intermediary of central government and the direct agent of the Home Office' (1994:232), reflecting 'a long-term trend of centralisation of the police service' (1994:221), and representing a fundamental shift in the constitutional position of the police from a 'local service' to a 'State police' with the Home Office increasingly in control (1995:156). Indeed Alderson, a former chief constable, caricaturised the Home Secretary as the 'new Cromwell' overseeing an increasingly centralised police service (1994:1). This 'centralisation thesis' has a long tradition, and can be traced back to the establishment of a uniformed police service under the County and Borough Police Act 1856 (Reiner, 1992:248). This thesis resurfaced as the 'authoritarian State thesis' in the late 1970s and 1980s with the election of the Thatcher Government and moves towards a 'law and order society' and 'strong State' (Gamble, 1994; Hall, 1979); for example, several writers noted the increasing centralisation of the policing of the National Union of Mineworkers' strike of 1984–85 (McCabe and Wallington, 1988; Scraton, 1985). Furthermore, the 'centralisation thesis' was also suggested by other writers when observing that since the mid-1980s the management of the police has been increasingly centralised under the banner of new public management (Cope *et al.*, 1996; Cope *et al.*, 1997; Leishman *et al.*, 1995; Leishman *et al.*, 1996; Leishman and Savage, 1993; Popham, 1989; Savage *et al.*, 1996:96–98).

This chapter seeks to unravel this debate between the constitutional–legal accounts of and the 'centralisation thesis' on the nature of police governance and policing policy-making. We shall in due course return to the centralisation thesis within the specific context of the role of ACPO (see chapters 2 and 5). By adopting the policy networks approach, the chapter argues that police governance and policing policy-making, and ACPO's role therein, is far more complex than these two rival narratives suggest. The next section examines the policy networks approach generally as a prelude to specifically applying the policy networks approach to understand the governance of the police and the making of policing policy.

UNDERSTANDING GOVERNANCE: THE POLICY NETWORKS APPROACH

There is now a rich vein of literature on policy networks, reflecting the embeddedness of network analysis in policy analysis as well as sociological analysis (Bogason and Toonen, 1998; Jordan and Schubert, 1992; Kickert *et al.*, 1997a; Marin and Mayntz, 1991; Marsh, 1998a; Marsh and Rhodes, 1992a; Smith, 1993). The policy networks approach has been used extensively by political scientists initially as a way of understanding policy-making in government (particularly, intergovernmental relations and pressure group–government relations) and later as a way of understanding governance (Börzel, 1998). This section charts the evolution of the policy networks approach from its inception to its later refinements, and assesses its contributions to explaining policy-making and governance.

The rise of the policy networks approach coincided with the rise of governance, both as an empirical trend and as a theoretical perspective. In the words of Pierre:

Governance has a dual meaning; on the one hand it refers to the empirical manifestations of State adaptation to its external environment as it emerges in the late twentieth century. On the other hand, governance also denotes a conceptual or theoretical representation of coordination of social systems and, for the most part, the role of the State in that process (2000:3).

Rhodes argued that Britain is no longer a unitary State but a ' "differentiated polity" ... characterised by functional and institutional specialization and the fragmentation of policies and politics' (1997:7). Governance reflects the view that Britain is no longer governed from one place, but instead is governed from many places. The traditional, largely hierarchical and monolithic system of government, as depicted by the Westminster model, has been challenged as a result of globalisation, Europeanisation, privatisation and decentralisation (Cope, 1999; Jessop, 1993; Rhodes, 1994; Rhodes, 1997). Following Pierre and Stoker:

> Governing Britain — and indeed any other advanced western democratic State — has thus become a matter of multi-level governance. To understand the challenge of governing requires a focus on multiple locations of decision-making — in both spatial and sectoral terms — and the way in which exchanges between actors in those locations are conducted and managed (2000:29–30).

There is thus a highly complex and dynamic set of interdependent and consequently interconnected actors, cutting across different levels of government and different sectors of society, involved in governing. Governance, according to Kooiman, 'takes place in interactions between actors on micro-, meso- and macro-levels of social-political aggregation' (1993:41). Governments do not govern on their own; they increasingly rely on other actors to govern society.

Gamble wrote:

> The separation of governing as a process from government, a particular agent, explains the popularity of the term, governance. Governance denotes the steering capacities of a political system, the ways in which governing is carried out, without making any assumption as to which institutions or agents do the steering. . . . The State is always involved in governance, but often in an enabling rather than a directing role, helping to establish and sustain the institutions in society, including crucially markets, which make steering possible (2000:110–111).

For Rhodes, networks are 'central to the analysis of governance' (2000:54), and governance can be seen as 'self-organising inter-organisational networks' (1997:51). Governance, then, is all about steering a myriad of networks, consisting of a maze of interconnected actors. It is 'a new process of governing' (Rhodes, 1997:46).

The Old Policy Networks Approach

Policy networks are specific forms of networks within governance. The policy networks approach originated in an attempt to explain relations between central and local government (Rhodes, 1988), and between government and pressure groups (Smith, 1993). It stresses the importance of disaggregating the policy-making process into discrete policy sectors. Benson defined a policy sector as 'a cluster or complex of organizations connected to each other by resource dependencies and distinguished from other clusters or complexes by breaks in the structure of resource dependencies' (1982:148). The power-dependence model of interorganisational relations is central in understanding the policy networks approach. This model assumes that all organisations are dependent on others for resources, and, therefore, organisations need to exchange resources for them to achieve their goals; such exchanges of resources involves bargaining within and between organisations (Rhodes, 1981:97–133). This interdependence facilitates the construction of policy networks, because actors within a policy sector are dependent upon each other for resources and are thus connected together as a network.

The policy networks approach acknowledges that policy-making is not uniform across government, because network structures vary considerably between policy sectors. The number of interested policy actors, their goals and resources, and their consequent relations will depend significantly upon the different traditions, routines and environments of policy sectors, as well as issues within policy sectors (Marsh, 1998a; Marsh and Rhodes, 1992a; Smith, 1993). As policy-making has become more complex, governments rely increasingly upon professional associations, pressure groups, think-tanks and private sector companies for the formulation and implementation of policies. Indeed Weir and Beetham argued that 'organised interests and professional groups play a significant and often dominant role in government policy-making' (1999:271). Following Kickert:

> The control capacity of government is limited for a number of reasons: lack of legitimacy, complexity of policy processes, complexity and multitude of institution etc. Government is only one of many actors that influence the course of events in a societal system. Government does not have enough power to exert its will on other

actors. Other social institutions are, to a great extent, autonomous (1993:275).

Furthermore, government is not monolithic, and within government there exist many agencies, both elected and appointed, operating at different levels (e.g., local, regional, national, international), and with different goals and resources. In the words of Smith:

> It is not the State that acts but State actors within particular parts of the State. The State does not have a unified set of interests. Different State agencies have various interests, and individuals within those agencies may also have conflicting interests (1993:50).

Government is thus fragmented, making the task of centrally steering government difficult. For example, within central government there is much conflict between the Treasury and spending departments (such as the Home Office) over public expenditure decisions, and between central government departments and local public sector agencies (such as local police authorities and police services) over the spending of such monies. This fragmentation within government reflects the lack of control that the core executive can exert over government. The core executive comprises 'all those organisations and structures which primarily serve to pull together and integrate central government policies, or act as final arbiters within the executive of conflicts between different elements of the government machine' (Dunleavy and Rhodes, 1990:4). The core executive (embracing such actors as the Prime Minister's Office, Cabinet Office and Treasury) can only attempt to 'police the functional policy networks' (Rhodes, 1997:14). The core executive is relatively weak, not strong, because 'power-dependence in policy networks is a cause of executive segmentation' (Rhodes, 1997:15).

As a result of segmented government and fragmented governance, a myriad of relationships of mutual dependence exist between actors within government and between government and non-government actors within a policy sector, involving exchanges of resources in the making of public policy. Following de Bruijn and ten Heuvelhof, a policy network is 'an entity consisting of public, quasi-public, or private actors who are dependent on each other and, as a consequence of this dependence, maintain relations with each other' (1995:163). A policy network consists of a set of interdependent actors sharing a common broad interest and operating within a functionally-defined policy area. Policy networks thus become '(more or less) stable patterns of social relations between interdependent actors, which take shape around policy problems and/or policy programmes' (Kickert *et al.*, 1997b:6).

Different Types of Policy Networks

Rhodes developed a typology of different kinds of policy networks along a continuum ranging from a policy community to an issue network (1988:235–366). A policy community represents a relatively closed, consensual and tightly-knit network of policy actors, that is character-ised by policy continuity, consensus, limited membership, significant resources held by all actors and a relative balance of power between actors. An issue network embraces a relatively open, conflictual and loosely-bound network of policy actors, that is characterised by policy instability, conflict, wide and relatively open membership, an imbalance of resources held by actors and unequal distribution of power between actors. The distinction between policy communities and issue networks is based upon 'their integration, stability and exclusiveness' (Rhodes, 1997:39) — see figure 1 (taken from Peterson, 1995:77).

Figure 1: Continuum of Policy Networks

POLICY COMMUNITY	ISSUE NETWORK
Stable membership	Fluid membership
Highly insular	Highly permeable
Strong dependencies	Weak dependencies

Policy communities are the most integrated type of policy network. They are characterised by limited membership of policy actors, involving perhaps a single government agency and a few privileged 'insider' interest groups insulated from other actors (including the public), and they 'are based on the major functional interests in and of government' (Rhodes, 1990:304). A policy community displays much continuity of policy, frequent interactions between participating policy actors, a high degree of consensus between actors, an exchange of resources between actors, and a 'positive-sum game' with all policy actors increasing their influence. Policy is thus made in a stable and regulated environment within which policy communities 'routinise relationships by incorporating the major interests to a "closed" world' (Rhodes, 1988:390). For example, the judicial policy network constitutes a policy community in that policy is traditionally made by an exclusive and small set of actors, namely, the Lord Chancellor's Department, the Home Office, the courts' system, the Crown Prosecution Service and the legal professions (Raine and Willson, 1993). Only occasionally and sporadically is this relatively closed network of 'insiders' open to 'semi-outsiders' (such as the police, prison, probation and social services) and 'outsiders' (such as pressure groups and the mass media), and often only when a perceived crisis has occurred within this otherwise routinised world of judicial policy-making.

Issue networks are the least integrated type of policy networks. They are characterised by a 'large number of participants and their limited degree of interdependence' (Rhodes, 1990:305). The membership of issue networks is fluid with actors freely joining and leaving the policy arena. An issue network displays a lack of continuity of policy, erratic interactions between participating actors (especially between government agencies and interest groups), a low degree of consensus between actors, a limited exchange of resources between actors and a 'zero-sum game' with some policy actors gaining influence at the expense of other actors. Relations between government and pressure groups are more likely to be characterised by informal consultation and lobbying, conflict between policy actors, policy instability, and even 'policy messes' (Rhodes, 1988:87). Issue networks embody 'relationships that are distinguished from the general pressure group universe' because their participating groups possess 'some interest in the area and minimal resources to exchange' (Smith, 1993:65). They thus display regularised (albeit informal rather than formal) contact between many loosely-connected actors. An example of an issue network would be that which emerged over gun reform in the aftermath of the Dunblane massacre in the mid-1990s. The Snowdrop Campaign was launched by many parents of the gunned-down children to restrict the possession and use of guns, which enjoyed considerable popular support and media attention. The issue also attracted other interested actors, such as the Home Office, police service, and political parties, as well as the gun, sports and civil liberties lobbies. This inclusive and open network was characterised by a conflict of goals between many of the actors, and once the issue disappeared from the political agenda, after the Labour Government implemented some limited gun reform measures, the network also disappeared (though perhaps to return if and when another shooting spree takes place).

The New Policy Networks Approach

The policy networks approach has become the dominant approach in understanding policy-making in government. It captures the complexity and interdependence of actors involved in shaping public policy, and sees policy as being made within a series of interconnected policy networks comprising interested and interdependent actors drawn from inside and outside government, though mediated by the core executive. Policy-making in government is fragmented, though there is interdependence within the fragments. The policy networks approach acknowledges such fragmentation between policy sectors and the influence of key actors transcending government and non-government agencies in shaping policy. The approach appreciates the myriad of formal and informal relations between interdependent actors within the complex world of multi-level governance.

Though the policy networks approach provides useful insights into how policy is made (and not made), there is an emerging critique of its validity (Dowding, 1995; Hay, 1998; Hay and Richards, 2000; Kassim, 1994; Klijn, 1996; Peters, 1998). Dowding argued that the policy networks approach is 'essentially metaphorical', relying on a set of images to visualise relations between actors within a policy network (1995:137). Börzel argued that 'the concept of policy networks as a specific form of governance does not constitute a proper theory' (1998:263). The policy networks approach is useful in understanding the policy-making process, but there are limits to its usefulness. It is far better at describing than explaining policy change. The approach is useful in making sense of a seemingly complex and chaotic policy-making process, often characterised by inclusion and exclusion of actors, interdependence of actors, and exchange of resources between actors. However, the policy networks approach cannot provide answers to questions about the formation of preferences of actors and the distribution of resources between actors. It is useful in understanding how things get done (or not done) but not very useful in understanding why things get done (or not done). Nonetheless, the approach captures, by describing without explaining, the complexity and interdependence of policy-making that is characterised by 'relatively stable relationships which are of non-hierarchical and interdependent nature linking a variety of actors, who share common interests with regard to a policy and who exchange resources to pursue these shared interests acknowledging that cooperation is the best way to achieve common goals' (Börzel, 1998:254).

The old policy networks approach is meso-level in that it examines relations between actors within the State, and also between State and non-State actors, in making public policy (Marsh, 1998b:15). The approach is firmly consistent with the neo-pluralist tradition from which it stemmed, that stresses the significance of pressure groups in the policy-making process and the importance of disaggregating the State to explain policy-making. The policy networks approach is weak at understanding how individual actors set goals and exchange resources in their pursuit of goals. For example, Dowding argued that 'the explanation lies in the characteristics of the actors' within a policy network and not with the characteristics of the network itself (1995:142). Moreover, the policy networks approach, though seeing policy networks as 'structures of resource dependency' (Marsh, 1998b:11), is weak at placing such structures within wider structures (such as economic ones) that shape patterns of power relations between actors within policy networks. Increasing globalisation, Europeanisation, privatisation and managerialisation of policy-making have had a significant impact on policy networks (Cope, 1999), yet the old policy networks approach largely regarded these developments as exogenous factors impacting upon a policy network, without unravelling how these factors actually impact upon a network and, moreover, how actors within a network impact upon these so-called exogenous pressures. The approach, if it is to fully explain policy-making within governance, needs to embrace more micro-level and macro-level forms of theoretical analysis. Following Marsh, the policy networks approach 'has little utility as an explanatory concept unless it is integrated with macro-level and micro-level analysis' (1998b:15). This multi-theoretical analysis is beginning slowly to take shape in the form of the new policy networks approach (Börzel, 1998; Daugbjerg and Marsh, 1998; Hay, 1998; Hay and Richards, 2000; Marsh, 1998c:192–197; Marsh and Smith, 2000). The new policy networks approach is developing mainly in response to the widespread criticism that the old policy networks approach is unable to explain both policy change and changes within policy networks.

In the earlier literature it was easy to leave with the impression that policy was made by a relatively exclusive set of interdependent and entrenched actors within a policy network, and that because policy-making was closed, routinised and stable, policy change was very difficult. Hay and Richards observed that policy networks are often portrayed as 'static, indeed torpid phenomena' (2000:2), and that a policy network is often seen as 'a static and invariant structure' (2000:4). This impression was not consciously sought by the proponents of the old policy networks approach, who have long noted, particularly within issue networks, that policy change takes place as a result of both endogenous and, moreover, exogenous pressures (Marsh and Rhodes, 1992b:257–261; Rhodes and Marsh, 1992:193–197; Smith, 1993:76–98). However, what was problematic was not the misplaced criticism that the policy networks approach denied that change takes place, but that the approach fails to sufficiently explain change within policy-making. If change is brought about by endogenous and/or exogenous pressures, then, the policy networks approach lacked theoretical power to explain such changes, not least because 'the distinction between exogenous and endogenous factors is difficult to sustain' (Marsh and Smith, 2000:7). As a meso-level approach, it found itself in 'no-man's land'; it did not have the conceptual tools to explain policy change and consequently failed to understand how policy networks sponsor, resist and react to change by precisely specifying 'the mechanisms through which change occurs' (Smith, 1993:97). In response to this static representation of policy networks, two refined models of policy networks have been formulated as a way of explaining change within policy networks, both of these models constitute the new policy networks approach.

First, Hay and Richards developed a strategic-relational model of policy networks that recognised 'the observable sequence of network formation, development and termination' (2000:5). There was an assumption in the earlier literature on policy networks that such networks were given entities; they just existed. This assumption was far more apparent in the discussion of the more stable policy communities than the more fluid issue networks. However, there was little discussion, never mind explanation, of how and why policy networks form. Following Hay and Richards, the idea of a network 'is neither a neutral nor an uncontested concept' (2000:12). They argued that 'decisions to participate in networks are, in some sense, strategic' (2000:13), and posited the following three strategic and contextual conditions for network formation:

(a)   The recognition of the potential for mutual advantage through collective (as opposed to individual) action, i.e., a positive-sum game for all those participating in a particular network form.
(b)   The recognition of the potential for enhancing the strategic capacities of participant organisations through the pooling of strategic resources. . . .
(c)   The recognition and/or establishment of the conditions of network feasibility . . . (2000:17).

This criticism, though valid, does not make the old policy networks approach redundant, rather it highlights a significant omission in the earlier literature. Marsh and Smith admitted that policy networks 'are structures that cannot be treated as given' and 'are inscribed with other structural divisions' (2000:7).

Second, Marsh and Smith offered a dialectical model of policy networks recognising 'a dialectical relationship between the network and the broader context within which it is located' (2000:7). Their model recognises that 'networks are structures which constrain and facilitate agents' and that 'the culture of a network acts as a constraint and/or opportunity on/for its members' (2000:5). However, unlike the old policy networks approach that tended to assume that network structures largely determine policy outcomes (Marsh and Rhodes, 1992b:262; Rhodes and Marsh, 1992:197), Marsh and Smith argued that both structures and agents matter. They noted that 'outcomes cannot be explained solely by reference to the structure of the network; they are the result of the actions of strategically calculating subjects', but they added that 'these agents are located within a structured context, which is provided by both the network and the broader political and social-structural context within which the network operates and those contexts clearly affect the actor's resources' (2000:6–7). This dialectical model of policy networks acknowledges that:

(a)   The broader structural context affects both the network structure and the resources that actors have to utilise within the network.

(b)   The skill that an actor has to utilise in bargaining is a product of their innate skill and the learning process through which they go.

(c)   The network interaction and bargaining reflects a combination of the actor's resources, the actor's skill, the network structure and the policy interaction.

(d)   The network structure is a reflection of the structural context, the actor's resources, the network interaction and the policy outcome.

(e)   The policy outcome reflects the interaction between the network structure and network interaction (Marsh and Smith, 2000:9–10).

Marsh and Smith explicitly argued that relations between actors within a policy network, the structure of a policy network and the wider structural context surrounding a policy network are 'interactive or dialectical' (2000:10), thus accepting that micro-level and macro-level, as well as meso-level, forms of analysis are necessary in understanding how policy networks change.

The new policy networks approach — both the strategic–relational and dialectical models of policy networks — represents a significant advance in understanding and explaining change within policy networks. The policy networks approach is thus a very useful way of understanding governance, and constitutes a relatively robust and sophisticated theory of policy-making. The policy networks approach, as a result of concerted empirical application and considerable theoretical critique, has moved from descriptive to explanatory analysis. It is a useful antidote to the belief that governance is government; more often government is only part of governance, and sometimes governance is 'governing without Government' (Rhodes, 1997:47). The policy networks approach challenges and indeed rejects the simplistic and misplaced belief that governments govern.

MAKING POLICING POLICY: REFORMING
RESISTANT POLICY NETWORKS?

This section maps out the policing policy network and discusses the roles of and relations between key policy actors within this network, before examining government-sponsored attempts to reform the policing policy network. The policing policy network comprises a set of interdependent actors, drawn from different levels of government and from the public and private sectors, involved in the formulation and implementation of policing policy. Figure 2 portrays the policing policy network.

By mapping out the terrain of the policing policy network, it is clear that the constitutional metaphor of the tripartite structure of police

Figure 2: The Policing Policy Network

	PUBLIC		PRIVATE
S **U** **P** **R** **A** **N** **A** **T** **I** **O** **N** **A** **L**	UNITED NATIONS INTERPOL EUROPOL		INTERNATIONAL ASSOCIATION OF CHIEFS OF POLICE
N **A** **T** **I** **O** **N** **A** **L**	HOME OFFICE HOME AFFAIRS SELECT COMMITTEE MI5 HM INSPECTORATE OF CONSTABULARY AUDIT COMMISSION NATIONAL AUDIT OFFICE NATIONAL CRIMINAL INTELLIGENCE SERVICE NATIONAL CRIME SQUAD CROWN PROSECUTION SERVICE POLICE COMPLAINTS AUTHORITY POLICE NEGOTIATING BOARD ASSOCIATION OF POLICE AUTHORITIES	ACPO POLICE SUPERINTENDENTS' ASSOCIATION POLICE FEDERATION CHIEF POLICE OFFICERS' STAFF ASSOCIATION ACADEMICS/RESEARCHERS	BRITISH SECURITY INDUSTRY PRIVATE SECURITY INDUSTRY NATIONAL MEDIA PRESSURE GROUPS THINK TANKS
S **U** **B** **N** **A** **T** **I** **O** **N** **A** **L**	POLICE AUTHORITIES POLICE SERVICES LOCAL AUTHORITIES	 POLICE-COMMUNITY LIAISON GROUPS	 LOCAL MEDIA

governance, established by the Police Act 1964 and revamped by the Police and the Magistrates' Courts Act 1994, fails to capture the myriad of policy actors involved in the multi-level governance of the police. The interdependence of policy actors in the policing policy network is asymmetrical; some actors are more powerful than others because of the uneven distribution of resources between actors within the network. Within this broader policy network there exists a smaller policy community consisting of the following key policy actors:

(a) Home Office.
(b) Local police authorities.
(c) Local police services.
(d) National Criminal Intelligence Service.
(e) National Crime Squad.
(f) MI5.
(g) European Police Office (Europol).
(h) HM Inspectorate of Constabulary.
(i) Audit Commission.
(j) National Audit Office.
(k) Association of Police Authorities.
(l) Association of Chief Police Officers.
(m) Police Superintendents' Association.
(n) Police Federation.

These actors are the 'insiders' that dominate the routines of making policing policy. However, even membership of this relatively stable policy community changes over time. For example, local authorities were once 'insiders' as police authorities were effectively committees of local authorities, with elected councillors forming the majority of their membership. But the Police and Magistrates' Courts Act 1994 made police authorities formally independent of local government, though councillors form half of their membership with magistrates and independent members forming the other half. However, under the Crime and Disorder Act 1998, local authorities have been given a partnership role with local police services and other agencies to prevent crime (Loveday, 1999:225–226). Moreover, Parliament, the judiciary, the mass media, pressure groups and the public, though normally 'outsiders', sometimes influence the policing policy agenda when policy-making has become unsuccessful, more politicised or crisis-ridden. For example, in 2000, ACPO reversed its policy guidance, issued to its membership, not to prosecute motorists who slightly exceed speeding limits in light of a pressure group campaign and threatened legal challenge sponsored by Transport 2000, which was widely reported in the media (*The Guardian*, 25 July 2000; Travis, 2000). These two examples demonstrate the relatively fluid nature of membership within the policing policy network.

The policing policy network exhibits the characteristics of a relatively tightly integrated and State-dominated policy community, which is not surprising given that the police are the domestic guardians of 'the legitimate force which the State seeks to monopolise' (Reiner, 1994:29). Arguably the lead policy actor within the policing policy actor is the Home Office, led by the Home Secretary. According to Hennessy:

> The Home Office is, the premiership apart, one of the most glittering trophies in political life and yet, in ministerial terms, it is a poisoned chalice. A Home Secretary simply cannot win. It is a casework-dominated department and ... one section of society will maintain that the Home Secretary has been too hard or too soft, too reactionary or too liberal, whatever he decides' (1989:458).

Established in 1782, the Home Office is the central government department responsible for policing policy. Though the Home Office cannot formally interfere with the operational independence of chief constables, its influence over other policing policy actors has substantially increased. Reiner found:

> The Home Office is evidently seen by chief constables as the most influential central body in their decision-making. This is despite the fact that chiefs know that the formal status of its circulars is advisory only, and that they have no legal authority to direct any operational decision. Nevertheless most chiefs almost automatically implement the advice of its circulars, and take heed of interventions in particular operations. There are two basic reasons for this. First, the Home Office is seen as having available to it a battery of sanctions, formal and informal. Second, it is regarded as the legitimate expression of the popular will, that is, enjoying an electoral mandate (1991:267–268).

The Home Office exercises considerable financial and patronage powers over local police authorities and local police services. Also the Police and Magistrates' Courts Act 1994 gave the Home Secretary new powers to set national policing objectives which local police authorities and local police services must embrace, though there is little evidence yet that these objectives have significantly influenced the provision of local policing (Jones and Newburn, 1997; see chapter 5). Indeed the publication of national policing objectives may be aimed more towards media and public (and less towards police) consumption, given that Home Secretaries are the most sensitive of all cabinet ministers to media and public opinion (Marsh *et al.*, 2000:320).

Furthermore, the Home Office has established under its remit several national policing agencies, in particular the National Criminal Intelligence Service and National Crime Squad, though both these specialist agencies are not directed by the Home Office alone but by 'service authorities' with which the Home Office is closely involved (see chapter 7). More contentiously, MI5 has been granted policing powers to counter drugs trafficking, organised crime and terrorism, thus heralding the possibility of 'turf wars' between the security and police services and increasing Home Office influence over policing because MI5's Director-General is directly accountable to the Home Secretary (Alderson, 1996). Another specialist policing agency, though yet without any significant operational powers, is the European Police Office (Europol) established by the Maastricht Treaty as a way of combating cross-border crime. Its role is to analyse and exchange information concerning crimes like drugs trafficking and money laundering (Benyon, 1994), though there is some resistance by Member States of the European Union to establish common policing processes to facilitate Europol's mission (Guyomarch, 1995; Uçarer, 1999:254–256).

On the HM Inspectorate of Constabulary's influence over chief constables, Reiner commented that 'the HMI is seen not so much as a control, but as a useful senior colleague, and as a means of transmitting police views to officialdom' (1991:277). However, there is much evidence that the Home Office is using the HM Inspectorate of Constabulary, despite its formal independence, as a means of transmitting Home Office views to local police services. The inspection process has been revamped: the annual reports of the HM Inspectorate of Constabulary are publicised; inspectors are no longer drawn from the retired ranks of chief constables; lay inspectors have been appointed;

and a more rigorous three-tier inspection process has been installed (Hughes *et al.*, 1997:304–307; see chapter 5). The HM Inspectorate of Constabulary is increasingly seen as an enforcer of Home Office circulars (Savage *et al.*, 1996:97), and is increasingly getting into the business, sometimes in tandem with the Audit Commission, of measuring and publicising police performance. The Audit Commission (and the National Audit Office that audits the Metropolitan Police only) are less specialist regulatory agencies than the HM Inspectorate of Constabulary, are thus more reliant on local police services for information and expertise, and consequently exercise less, though far from insignificant, influence over policing through their value-for-money studies. Under the Local Government Act 1999, the Audit Commission's remit has been extended to oversee the implementation of Best Value within the police and other public services, replacing compulsory competitive tendering (Martin, 2000).

Local police authorities were always the 'Cinderella' in the tripartite structure established by the Police Act 1964, which 'strengthened the power of the Chief Constable and the Home Office at the expense of the local authority' (Reiner, 1992:237). Police authorities had very little influence over local policing, not least because operational decisions were the sole preserve of chief constables (Marshall and Loveday, 1994:296–303). In the words of Reiner, a chief constable 'had to be adroit in Machiavellian techniques for "educating" police authorities to their correct way of thinking' because 'there could be no question of allowing the authority to prevail on any policy matters' (1991:254). Police authorities were largely moribund, exercising negligible influence over their local police forces (Jones and Newburn, 1995:449–452; Jones *et al.*, 1994:271–277; Loveday, 1994:222–223). The Police and Magistrates' Courts Act 1994 removed police authorities from local government control to effectively become appointed quangos 'in which nomination replaces election as the mechanism for selection' (Loveday, 1994:221). The Act gave them new powers to formulate a local policing plan and to set an annual budget, though their plans have to be consistent with the national policing objectives laid down by the Home Secretary and their budgets are effectively controlled by central government (Loveday, 1997a). However, both these new powers have to be undertaken in consultation with the chief constable. Though the chief constable must have 'regard to the local policing plan', provisions of the plan can be disregarded if they 'are deemed to impinge on the chief constable's operational autonomy' (Loveday, 1997a:81). Generally the police authorities' local policing plans are their chief constables' plans because police authorities lack the wherewithal to formulate their own plans; however, there is some evidence that police authorities are exercising more influence over the formulation of plans as their experience and expertise increases (Jones and Newburn, 1997:222–223; Loveday, 1997a; see chapter 5). In 1997 the new police authorities formed the Association of Police Authorities, not part of the Local Government Association; beforehand they belonged to the Association of County Councils (as the Committee of Local Police Authorities) or the Association of Metropolitan Authorities. There is now a single national voice for all local police authorities, unlike local police services that have three national voices representing different ranks of police officers — namely, the Police Federation, the Police Superintendents' Association, and ACPO. However, arguably these three voices and particularly that of ACPO, are still far more powerful, because of the resources they command, than that of the Association of Police Authorities. Ritchie commented that 'the Association of Chief Police Officers (ACPO) and the Police Federation are consulted about policing policy and new legislation ... [and are] ... seen as vital partners in the policy-making process' (1992:204).

This policing policy community consists of a set of interconnected actors that exchange a variety of resources (such as legal, financial, informational, organisational and political resources) in the shaping of policing policy. More widely, the policing policy network is part of the wider criminal justice policy network, embracing a series of interconnected and overlapping policy communities and issue networks (such as judicial and penal policy networks comprising actors like judges, lawyers, probation officers, prison officers, social workers, academics and journalists). Moreover, as successive governments have adopted a multi-agency approach to tackle crime the policing policy network is increasingly connected to key actors in other criminal justice networks, furthering the creation of a single criminal justice policy network. For example, in 1991 the Home Office established the Criminal Justice Consultative Council, comprising actors drawn from central government, the courts and the police and social services. Furthermore, Rose claimed that under one former Home Secretary, Michael Howard, ACPO 'found itself in the unfamiliar position of actually being asked to draft Government policy' on certain criminal justice matters (1996:327;

see chapter 6). McLeay claimed that 'the autonomy of the traditional policing policy State network has been challenged; "policing" has increasingly been subsumed into the broader sector of "criminal justice", introducing further influential agencies and, moreover, groups outside the State', and, as a possible consequence, 'policing policy in future becomes part of this wider sectoral network' (1998:131). A policy network thus both comprises of subpolicy networks and forms part of wider suprapolicy networks; policy networks are thus nested.

The constitutional–legal account of police governance tends to stress the statutory roles of and relations between the Home Secretary, local police authorities and chief constables, as the key actors of the tripartite structure as laid out by statute. However, this account, though valid within its legalistic terms, fails to fully capture the multitude of policy actors, the multiplicity of their relations, and complexity within the governance of the police. For example, Reiner argued:

> The myth of a tripartite structure of governance for essentially local policing, with constabulary independence for operational decisions, is useful for legitimating a system of *de facto* national control (1992:249).

Though there is much evidence to support this 'centralisation thesis', it assumes that the Home Office is the dominant and independent actor able to autonomously impose its wishes upon other policing actors. The policy networks approach provides an antidote to this view, and, as will be argued in the case study on police reform below, suggests that the Home Office, though still a relatively powerful actor, is constrained in what it can do within the policing policy network.

Reforming the Police: The Rise of New Public Management

This case study examines the processes of police reform launched by the Conservative Government in the early 1990s, which have been not just accepted but embraced by the present Labour Government; and argues that the Government was unable completely to fully implement its reform plans. Moreover, the package of police reforms was significantly shaped by both macro-pressures transcending and micro-pressures emanating from within the policing policy network. The case study argues that increasing globalisation prompted States to restructure the way they provided public services, including the police service, and paved the way for a series of new public management reforms of police governance and policing policy-making, but that these reforms were mediated by key actors within the policing policy network.

Globalisation reflects 'the increasing interdependence of world society' (Giddens, 1993:528), embodying a complex set of processes — economic, financial, technological, political and cultural — that increasingly connect the local with the global. It is wrong to simply read off from the global to understand what is happening locally, and wrong to assume the local is detached from what is happening globally, since States have both sponsored and been affected by globalisation. Globalisation has had profound, though uneven, effects upon States worldwide. As a result of increasing interconnectedness and interdependence, the policy-making capacity of States has been both constrained and enhanced, because 'events, decisions and activities in one part of the world can come to have immediate significance for individuals and communities in quite distant parts of the global system' (Held and McGrew, 1993:262). As a result of increasing globalisation, States are restructuring themselves and the societies they govern to remain competitive in 'the global marketplace' (Dahrendorf, 1995:41), in which goods, services, capital and persons can move more freely than before.

Globalisation has thus challenged the autonomy of States in managing their economies and governing their societies. Generally States have moved away from being 'welfare States' towards becoming 'competition States', less concerned with satisfying the welfare needs of their citizens and more concerned with retaining and attracting business to their territories in the face of competition from other States (Cerny, 1993; Jessop, 1993). Jessop argued that the capacities of States 'to project power even within its own national borders are becoming ever more limited due to a complex triple displacement of powers upward, downward, and, to some extent, outward' (1993:10). In Britain this displacement has manifested itself in the forms of increasing *Europeanisation* (as witnessed by the increasing, though still embryonic, influence of the European Union upon policing matters, for example, by the establishment of Europol (Norman, 1999)), increasing privatisation (as witnessed by the growing private security industry (Johnston, 1992; Johnston, 1996)), and increasing managerialisation (as witnessed by the rise of new public management in the police service (McLaughlin and Murji, 1995)).

As States have restructured in response to globalisation, new public management has been a very prominent form of restructuring in most western governments, though its impact has been uneven between countries and between policy sectors within the same country. The British Government is very much on the crest of this new public management wave, though some policy sectors (such as education and health care) have been exposed to new public management more than other policy sectors (such as policing). Essentially new public management rests on the twin doctrines of removing differences between the public and private sectors, and of shifting 'methods of doing business in public organisations' away from complying with procedural rules towards 'getting results' (Hood, 1994:129), thus heralding a new 'performance culture' in government. New public management has manifested itself generally as a series of interconnected managerial traits — 'private good, public bad'; centralisation; decentralisation; and competition. These traits represented key elements within the Conservative Government's police reform plans; and, to a significant extent, the reforms constituted an attempt to restructure, by introducing new public management, the policing policy network.

First, new public management often embodies an ideological commitment asserting the superiority of the market over the State. With its emphasis on injecting market forces into government, it represents the New Right way of managing the public sector by 'reorganising public sector bodies to bring their management, reporting, and accounting approaches closer to (a particular perception of) business methods' (Dunleavy and Hood, 1994:9). There was much evidence of this new public management thinking underpinning the Conservative Government's police reforms, demonstrating its keenness to inject business ideas into the management of the police service. For example, the membership of the Sheehy Inquiry, established to examine police pay and conditions of service, embraced 'considerable experience of commerce but little of public service' (Morgan and Newburn, 1997:5), thus facilitating recommendations that imitated the private sector (such as performance-related pay, fixed-term contracts of employment, more flexible and de-layered management structures) (Home Office, 1993a). However, there is evidence that since the police-led campaign against the Sheehy recommendations, supported by ACPO, and the subsequent climbdowns in implementing Sheehy, that the Conservative Government, when launching the Posen Inquiry to examine police tasks, became less keen to introduce business methods into the police. This Inquiry was led not by a businessman as Sheehy was, but by a civil servant; and despite police fears of a privatisation agenda the Inquiry consulted extensively with the police (especially ACPO), did not consult with the private security industry, and did not recommend the privatisation of core policing tasks (Home Office, 1995a).

Second, new public management centralises the making of policy strategy, especially policy goals and budgets, increasingly in the hands of the core executive at the heart of government. It separates 'steering from rowing', leaving the centre to steer while other agencies row (Osborne and Gaebler, 1992:34). Essentially new public management asserts that the centre is best left to formulate policy strategy, while other decentralised bodies manage policy delivery within a centrally-determined strategy (Foster and Plowden, 1996:63–81; Osborne and Gaebler, 1992:25–48). In the case of policing, the centre is effectively represented by the Home Office, though there are other policing policy actors performing on this central stage. However, given its dominant position in the policing policy process and its effective control of the legislative process, the Home Office can be fairly characterised as the centre within the governance of the police. The Conservative Government's police reforms significantly enhanced the capacity of the Home Office to steer the police in determining policy goals, controlling resources (especially budgets) and regulating policy delivery. It believed that the Home Secretary should give the police 'a clear steer on priorities' by setting 'key objectives for policing which will provide the strategic framework within which police authorities and Chief Constables will operate' (Home Office, 1993b:24). The Home Secretary also has powers to control the spending of local police authorities, though his/her powers to control police establishment and capital spending have been substantially relaxed. As well as having powers to call for reports from police authorities and chief constables, the Home Secretary is advised by the strengthened HM Inspectorate of Constabulary on police performance matters and can use a range of performance indicators developed by the Audit Commission to assess police performance (Audit Commission, 1997). Furthermore, the Home Secretary has been given greater influence over the appointment of independent members to police authorities, though he/she has not been given powers of direct nomination as originally proposed (Loveday, 1997b:221). These powers given to the Home Office have considerably strengthened its capacity to formulate policing policy strategy, though moves to centralise policy strategy have been accompanied by moves to decentralise policy delivery within the police service.

Third, new public management decentralises the delivery of public policy to a plethora of agencies, including local authorities, quangos (such as police authorities) and private contractors, that exercise managerial and operational discretion within the limits of policy strategy set by the centre. These delivery agencies, regulated by the centre, thus possess '"freedom within boundaries"' (Hoggett, 1991:251). By providing centralised leadership, it is argued, governments can decentralise policy delivery as a way of empowering consumers of public services (Foster and Plowden, 1996:52–53, 126–146; Osborne and Gaebler, 1992:49–75, 250–279), as a 'remote agency is less likely to give customers the public services they want' (Foster and Plowden, 1996:52). With the Conservative Government's police reforms there were significant moves to centralise the steering and decentralise the rowing of the police — in other words, while policing policy strategy has been centralised, policy delivery has been decentralised. For example, both the White Paper on police reform and the Sheehy Inquiry recommended that chief constables have greater management powers in deploying resources (including personnel) within their police forces (Home Office, 1993b:9–16). However, chief constables, as newly empowered chief executives, must operate within a national steer set by the Home Office and a local steer set by their police authorities. The Police and Magistrates' Courts Act 1994 required each local police authority to approve an annual and costed policing plan drafted by its chief constable, reflecting not only the national policing objectives but also 'its own local objectives, which will reflect what local people want' (Home Office, 1993b:19). Furthermore, each police authority will set its own budget 'in close collaboration with the Chief Constable, to ensure that the budget set properly reflects policing needs' (Home Office, 1993b:18). The augmented role of local police authorities is further reinforced by plans of the present Labour Government to establish police authorities for London and Northern Ireland. However, there are significant limits to such moves towards greater decentralisation, not least the statutory powers of the Home Secretary to set national policing objectives and control police budgets. Furthermore, the purchaser/provider split — a key tenet of new public management — found in most other public services is not fully replicated within the police service; the local police authority acting on behalf of police-consumers cannot act as a genuine police-purchaser in the internal police-market because of the powers of the chief constable, also acting as the police-provider, in formulating local policing plans and budgets (Loveday, 1996a:31). Also police authorities are not directly elected, though elected councillors can comprise just over half of their membership, and consequently are not directly accountable to local people. They are required to consult with the public in setting their local policing plans, which usually takes the form of police-community liaison groups, public meetings and public surveys, but such consultation is relatively embryonic and limited (Weatheritt, 1995:16–19). Moreover, though the police, with the encouragement of the Audit Commission and HM Inspectorate of Constabulary, have attempted to make policing more consumer responsive by embracing the 'performance culture' (Butler, 1992; Savage, Cope and Charman, 1997; Savage and Leishman, 1996; Waters, 1996), there are political limits to how far consumers can be empowered with regard to policing because of 'the police monopoly of the use of legitimate force' (Home Office *et al.*, 1993b:3).

Fourth, new public management reflects the view that greater competition between the public and private sectors and within the public sector promotes greater efficiency by making public sector agencies more consumer responsive. The Conservative Government's package of police reforms reflected the new public management view that greater competition between the police and other providers of 'policing' (such as private security companies and local authorities) and within the police will make the police service more efficient and more consumer responsive. For example, the Sheehy Inquiry recommended that fixed-term contracts of employment should be introduced for all police ranks (later reduced to ACPO ranks only), performance-related pay introduced for ACPO ranks, and civilianisation extended within the police service (Home Office, 1993a), all of which inject greater competition within the police service. In particular, given that the Home Secretary must approve the appointment of chief constables selected by police authorities, there is a 'fear that chief constables on fixed-term contracts will feel compelled to follow centrally laid down and narrowly conceived measures of performance, rather than local needs and priorities' (Jones and Newburn, 1995:453): mechanisms of competition may thus become disguised mechanisms of centralisation. Furthermore, the White Paper on police reform recommended the extension of compulsory competitive tendering and special constables within the police service (Home Office, 1993b:16, 27–28), and the Posen Inquiry identified many ancillary tasks where 'police effort could be streamlined or reduced' (Home Office, 1995a:13). These recommendations need to be set against existing trends of greater 'municipal policing' provided by local authorities and greater 'private policing' undertaken by private security companies, whose employees already exceed the number of uniformed police officers (Johnston, 1996:60). The rise of 'municipal policing' and 'private policing' indicate there exists significant policing capacity outside the public police, thus potentially challenging its monopoly position in policing.

The police play a key role in policy-making because governments need their consent for many policies to be implemented. For example, in the wake of football hooliganism at the European Championships in 2000, the Prime Minister, Tony Blair, suggested that the police be given new powers to impose on-the-spot fines, but these proposals were soon watered down on the advice of senior police officers. As outlined above, in the early 1990s the previous Conservative Government, concerned about rising crime despite spending heavily on the police (Baker, 1993:450; Morgan and Newburn, 1997:1–3), attempted to restructure the policing policy network by overriding the traditional consultative mechanisms of making policy, and generally wanted to impose rather than negotiate reform. Leishman, Cope and Starie argued that the Government 'attempted to use "despotic power", involving the capacity to implement its policy without consultation and negotiation with affected groups; rather than "infrastructural power", involving the capacity to intervene in society via its interdependent relationships with groups' (1996:18–19; on the distinction between despotic and infras- tructural power, see Mann, 1984). These reforms represented an attack upon the police, which constitute a significant part of the highly integrated and relatively powerful policing policy network that tradi- tionally exercised a dominant influence over policy-making. However, many reform measures were dropped or diluted because of parliamen- tary and police resistance (see chapter 6). For example, the then Home Secretary, under pressure from the police, conceded that fixed-term contracts should be introduced only for senior and not all police officers and that he should not appoint the chairpersons of police authorities. The implementation of police reform was less than smooth, mainly because of resistance from the police (especially ACPO and the Police Federation), supported by many in Parliament and local government. The Conservative Government was unable to stand firm against this campaign not least because of its small parliamentary majority. The case study on police reform demonstrates that the Conservative Government was unable to fully implement its reform plans because of resistance from elsewhere within the policing policy network. It illustrates the interdependent world of the policing policy network embracing a few relatively powerful actors who together shape policing policy. The failure of the Conservative Government to get its reforms through Parliament can be understood by using the policy networks approach. The policing policy network is highly integrated as witnessed by the ease with which many of its constituent parts were welded together to block the reforms. The Home Office, and especially the Home Secretary, were left stranded as other formidable parts of the network mobilised political support amongst politicians and the media against its proposals. The mobilisation of the many actors within the policy network was facilitated by the hierarchical structure of the police, popular concern over rising crime rates, the small parliamentary majority of the Conservative Government, and government dependence upon the police to implement law and order and other policies. The reforms represented an attempt by the Conservative Government to restructure an obdurate policy network. However, the strength of the police within the policing policy network and the consequent weakness of the Conservative Government meant that the police reforms were always likely to be (at least temporarily) blocked. The case study demonstrates the difficulties in implementing reform in a policy arena dominated by a highly integrated and relatively closed policy community. The Home Office, constrained from above and below, was unable to use 'despotic power', and was only able to wield its, albeit significant, 'infrastructural power' to reform the police.

CONCLUSION: FROM 'STEERING NOT ROWING' TO 'DRIVING NOT PLODDING'?

This case study on police reform demonstrates the interdependent world of police governance and the interplay of interconnected actors in the making of policing policy. In reforming the police, the Home Office was not all-powerful, as supposed by the 'centralisation thesis'; and the Home Secretary, police authorities and chief constables together did not make policy alone, as imagined by constitutional–legal accounts on the tripartite structure of police governance. These two interpretations are too simplistic. The policy networks approach allows for far more multidimensional and sophisticated analysis of police reform, stressing the interdependence of key actors, exchange of resources in shaping reform, asymmetrical distribution of power resources, and consequent inclusion and exclusion of actors. Moreover, both Hay and Richards' strategic-relational and Marsh and Smith's dialectical models of policy networks, representing the new policy networks approach, stress the dynamic nature of policy networks and interactive relations between structures surrounding and agents operating within policy networks. Police reform was a dynamic process that involved the interplay of actors, building strategic alliances to defend and promote their interests and operating within constraining structures. Furthermore, reforms implemented both strengthened and weakened the positions of different actors within the policing policy network, thus reshaping the contours upon which subsequent reforms have been and will be moulded. New public management reform, despite its anodyne discourse, is political, because it favours certain actors, such as ACPO, over others.

The steering–rowing split is a relatively useful way in which to understand many recent police reforms inspired by new public management thinking, with the Home Office enhancing its steering capacity and police authorities and chief constables increasing their rowing capacity. However, there are three significant limits to this metaphor as a way of visualising police reform, which can be illustrated by examining the position of ACPO within the policing policy process. First, it is too simplistic to argue that the Home Office steers the police. This Home Office steer is influenced by other policing policy actors, such as ACPO. By representing the interests of the policing elite, ACPO has become a key member of the policing policy elite, exercising considerable influence on policing and wider criminal justice policy (Savage et al., 1996:102–103; Savage, Cope and Charman, 1997). It has been increasingly incorporated into government, perhaps to a point where it has become part of government; ACPO is mainly funded by public monies and consists of key public officials. ACPO is therefore seen as a useful conduit of influence to those who are rowing within the police, as well as a vital influence upon its national steer. Furthermore, there are other steers on the police coming from national policing policy actors other than the Home Office, such as the HMIC and Audit Commission. Both actors have influenced the Home Office, but more important both have influenced and have been influenced by ACPO and its members (Hughes *et al.*, 1997:304–307; Savage and Charman, 1997). Second, police authorities provide a local steer on police forces. However, ACPO members exercise significant influence over this local steer. Chief constables, and assistant chief constables, exercise substantial influence over the policing plans and budgets formulated by local police authorities, which are highly dependent upon the police for advice and information, though their influence has marginally declined over time. Third, ACPO, with its 'new corporacy' embodied in the principle of *'presumption in favour of compliance'* of ACPO policy guidance by chief constables locally (see chapter 3), effectively has its own national steer, though formulated in a bottom-up manner to reflect the wishes of its members working in local police services. It may be tempting to suggest that ACPO steers, while its members row (or at least that ACPO is part of the steering process), but this temptation should be resisted.

The rise of new public management can be seen, in part, as an attack on the entrenched and relatively autonomous position of many professions within government that tend to be mission-oriented with little regard to the costs of providing public services (Pollitt, 1993). However, it is possible to argue that its rise has enhanced, in many ways, the status of ACPO within the policing policy network. Government desire to deal increasingly with ACPO stems in part from the fact that ACPO represents senior police managers, whose support is often necessary, and certainly useful, in implementing police and other reforms. New public management exacerbates differences between the interests of managers (in this case, senior police officers represented by ACPO) and those of workers (police officers represented by the Police Federation); consequently, the steering–rowing split inherent within new public management, has arguably strengthened the position of ACPO within the new police governance. However, ACPO is very much caught up in the middle of this steering–rowing split; perhaps a driving–plodding metaphor is more useful in understanding the position of ACPO within police governance. ACPO drives while police officers plod; driving is more hands-on than steering (as undertaken by the Home Office and local police authorities) but more hands-off than rowing (as undertaken by police officers on the frontline).

Chapter 2
ACPO: An Introduction

THE HISTORY OF ACPO

What we now know as the Association of Chief Police Officers (ACPO) is an organisation which has changed immeasurably since its inception in 1948. Up until that point, chief officer representation functioned through two quite separate bodies which mirrored the geographical and political structures which framed British policing at that time. In this chapter we shall chart the historical development of ACPO as it grew from those foundations and the factors which contributed to that development.

In 1858 the chief constables of the then county police forces founded the County Chief Constables' Club followed in 1896 by the formation of the Chief Constables' Association of England and Wales, a similar organisation for the then city and borough police forces (established by the County Police Acts 1839 and 1840 and the Municipal Corporations Act 1835 respectively). Each of the clubs functioned independently and there was little communication between them, the County Chief Constables' Club believing themselves to be 'superior' to the Chief Constables' Association (Wall, 1998:53). The two associations were widely thought of as functioning for the benefit of social contact although issues such as operational duty and the application of law were considered though this was certainly a secondary issue:

... the object of both organisations was largely to encourage social contact, addressing issues of more personal interest to members such as their tenure in office, the colour of their sword knots and the design of their tassels and braid on their cocked hats (Johnson, 1992:193).

But however trivial the discussions that took place at these meetings now appears, the important feature is that these meetings took place at all. Before this there was virtually no contact between chief officers in the vast amount of forces around the country (over 200 for a significant part of the late nineteenth century). What was being witnessed was the tiny beginnings of corporacy amongst senior police officers:

... it was first and foremost, a professional policemen's organisation (Emsley, 1991:95).

It must also be noted that the life of these representative organisations reflected the lives of the individual chief constables. The role of chief officers in the nineteenth century is far removed from the multi-tasked, budget-holding managers and employers of the twenty first century. Wall provides an illustration of the life of a chief constable:

When he arrived 'any letters?' was his first query. 'No letters sir', was the stereotyped reply. 'Suppose we go along to the club', the Captain would say, and along we went. 'Two small whiskies' was the order promptly given and promptly executed. After disposing of them we played billiard, or took a walk till luncheon time and then back to the office. 'Any letters'? 'None this afternoon, sir'. In fact there seldom were any (Smith, 1910; quoted in Wall, 1998:115).

This situation continued much in the same vein until the twentieth century when small but significant changes began to emerge. The first of these, and one which to this day remains controversial and is often greeted with suspicion, were moves to create closer and more constructive cooperation between the chief officer associations and the Home Office. This was surprisingly a fairly radical suggestion. One might see cooperation as a stage further than communication yet even communication did not exist between forces and associations and was also not to be found between police forces and the Home Office. One problem was that the County Chief Constables' Club regarded themselves as superior to the Chief Constables' Association, a feeling replicated from the view that county forces were further up the police hierarchy than city and borough forces (Wall, 1998:53). In fact, one of the few publicised achievements of the County Chief Constables' Club was its efforts and success in arguing for special uniforms in order to distinguish themselves from the borough and city chief constables. Not to be outdone, members of the Chief Constables' Association who commanded larger forces then wanted a uniform to distinguish themselves from those commanding smaller forces (Wall, 1998:53). Such was the business of the two associations.

For the purpose of this closer cooperation England and Wales was divided into eight regions or districts in 1918. Every chief constable then became a member of his District Conference. The Home Office and Her Majesty's Inspectorate of Constabulary also attended these conferences with the Home Office acting as the chair (Johnson, 1992:193). Critchley describes the aim of these conferences as an 'exchange of ideas and experiences' which remains much the same today (Critchley, 1978:183). We may have seen dramatic changes in the nature and function of police representative groups since the early twentieth century (which will be documented later) but in essence the technique of exchanging ideas has remained a staple part of even the focused seminars that we now see today. The organisational mechanics may have changed, the purpose of communication and collaboration has not.

The official objectives of the District Conferences were for closer contact between the police and the Home Office and the police and government departments generally. In addition the meetings were designed to help the Home Office in issuing instructions to the police (presumably through explanation) (Johnson, 1992:193). However, these beginnings of a new corporacy and collectiveness with senior police officers appeared to last an extremely short time (Johnson cites the regional divide as taking place in 1918, Wall cites the end of cooperation as the end of the First World War! (Johnson, 1992:193; Wall, 1998:54)). It is interesting to note that neither the official history of ACPO nor the article written by Johnson (ex-President of ACPO) mentions the rather turbulent beginnings of a corporate culture. The organisational changes are charted, the fact that neither association actually met for 30 years is not.

Although the mechanics existed for the two associations to meet, this did not officially happen again until 1948. There had been a recommendation five years previously that the two bodies should amalgamate as difficulties were evident in the formulation of national policing policy. However, efforts proved fruitless, mainly due to unwillingness on the part of the County Chief Constables' Club, therefore the two bodies remained separate. This 'stubbornness' displayed by chief constables is not a feature that has completely disappeared and will return periodically throughout this study. The two organisations were involving themselves more and more in matters of national policing policy yet approaches to the Home Secretary were dependent entirely on informal liaison between the two bodies. The date of 1948 is an historically important one as it was the year when the two bodies met again, not through choice but rather through the insistence of Lord Oaksey. This was probably not the first and was certainly not the last time that civil servants involved with policing matters voiced their frustration at the many and varied 'police voices' clamouring to be heard as we shall see in subsequent chapters. Lord Oaksey was chairing a special committee of general inquiry into the police and asked to meet with representatives of chief constables. On hearing that there were in fact two bodies representing chief constables, Lord Oaksey argued that he would only meet one (Johnson, 1992:194). Very swiftly, in July 1948, the Association of Chief Police Officers of England and Wales was formed, representing chief constables of both county and borough forces.

The 'history' of ACPO begins to suffer at this point. Johnson (1992) mentions honorary secretaries and the burden of administration before we arrive at 1968. The document entitled *From Club to Professional Police Policy-Making Body*, provided by ACPO, mentions nothing until 1970. It is, we have to assume, safe to conclude that ACPO's activities were as robust as their predecessors. In 1968, ACPO established a Secretariat with a full-time General Secretary (a retired ACPO member). In 1970, ACPO welcomed the Royal Ulster Constabulary and the association became the Association of Chief Police Officers of England, Wales and Northern Ireland, a title it has kept until this day. The statement of objectives of the Association changed little from 1948 until the split in the organisation in 1995 (see chapter 3):

(1)   To promote the effectiveness, efficiency and professional interests of the Police Service within England, Wales and Northern Ireland; and

(2)   To safeguard the individual and collective interests of members of the Association. (ACPO, 'Rules of the Association', 1993 unpublished).

These aims described activities from the Association's past whilst at the same time providing for more political intervention in the future (Brogden, 1982). Whilst the second statement would appear to be straightforward, the first is more ambiguous. What are, 'the professional interests' of the police? This could cover a range of activities and as such it is not particularly clear. It could potentially include a range of issues from developing professional standards to acting as the 'mouthpiece' of policing nationally. Interestingly by the fiftieth anniversary of ACPO, its official purpose had changed to promoting the 'effectiveness, efficiency and *professionalism*' (italics added) of the police rather than the 'professional interests'. ACPO argue that:

> In 50 years ACPO has travelled a long way. Beginning as essentially a club for Chief Officers, it has developed into a major policy discussion and development forum, influencing the debate on policing issues (ACPO, 1998).

It is the aim of this chapter and what follows to establish what happened along those travels and how ACPO moved from a club to a professional body in the manner in which ACPO describe themselves above, if indeed this is what they have achieved.

Full details of ACPO's organisational structure will be provided in chapter 3 but at this stage a very brief synopsis of the organisation would seem helpful. ACPO consists of senior police officers from the rank of assistant chief constable upwards in the provincial forces and from commander upwards in the London forces. There are therefore approximately 230 full members with in addition 'life' members (retired members) and associate members coming from the 'Home Office' forces, e.g., the National Criminal Intelligence Service. At the beginning of 2000 there were only 13 full female members of ACPO. The Association is funded through four means: a Home Office grant, contributions from police authorities, membership subscriptions and more recently from proceeds from conferences. The work of the Association is carried out via a complicated organisational structure which will be considered later. It consists of an Executive Committee, a Chief Constables' Council, 10 permanent committees and various *ad hoc* committees and subcommittees. This is supported by a network of regional committees, whose recommendations and resolutions are forwarded to either the Chief Constables' Council or the Executive

Committee. ACPO is serviced by a Secretariat in London, headed by a former civil servant. ACPO has a President who serves for one year alongside his (there has yet to be a female President of ACPO) duties as chief constable. ACPO does not have a statutory footing and claims that 'policy development work has taken centre stage'. Since 1996 the Association has split its functions between two separate organisations: the Chief Police Officers' Staff Association (CPOSA) which considers issues surrounding the pay and conditions of senior police officers and ACPO which concentrates on its role as a 'policy consideration forum' (ACPO, 1998).

The history of ACPO has illustrated, in part, that policing cooperation and the activities of senior members of the police force were fairly limited. In order to appreciate the position of police representative bodies at this point in time, it is necessary to understand some of the wider changes that have taken place within policing. It is not possible, nor would it be necessary, to chart in detail all of the major developments we have witnessed within policing this century but some changes are worthy of further consideration. Most notably we need some further understanding and appreciation of the role that political factors have played within policing and the apparent 'politicisation' of the police themselves. In addition, we need to investigate the accountability issue in relation to the police (see chapter 1) and more specifically to ACPO. In order to understand the vast and varied criticisms that have been levelled at the Association these issues need to be addressed.

ACPO UNDER FIRE

The Politicisation of the Police

What surprises many commentators is not that the police have become more and more involved with politics over the years but the fact that they arrived on the political scene so late in the day (McLeay, 1990:624). This can be attributed, in part, to the late arrival of 'law and order' itself as an important political, and perhaps more importantly electoral, issue. During the immediate post war period Britain was heavily involved in rebuilding the country and establishing the 'welfare State' — crime was not considered to be a serious problem. This period was also characterised by political consensus and criminal justice policy was part of that consensus (Downes and Morgan, 1997:89). Indeed, it was not until 1959 that the Conservative Party mentioned 'law and order' in their election manifesto (ibid:89). This situation began to change with increases in law and order coverage in every manifesto, although the Labour Party were not embracing law and order as an issue quite so enthusiastically. As the political parties began to discuss law and order as an issue so did the media with intense coverage, discussion and analysis. Policing formed a significant part of this debate.

It was the Police Federation (representing the vast majority of police officers of Chief Inspector and below, discussed further in chapter 6) rather than one of the organisations representing the senior levels of the police service which first became openly involved in the politics of policing. Indeed it was as early as the 1950s when they appointed a parliamentary consultant. However, 1965 signalled the real beginnings of politicking. They produced a document entitled *The Problem*, which argued that the British police were in danger of losing the fight against crime and were in need of higher wages, better equipment and a change in managerial style. Although the authorities were furious, Roy Jenkins, the new Home Secretary, established three working parties to consider manpower, equipment and efficiency. Each was attended by Federation representatives. The early part of the 1970s showed the Federation relatively happy with the favourable treatment regarding pay negotiations. Concern about law and order saw them in a very strong bargaining position. A rapid growth in unemployment in the mid-1970s, however, saw that strong position change considerably. The Federation were becoming increasingly frustrated at the apparent leniency of the criminal justice system and the emergence of a strong 'antipolice' element. In 1975 they launched a 'law and order' campaign aiming to turn public concern into positive action. In particular they wanted to halt the spread of liberal reforms such as those seeking the abolition of capital punishment and changes to the homosexuality laws. The campaign established the Federation's influence and signalled its departure from political non-involvement. It involved letters to trade unions, the Confederation of British Industry and political parties around the country and was supported by certain chief constables and the Superintendents' Association.

Many sectors condemned this departure from operational police work and 25 Labour MPs laid down a parliamentary motion regretting the campaign and the Federation's political involvement. The Federation defended itself:

> The Federation has a right to comment on legislation and on crime, which affected the working lives of police officers who might have strong views on it. (*Police*, December 1975, p. 3).

Although the Federation remain an organisation without full union status or independence there have been repeated calls for the right to strike. In May 1977, this reached a climax when at the annual conference resolutions were passed demanding the right to strike. However, the Government appointed a commission under Lord Edmund-Davies to consider pay and negotiations and the matter cooled off.

The 'law and order' campaign was revived in 1978 with the Federation wanting the issue to be at the forefront of any election manifesto. Reiner (1983) has noticed the apparent similarities between the Federation's declarations on law and order and those of Conservative politicians. The Federation intervened one step further when two weeks before the General Election of 1979 they placed £21,000 worth of advertisements in the national press addressed to prospective parliamentary candidates outlining the 'problems' of crime and the possible 'solutions'. Four days later the Conservatives outlined their plans to tackle crime which, not surprisingly, matched the Federation's demands. Immediately following the Conservative victory the Federation were rewarded with a 20 per cent pay increase followed three months later (more quickly than Labour had intended had they retained their majority in Parliament) by a further 13.5 per cent as a result of the recommendations of the Edmund-Davies Inquiry, set up by the previous Labour Government, which intended to compensate the police for sacrificing the right to strike.

In addition to this we began to see the higher involvement of chief constables, particularly outspoken chief constables, entering the fray. The Conservative leader of Merseyside County Council was quoted as saying:

> Political direction of a police force or of a single policeman is unacceptable. Increasingly unacceptable is the distant authoritarianism of certain ego-inflated chief police officers ... a small group of intriguers who shape public opinion (quoted in Spencer, 1985a:64).

As more and more criticisms began to emerge concerning the police and as policing became more and more an open debate so chiefs began firstly to defend themselves and subsequently to argue their case for successful policing. Traditional support for the police began to wane. There were accusations of police malpractice and corruption and concerns about police powers and accountability (Reiner, 1992:203). In the late 1970s Britain had witnessed the murder of a well-known Conservative MP, the riots at Southall and increasingly strong statements from Robert Mark the then Commissioner of the Metropolitan Police and Lord Denning, Master of the Rolls (Downes and Morgan, 1997:98). In the 1980s there were the urban riots of 1981, most particularly at Brixton and the miners' strike of 1984–85 (this will be analysed as a case study of the increasing link between politics and policing later in this chapter). The police were under attack and the post war consensus on law and order had turned into a fiery political contest. The Conservative Party clearly had the upper hand, press coverage was largely in their favour and the police battled on, becoming more and more loudly political. The police were largely successful in becoming a powerful voice to be listened to. They were the coercive arm of the State (the 'thin blue line'), they were 'accountable through the law' and therefore could be allowed wide discretion and they had direct access to government decision-making processes (McLeay, 1990:625). These structural advantages coupled with group advantages and the close support of the Government meant that their involvement in the political world was largely welcomed. It could be argued that the police embraced this new world of politicking too enthusiastically. It went firmly against the advice of a retired Commissioner of Police, Robert Mark, who argued that political 'independence' was one of three conditions that needed to be laid down in order to achieve policing by consent (1978).

This movement into politics clearly upset many commentators who argued that the split between making policy and enforcing policy needed to be considerably clearer (Hall, 1980:17; Sullivan, 1998:315; Fielding, 1991:168). Stuart Hall was particularly vociferous:

> With the ideological mobilisation of the police as the best informed, more knowledgeable and now most organised voice, campaigning in a consistently 'Law and Order' direction, forming a core element in the law and order bloc, that strict separation of powers and functions is becoming seriously blurred. The police themselves are beginning

to shape the identity of public opinion on these crucial questions. They are beginning to wield a deep ideological influence and they are consistently exerting that influence in the disciplinary direction (1980:16).

As the police continued to voice their concerns about society's ills, so they also continued to express their ideas about change. ACPO began to assert itself in two ways, first, by attempting to prevent any encroachment on their powers and second, by raising unnecessary concern about rising crime rates and labelling those who wished to see more control over the police as subversive (Campbell, 1987; Cashmore and McLaughlin, 1991; Hall, 1980:17). Their success should not be underestimated:

This is formidable. As a historian, I can say that I know of no period in which the police have had such a loud and didactic public presence, and when they have offered themselves as a distinct interest, as one of the great 'institutions' and perhaps the first in the realm. And I know of no period in which politicians and editors have submitted so abjectly or ardently to their persuasions (Thompson, 1979:379).

This will all be discussed in more detail later in this study, however, it is necessary to establish how the politicisation of the police developed. The climax of this situation came in the 1984 party conference season (Reiner, 1992:xv). The Labour Party conference was at this time extremely critical of the police and this year was no exception. After some very bitter exchanges and motions passed, the Chairman of the Police Federation questioned whether the police service would be able to provide as loyal a service to a Labour Government as a Conservative one. The Conservative conference the following week then warmly praised the police and added proposals to increase their powers.

However, it cannot be argued that the police single handedly masterminded their emergence onto the political stage. The Conservative Government saw value in gaining the support of the police and indeed exploited it in their 1979 election success. During the 1980s and the miners' strike, as we shall see later, the Government's 'success' during the conflict was in part due to the role that the police played. The Government were also very keen to 'professionalise' the police and coupled with that professionalism came a greater awareness of the political process and a greater willingness on the part of the police to engage with that process.

During this period the dangers inherent in the politicisation of policing were becoming apparent to some (Reiner, 1992:xvi). By the time one of the more outspoken chief constables, James Anderton, had retired in 1991, there was a realisation from within the police that political interventions were dangerous. However, the fact that the police had involved themselves so readily and so fundamentally in the political process meant that a retreat was never going to be easy. To claim once again the political 'independence' of the police service was always going to be difficult.

Accountability

A second and related issue is that of accountability (examined in part in chapter 1). Questions about police accountability have tended to focus on three issues: the relative powerlessness of the local police authorities, political control over the police and, what has just been discussed, the politicisation of the police (McLeay, 1990:622). Police accountability has been an important issue throughout the history of modern policing but most especially in the past two decades. The legal and constitutional standing of the police had changed dramatically in recent years leaving the position of accountability an ambiguous and contentious issue. Political thought defines that democracy is not only concerned with those who are elected to power running society's affairs, it is also concerned with their ongoing responsibility to justify and account for their conduct. There are different forms of accountability, different approaches towards accountability and different opinions as to what accountability actually means. There is often confusion over the difference between 'control' and 'accountability' and much of the disagreement is concerned with how much control particular political institutions have over the police (Lustgarten, 1986). Baldwin and Kinsey offer a clear distinction:

> ... accountability is liability to account for a decision after it has been taken; control, on the other hand, exists where influence is exerted in making a decision (1982:106).

Accountability therefore implies a duty to account for actions. The police, therefore, must be accountable for their actions and be able to provide that accountability to some external, independent authority

(Turpin, 1995:69). The issue of accountability is a vast one (and is examined elsewhere in this study) but here we offer a brief discussion of the issue. The debate surrounding whether accountability should be retrospective (Brogden *et al.*, 1988), after the fact (Day and Klein, 1987) or explanatory (Marshall, 1984), for example, will not be discussed here. The important issue is that accountability has always caused a certain amount of consternation amongst commentators and this has spilled over into discussions about ACPO. The starting point is the 'office of constable'. The traditional premise has been that this office, by its very nature, renders the constable uniquely independent, answerable only to the law. The most commonly cited case law is *Fisher v Oldham Corporation* [1930] 1 KB 210, which was a claim for compensation from Oldham Corporation by a victim of wrongful arrest. The claim failed primarily due to the ruling that the Watch Committee (pre-1964 version of the police authority) was not in a position of power over police constables and could not be responsible for their actions. If that happened then the Watch Committee would have to take complete charge of all areas of policing, which it warned would be extremely dangerous.

There has been more contention, however, over the office of *chief constable*. What further complicates the issue of accountability is the issue of *constabulary independence*. This is a common law doctrine which was formally recognised by the 1960 Royal Commission and is constantly referred to as evidence of the independence of the police, on the basis that since the authority stemming from the office of constable 'is original, not delegated and is exercised at his own discretion by virtue of his office' a police officer is answerable only to the law and not to any other authority. The argument, quite simply, has been centred around calls from outside the police for more accountability from chief constables and calls from inside the police to resist them, as exemplified by these quotes:

[chief constables] are united in rejecting demands that they be made more accountable to elected representatives for their actions (Spencer, 1985a:4).

... the two great problems for the next generation of policemen. Resistance to political encroachment on their operational freedom, and exposure to the brunt of social change (Mark, 1978:308).

The concept of constabulary independence has been a well used one throughout policing circles and will be examined in more detail later in this study; what is necessary now is a brief explanation. The tripartite structure of policing established under the Police Act 1964 gave powers and responsibilities to local police authorities and the Home Secretary as a means of redress against the actions of chief constables. The police were therefore accountable in theory to their police authorities, who were in the most part elected representatives. This was reinforced by accountability to the Home Secretary, thereby ensuring accountability at both the local and the national level. However, this framework has always been unclear. Should the chief constable either take orders from or even consult with the police authority or the Home Secretary, or should the chief constable merely answer for already taken actions? Many writers have considered these debates in detail (see Marshall, 1984; Reiner, 1992), however a number of problems stand out. First, what is the sanction for an unsatisfactory explanation to the police authority? Secondly, does that allow the police to withhold information based on that information not being in the public interest? Thirdly, if police officers are answerable only to the law then the means of redress for the local police authority or the Home Secretary are severely limited. None of this is helped by the ruling in the Royal Commission on the Police which argued that the chief constable was 'accountable to no-one, and subject to no-one's orders' (1962:para. 89). These issues will be addressed later, but they act at this stage as an important reference point for further discussion of ACPO, to which we now turn.

Growing Criticism of ACPO

The debates surrounding the accountability of the police and their growing politicisation were taking place alongside fairly major events in not only policing history but British history. One of these was the National Union of Mineworker's Strike in 1984–85. Concerns about the constitutional status of ACPO, the power of ACPO, the increasing 'closeness' between ACPO and the Home Office and the growing isolation of local police authorities all came to the fore during this period. As this chapter has attempted to illustrate so far, relatively little was known of the Association until this point and although some commentators had voiced some dissent this was largely subsumed by other debates. The events of the mid-1980s, the Thatcher administration and the activities of ACPO began to arouse interest, but most notably, suspicion. Concern appears to have centred on two opposing arguments. The first was that ACPO was beginning to 'control' the policing agenda, therefore playing an important role in defining policy and then enforcing it, summed up by Campbell who argued that, 'The feeling that the ACPO tail is wagging the Home Office dog remains hard to dispel' (1987). The second criticism is very different to the first and argues that the Home Office was using ACPO in order to advance its policies of centralisation and in order to avoid difficult issues of accountability during the miners' strike, summed up by McCabe and Wallington, '[ACPO are] the major conduit for Home Office influence on policing' (1988:138). However, all criticism is united in agreement that both organisations were attempting to wrestle any control over policing from the local police authorities. These arguments will be examined in detail.

The miners' strike started at the beginning of 1984 after Government announcements of a pit closure programme. The National Union of Mineworkers' was prepared for this. In 1972, the miners effectively defeated the Government by forcing them to concede to a pay rise by preventing coke from reaching the power stations. Their success had been aided by 'flying pickets' who had arrived at Saltley from all over the country. At times there were up to 15,000 pickets and nearly 1,000 police officers (Scraton, 1985:142). The Government, it is argued, were not going to be defeated again (ibid:1), and the police, in particular, were to be prepared for the well-organised mass picket. In preparation for any similar incident, a policy of mutual aid was established between police forces which would be coordinated by the 'National Reporting Centre' from where national policing operations could be directed. The Centre was to be headed by the President of ACPO. In the event of the 1984–85 miners' strike the police were prepared. What followed was a massive coordinated police approach to the picketing of mines. The policing methods used have been termed 'controversial' (Spencer, 1985a:3), 'offensive, and often brutal' (Scraton, 1985:3) and 'menacing' (Jefferson, 1990:1). The police tactics that were used emanated from the then unpublished *ACPO Public Order Manual of Tactical Options and Related Matters* (based on paramilitary policing in Hong Kong) and involved much more hardware (or riot equipment) than had previously been seen, shields, batons of every length and the use of mounted police to charge into crowds of pickets. The mutual aid operation saw huge numbers of police officers removed from their home forces and transported into mining areas to deal with picket lines. As many commentators saw it, local policing became an anomaly.

The role of the President of ACPO as coordinator of the National Reporting Centre drew huge criticism. Commentators argued that what could be seen to be a national police force had been established without any consultation and was headed by the President of an organisation with no statutory footing (Kinsey *et al.*, 1986:182; Lustgarten, 1986:109). If such a decision had already been made then the Centre at least needed to be under full Parliamentary control. Instead the Centre was controlled by a chief constable who, as we learned earlier, is 'accountable to no-one, and subject to no-one's orders' (Royal Commission on the Police, 1962: para. 89). Had the Home Secretary nominated himself to direct the Centre then he would have been answerable to Parliament for its actions. Clearly with this in mind, power was handed to the President of ACPO and the Government could effectively bypass Parliamentary scrutiny of the policing of the miners. The effect was that no democratically elected body was responsible for how an industrial dispute was policed and no-one was accountable to any democratically elected body either (Morgan and Newburn, 1997: 198). As one commentator saw it:

> Placing the running of the NRC in the hands of the president of ACPO gets the Home Office off the political and ideological hook, whilst ensuring achievement of the end it seeks (Lustgarten, 1986:110).

The same could be said for the production of the public order manual referred to earlier. It was clearly produced in consultation with the Home Office but again emerged under the auspices of ACPO, and was for a considerable time a secret document. The Home Office could again avoid direct political responsibility for its contents. Whilst the Centre were effectively bypassing responsibility for the policing of the miners' strike, local authorities were forcibly removed from the argument. They were not consulted about the movement of officers from their force areas to mining areas (Spencer, 1985a:7), they were not consulted with regard to the supposed 'blank cheque' offered to the police for managing the dispute (Scraton, 1985:157; Jenkins, 1995:98; Spencer, 1985b:9) and they found that a variety of other matters were termed as 'operational' (Spencer, 1985a:23).

One of the central concerns for our purposes, in terms of criticism over the policing of the miners' strike, was the allegation of the undemocratic position of ACPO, 'its influence with governments ... fundamentally undermines the democratic process' (Scraton, 1985:121). This means two things, first the lack of a statutory footing for the Association (which cannot be disputed) and second, the often undemocratic nature of decision-making within the organisation (which can and later will be disputed). As a voluntary association and a non-governmental organisation, ACPO is not obliged to discuss its affairs with anyone outside of senior police officer rank. This concerns many commentators who believe that if ACPO are to take an increasingly prominent role in formulating policing policy then they need to be made more accountable and more responsible for their activities (McCabe and Wallington, 1988:138; see chapter 7). The policing of the miners' strike served only as an indication that democratic accountability could be ignored and the police could be left to their own devices (Fine and Millar, 1985:13). As Thompson noted:

> ... the undermining of democracy is certainly going on, and at an inflammatory rate. And it is becoming clear from which quarter the wind is blowing. It is blowing from the quarters of ACPO ... (1979:380).

The case advanced was, that if the police wish to become heavily involved in political debates about policing policy then there must first be an acceptance that policing policy be decided by the political authorities (Lustgarten, 1985:142) and second that ACPO stop resisting calls for it to become more accountable (Robertson, 1989:25). Unless this happened then the police were seen to undermine the notion that they should remain independent of the political process (Lustgarten, 1985:142).

Critics follow this argument about the 'democratic deficit' (Jenkins, 1995:95) of ACPO by stating that even within the organisation itself there are a handful of extremely powerful chief constables who hold sway within the organisation. They are referred to as a 'self-perpetuating elite' (Campbell, 1987). Whilst it is true to say that chief constables within ACPO do exercise more power than, for example, assistant chief constables and there is a fairly substantial hierarchical structure within ACPO, it can be disputed that the organisation, at least internally, is 'undemocratic'. Indeed later in this study, the often over bureaucratic and extremely democratic nature of the organisation will be examined.

As mentioned earlier, however, it was the two opposing arguments about the increasing status of ACPO that caused much concern. The first of those was that the Home Office were 'using' ACPO (in much the way we saw with the National Reporting Centre) in order to further one of its long-term aims, the centralisation of policing. As Kettle states:

> ACPO [is] ... a key body in the gradual *centralisation* of parts of Britain's policing system (1984; cited in Spencer, 1985a:25).

The concern was that British policing is, in principle, a local service independent of direct political control and that too much power in the hands of too few in the centre will result in an erosion in this service. In terms of ACPO's role in this, the concern is that too much power will rest with an unelected body (Brogden, 1982:20). The essence of the centralisation debate is that the Home Office, over a long period of time, have been trying to centralise police policy and police practice (see Jefferson and Grimshaw, 1984; Loveday,1995; Reiner, 1991, 1992; Wall, 1998). Central control is seen by most commentators to be an undesirable move, although certain aspects, such as coordination and uniformity, are welcomed. The Home Office have, according to some, used many devices in order to achieve central control, including reducing the number of forces in the Police Act 1964, reducing the powers of the local police authorities (arguments continue as to whether this was the main function of the Police and Magistrates' Court Act 1994 (Loveday, 1995)), the establishment of specialised national policing bodies, e.g., the National Crime Squad, greater use and greater assertiveness of Home Office Circulars and, in relation to the circulars, strengthening the role of Her Majesty's Inspectorate of Constabulary (HMIC) as 'enforcer' of Home Office policy as reflected in the guidelines. In addition to HMIC's role as enforcers there has been a general strengthening of the regulatory agencies related to the police service. HMIC is now accompanied by the Audit Commission which in addition to conducting a series of influential thematic reviews of police management has also worked with HMIC in establishing performance indicators for the police service which the Home Office has translated into national league tables of performance. These have all been significant changes for the police service which have been examined earlier in this study. For the moment our attention will focus on how centralisation processes relate to ACPO specifically.

What is difficult to dispute is that we have witnessed a process of centralisation in British policing since the end of the Second World War, and especially during the 1980s and 1990s Conservative administrations under Home Secretaries Baker (1990–92), Clarke (1992–93) and Howard (1993–97). Kenneth Clarke, for example, was quite explicit in his preference for central controls over policing. He was, 'shameless in his contempt for local government of any sort' (Jenkins, 1995:101). What can be disputed however, and as will become clear later in this study, is the role of ACPO as complicit within this trend of centralisation. However, during the 1980s and 1990s commentators strongly believed that ACPO's involvement was a full and enthusiastic one.

Some cite the Home Office encouragement of ACPO to become more corporate as evidence of their using the Association for their own centralising ends (Reiner, 1992:243). This was seen as an easier and more politically acceptable solution than *nationalisation*. In addition to this, there had been some frustration by successive Home Secretaries that, unlike their European counterparts, they could at no time speak for 'policing' in Britain, they first had to consult with 43 forces. In 1989, Douglas Hurd, then Home Secretary, called on ACPO to begin to deliver policing in a much more coordinated and uniform manner. In a thinly veiled threat he added that regionalisation or nationalisation may be necessary if uniformity could not be achieved (ibid:243–44).

However, the role of ACPO within the miners' strike and especially their role within the National Reporting Centre alerted most writers to the view that the Home Office were using ACPO as a medium for centralisation. Whilst this thesis of ACPO's role within centralisation is not without its critics, there is little doubt from many writers that ACPO at the very least facilitated the process of 'standardisation' (Fine and Millar, 1985:13; Kettle, 1985:32) or as Scraton comments we can at least 'pretend' that that is all that was happening (1986:3). The language that is used by commentators on this apparent centralisation attempt does indicate the contempt that was felt by many towards the actions of the Home Office and ACPO. Scraton (ibid) and Thornton (1989:59) talk of pretence, Morris of the 'sly reshaping ... into a national force' (1985:363–64). Despite the fact that many commentators argue that ACPO was 'used' in this process of centralisation, it is ACPO who have been left very much with the image of the guilty party and, as we consider later in this study, have never quite managed to shed this unpopular image with policing commentators. What is clear from this brief discussion is that ACPO were seen by many to be a vital part of the centralising tendencies of the Conservative Government, and by no means a sleeping partner (Hebenton and Thomas, 1995:24; Hewitt, 1982:61; Fine and Millar, 1985:13; Newburn, 1995:78; Rutherford, 1993:30). What we were witnessing, according to some, was a clear 'coincidence of interests' (Green, 1990:87; Scraton, 1987:157).

The opposing argument to this, which was summed up by Campbell at the beginning of this section, still claimed the excessive influence and power of ACPO but did not link this with part of a grand Home Office 'plan'. Instead critics argued that it was ACPO that was *leading* the way on policing and indeed criminal justice policy and that the Home Office was only to keen to provide ACPO with anything that would assist it in its 'fight against crime'. There is little doubt that for much of the Conservative administration the views of the police service and the Government were clearly in tune.

Concern over the non-statutory standing of ACPO reaches fever pitch when commentators draw the conclusion that not only does ACPO have enormous power but it *directs* the Home Office as to what policies it would like to see. Campbell notes that Government Ministers suggested that it was up to Parliament to produce what the police want and not the other way round (1987:12). He cites a Home Office minister Giles Shaw who said, 'You the Chief Constables, are not slow to tell us if we are getting it wrong. And that is how it should be.' (ibid). Thompson agrees:

ACPO does not attend on governments; governments attend on it (1979:379).

What concerned commentators like Thompson was not that ACPO attempted to continually get its own way, as that is the function of pressure groups, but that every door that was pushed was wide open to them. He wryly noted:

What is decided by ACPO does not immediately have effect, as by royal prerogative. They are still at work on an enabling act for that (ibid:379).

As we shall see from our research interviews with ACPO members, (and confirmed by Reiner's study (1989;1991) the suggestions that ACPO was somehow in 'charge' of the Home Office and policing policy are seen as ludicrous, but these were also met with concern from members that ACPO's high profile could do irreparable damage to their supposed non-political stance (see chapter 6). As politics has moved on since those criticisms we have also seen changes in the relationship between the Home Office and ACPO; these will be examined later. ACPO did have enormous 'success' over a relatively short period of time which did lead critics to question ACPO's position but the idea that ACPO 'directed' the Home Office remains difficult to substantiate. It is true to say that ACPO also benefited from the lack of financial constraints placed on policing at this time which was certainly not the position of many other public sector bodies (Bradley *et al.*, 1986:91). ACPO's policies and ideas may well have conveniently fitted in with Government policy and Government were apparently happy to accept the advice of the police as 'expert practitioners', rather than following their own already decided 'hard line' on public spending.

Whilst a number of commentators led vociferous campaigns against the supposed unstoppable powers of ACPO and the Home Office, many others began to realise that although ACPO was thought to be some kind of secret association working by stealth to take over criminal justice policy-making, the reality was possibly less conspiratorial. ACPO's low profile was often taken to mean secrecy; what will be seen later on is that this low profile was probably more to do with lack of organisation. Likewise, Hills argues that theories about the police and Home Office working together may be a little too 'machiavellian' (Hills, 1995:455). Policy decisions she argues result more from 'confusion and ambiguity' than 'deviousness' (ibid). Some writers began to feel that the power of ACPO, at least in the rather disorganised form it was then in, was not such a threat. It was soon realised that the development of corporacy amongst 43 highly independent and highly territorial chief constables would not be very straightforward (Kettle, 1985:32). This is particularly the case with the Metropolitan Police, as we shall see later.

Where ACPO does manage to speak with one voice, it is argued that they do not automatically achieve what they want (Kettle, 1985:32; Lustgarten, 1986:109; Watts-Pope, 1981:31). When demands are compared with Government actions, it becomes clear that ACPO's influence over the policing agenda is sporadic. A further point about the activities of pressure groups must be remembered. Commentators looking at the influence of ACPO focus on the times when they hear ACPO's voice, either influencing public opinion or rallying the support of politicians. However, pressure groups 'under pressure' often resort to a more public voice, after failing through other, more effective, policy shaping channels. Schlesinger and Tumber (1994:167) thought that ACPO's more public voice could have more to do with losing some influence within the Home Office than an effective means of pressure group activity. Kettle goes as far as saying that many within the Home Office view ACPO with 'condescension' (1985:32). ACPO are also in the rather precarious position of being an advisory body with no executive authority. This goes relatively unnoticed when ACPO are commanding a successful relationship with Whitehall, but this can rapidly change when the mood and whim of the Home Office changes. They must:

'operate though negotiation and informal persuasion . . . [and] . . . tend to be in a position to encourage rather than to demand' (Walker, 1993:147–78).

As we have seen in this chapter, a number of often conflicting 'theses' surround ACPO and its relationship with government. However, even though some believe that ACPO 'control' the Home Office and others believe that the Home Office are 'using' ACPO and many other criticisms beyond, all of these complaints come down fundamentally to one: that of accountability. That ACPO comments on policing policy is seen by most to be a reasonable activity, that ACPO demands and is successful in achieving policy change is considered problematic. As has been noted the debate surrounding policing and accountability generally is a contentious one, but where an influential body such as ACPO is seen to be deciding policing policy, critics become even more hostile. Scraton is one of those:

There needs to be a rethinking of the financial and political structure of policing . . . to recommend ways to restore proper accountability to a system where ACPO is now accountable to nobody but itself. A State where the police are in effect only accountable to the police is a police State (1986:4).

Although many of the interpretations and criticisms of the role and status of ACPO considered in this chapter have become more muted in recent years ACPO, particularly in terms of its accountability relationships, is still a bone of contention (Johnston, 2000:76). On this basis we shall proceed in the following chapter to delve deeper into the organisation that is ACPO.

Chapter 3
The Changing Role of ACPO: Cultural and Organisational Formation

The image portrayed of ACPO from the literature, most of it written in the 1980s, pictured the organisation as a secret body wielding considerable influence in the world of policing and criminal justice over an unsuspecting public. ACPO was variously thought to be either a tool of the Home Office as part of its grand plan of centralisation or rather as a body manipulating a submissive Home Office and Parliament into legislating constantly in its favour. Alongside these issues was the question of accountability. ACPO was frequently portrayed as a powerful yet unaccountable organisation — exhibiting much power and little responsibility. This image of ACPO has been consistently maintained without any substantial disagreement. Reiner's study of chief constables (1991) was, as is to be expected, rather more interested in the specific rank of chief constable than the professional organisation that they belonged to. So it was armed with only these impressions of the Association that past Presidents of ACPO and the then Presidential Team (numbering 14) were interviewed. Details of the process of selection of subject and methodology plus the interviewing itself were outlined in the Introduction.

One difficulty with the criticisms of ACPO that have already been highlighted, is that they almost certainly exaggerate the degree to which

ACPO has in the past, and even in the recent past, been able to act in a cohesive and concerted fashion. The capacity of one body to coordinate the views and activities of 43 fiercely independent chief constables is not an issue to be taken lightly. Our research indicates that as far as key ACPO figures are concerned, the history of ACPO has been one of fragmentation rather than unity, and that it is only relatively recently that this situation has been transformed. This chapter is divided into three sections: first, there is a consideration of the views of ACPO from past Presidents of the Association, whose membership of ACPO dates back to the 1950s. This relies heavily on the words of those members. Secondly, an analysis of the forces for change, both organisational and cultural, that occurred within the organisation and thirdly, a consideration of the mechanisms of that change.

'THE WAY WE WERE'

The ACPO of the policing literature is not the ACPO that many of the past Presidents of the Association would easily recognise. As we have seen from the history of the organisation, the prime function of ACPO was as a 'gentleman's social club'. Although there is no doubt that that situation had changed by the time our respondents were in post, it is not unrealistic to suggest that the social aspect of the Association was still considered by many to be its most important function. This was coupled with its role as a staff association, concerned with the pay and conditions of its members, a role that caused ACPO to be criticised by many in subsequent years. One President recalled an extended debate within ACPO's annual meeting about the raising of subscriptions by £10. It was the longest debate of the meeting and questions were raised about whether subscriptions would be eligible for income tax relief:

> ... it was very much a staff association ... rather than a consultative group (P13).

ACPO Presidents felt that one of the biggest constraints on the development of corporacy was that although ACPO as an organisation could agree on policy, chief constables were under no real obligation to enforce this when back in their force areas. The ACPO still encounter this problem (see chapter 5) but attempt to circumvent it by agreements in principle that they will follow policy (see later in this chapter). The difference at this time was that the benefits of corporacy had not been established and the benefits of fierce independence seemed much more attractive. Past Presidents of ACPO found, at best, policy agreement and then non-compliance and, at worst, no agreement at all. In one force area, decisions that were made by ACPO were 'borne in mind' (P14) when making local policy. Others expressed similar sentiments:

... we were being made to look ineffective by not following policy issued by Council ... it was bringing the Association down in its strengths really, it was undermining the Association and also making it look ineffective, very ineffective (P08).

I'm not sure that they really paid much regard to the decisions that were taken by ACPO (P14).

... individual chief constables have to make up their own minds as to what is required even when it seems to cut against an ACPO policy (P10).

I remember putting forward some proposals to the ACPO Council and everyone said 'yes OK, that's going to be the common policy' and before they got up from the table two or three were saying 'I'm not going to do that', and that was the problem (P13).

I can think of instances where chief constables would be in Council and would see something go through without comment and over lunch would say, 'I can't possibly do that' (P08).

Some past Presidents referred to the committee structure at this stage, which was seen as a well intentioned but perhaps not terribly successful device of achieving corporacy. One argued that ACPO created committees and then sub-committees in the hope of involving as many people as possible. Doing this, it was argued, would achieve those elusive levels of consensus (P13). However, others realised that this was not as easy a solution as it appeared:

I bet ACPO is dealing with things now in committee that we were dealing with in committee when I was a committee member, simply because solutions are not always easy to achieve (P08).

The problems of non-compliance then spilled over into the public domain when chief constables publicly flouted ACPO policy. The difficulty lay in there being no sanctions for this. Asked if there was anything that could be done about this, one respondent argued:

> Yes, you'd ring them up and say 'what the hell did you say that for' and he'd say 'mind your own blinking business' (P13).

Clearly ACPO's difficulties in resolving this and agreeing not only to agree on ACPO policy but then to bide by that within force areas created a problem for relations with the media. The relationship between the media and ACPO will be considered in more detail later in this study but the early period and the opinions of past Presidents need to be established here. Again, the difficulties of the independent nature of chief constables brought problems. Not only did ACPO members feel that they alone could discuss policing within their force boundaries (ideas of specialism were some way off at this stage) but there was also the view that the greater evil was civilians being permitted to speak on behalf of the Association. Even though it often proved problematic to contact the President of the day to comment on an incident, (and in some ways contributed to losing out to the Police Federation as will be seen) a delay was seen as preferable to a civilian speaking on ACPO's behalf. In later years, with the appointment of a civilian as General Secretary of the organisation, this view was, and to some degree still is, maintained. This view of the police as the sole and unique experts on policing matters is used not only within the organisation but as we shall see in later chapters, forms the basis for their 'reluctant' foray into politics and lobbying activities.

The media has always been the 'Achilles' heel' (P09) of the Association. The main problem was that ACPO 'were not vocal enough' (P08). If they did respond to the media the response was usually too little, too late:

> ... the chances of getting a consensus and getting it speedily was virtually nil (P07).

ACPO was reluctant to respond to any issue that hit the headlines with any urgency. The strong independence of chief constables caused ACPO members to be extremely wary of responding to the media in case they encroached on the area of a colleague. It caused ACPO members to become:

... media shy, over cautious and indecisive (P08).

The media however needed comment from policing circles and if it was unavailable from one source the media would achieve their aim through other sources, the most popular alternative being the Police Federation. Again, this relationship will be explored in more detail later in this study but in an historical context, the Police Federation were already taking a lead within the media. The Federation had a number of advantages. First, as an organisation they agreed policy and acted upon it. Clearly this is not as problematic when the members of the organisation are not the makers of force policy but the enforcers of it, but this was still in media circles an advantage. Executive members of the Federation spoke on behalf of their colleagues without fear of recrimination from within their organisation. Secondly, the Federation were substantially more financially secure than ACPO. This was based on the huge revenues that could be collected from a membership of over 120,000. This enabled the Federation to employ press officers to coordinate their activities, a device that ACPO were relatively slow to copy. Being 'poor relations' (P10) to the Police Federation caused barely disguised annoyance. A further advantage of the Federation according to one past President is that the Federation only had to speak on behalf of its members. Whilst it would seem at face value that that is all that would be expected of ACPO, it was highlighted that ACPO had to consider 'society's wish' (P10) in addition to that of its membership. A criticism of the Federation which continued throughout the development of ACPO was that ACPO, as leaders of the service, could not act in the often 'irresponsible way' that the Federation did.

In relation to the organisational strengths of the Federation outlined above, the Federation could also rely on an impressive administrative support system within their organisation. ACPO could not. The arrival of a civilian General Secretary of ACPO did not occur until 1990 and before that date ACPO relied on sometimes part-time and sometimes full-time retired ACPO members to effectively run the organisation. Unsurprisingly, this did affect ACPO's abilities to organise themselves in an efficient and professional manner. According to one past President, the idea of a professional General Secretary was mooted as early as 1983 but there was reluctance on behalf of the Home Office, who were to fund the post, coupled with a general difficulty in making organisational decisions. This supportive/unsupportive see-saw with which the Home Office relate to ACPO will be examined later. The delay in strengthening the central support system of ACPO is cited by many past Presidents as a significant cause of their relatively slow progress towards corporacy, if indeed it has ever been achieved. Comments are numerous about the organisation's deficiencies:

> [ACPO] had no proper computer facilities, the filing systems were antiquated, bundles of papers on shelves (P10).

> As President of ACPO you'd find yourself with a letter, probably dictated two weeks previously but not posted or shifted down for various opinions or signatures, requiring you to respond in about three days (P09).

However the relationship which caused the most interest from outside commentators which was analysed in chapter 2 was that between ACPO and the Home Office. ACPO was variously believed to be either the driving force behind Government legislation or the pawn in the Home Office game of centralisation. Both propositions were put to the past Presidents of the Association. In the same way as there are two distinct views of the relationship between ACPO and the Home Office from outside commentators, so there are also two views from within the organisation about the Home Office view of ACPO. The rather confused messages that either come from the Home Office or are interpreted as such by ACPO members are that first, the Home Office want a strong, organised and coherent Association and secondly, that the Home Office are worried about 'too strong' an ACPO that will challenge its own powers. The views of past Presidents of the Association illustrate this issue.

At this stage of the development of the Association, problems of ACPO being too strong and too powerful for the Home Office were not a reality but only a possibility. However, we are beginning to see the fine line that the Home Office faced between wanting uniformity and cohesiveness on the one hand, without necessarily the corresponding increase in strength and power that might go along with this development on the other. Past Presidents have noted this:

I think there might have been times certainly when the Home Office would much prefer to deal with individual chief officers than they would with a strong Association (P07).

... there is a reluctance on the part of the establishment for ACPO to be too powerful because it might start to usurp the function of Home Office but Home Office could not exist effectively without ACPO (P12).

One past President referred to this difficulty facing the Home Office as the two organisations, 'genuinely struggling ... to reach an accommodation' (P10). However this past President and other past Presidents were keen to note that neither the Home Office or ACPO were 'in charge'. The relationship was not always an easy one but there was no clear master–servant connection.

Although it was felt that there was no dominance from either side in this relationship between the Home Office and ACPO, there were clearly feelings from past Presidents that the Home Office did not consider ACPO to be an effectively co-ordinated body. This frustration was felt by all levels at the Home Office, but most especially by the Home Secretary when representing the country in Europe as mentioned in chapter 2. Past Presidents of the Association were aware of this frustration:

[the Home Office were] frustrated because it would seem to them at ministerial level that ACPO had failed to deliver any cohesive view on a particular subject (P09).

... they [the Home Office] thought it [ACPO] was a minor thorn in their side, that they had got to pay lip service to it, but that it was a fairly ineffective organisation (P13).

In addition to this, ACPO felt that their influence within the Home Office was not significant:

If we didn't persuade them [the Home Office] then we'd lost the day and we gave up (P14).

They [the Home Office] hear what you say and they are sympathetic to what you are trying to do but I'm not sure that we influenced legislation or the direction that the Government or the Home Office was set upon (P08).

ACPO at this stage had not utilised any of its lobbying and pressure potential on the law and order stage, that was to come most apparently in the mid-1990s. What was noted by past Presidents at this juncture was a rather hit-and-miss approach with regard to the Home Office. They suggested to the Home Office what reform they would like to see, but it was not orchestrated in the coherent and convincing manner that was seen in the later stages of the development of ACPO. At this time the 'lobbying' activities (if they can be called this) of ACPO were at the fairly rudimentary stage:

ACPO never saw itself in my day as being a body which should go wildly public about its views.... If it didn't like legislation or it didn't like proposed legislation and had views that it wished to express, it was done with the Home Office in the hope that when the legislation got in front of Parliament their views would have been taken on board.... That clearly was not very influential (P14).

The key messages emanating from interviews with the past Presidents up to this point indicate an Association far removed from the one referred to by outside commentators and discussed in chapter 2. It would be misleading to suggest that ACPO had no influence at all. No matter what the internal state of the Association, the very fact that 43 chief constables and their assistants were part of even a loosely based Association meant that there would be some level of influence, they were after all the senior managers and leaders of the police service. It was also not the case that changes within ACPO happened very quickly. There was not a particular date after which ACPO suddenly became a corporate and powerful institution. The beginnings of development within the organisation therefore emerged slowly. However, the suggestions of the critics of the organisation should be borne in mind alongside the revelations from those who held key roles within ACPO itself. The past Presidents were not blind to the inert influence of the Association nor were they slow to pick up upon any signs that changes within the organisation could have a significant impact. The beginnings of corporacy amongst ACPO members were not overlooked:

We realised that we should spend more time starting the ball rolling rather than pulling back when it's rolled too long (P11).

Gradually it's becoming more and more professional and I think it was beginning to have more of an interest in ensuring better policing than necessarily being concerned with quite narrow issues, which I think had been the case hitherto (P07).

ACPO, it was argued, was keen to become more corporate and more consensual but often ran into the difficulties of operational independence and fiercely territorial chief constables. However, it was clear to many that the desire at least to change was emerging. This would indicate that cultural change can emanate from a desire from within to change rather than necessarily being imposed from outside. There was also an awareness that ACPO, although struggling with the mechanics of becoming a more corporate body, at least had the potential to do so:

... it was a desire to have an Association which was worthy of its name and one that would be an influence in policing matters (P07).

ACPO was getting its act together. There was a greater involvement of chief constables, there was a willingness to create agendas (P10).

The past President interviews that have been used for this stage of the research were from Presidents who held the role until 1990. That year signalled changes for the Association, which is why an artificial divide between the past President interviews has been drawn. These changes within the Association will now be discussed alongside the growing development of ACPO into a more consensual and efficient organisation.

FORCES FOR CHANGE

That ACPO has changed since this point there is no doubt. This fact alone defies traditional conceptions of police culture as unchanging. Waddington (1999) has argued that despite changes within policing itself, police culture has maintained a continuity. In terms of the culture of *senior* police officers, this argument cannot apply. However, assessment is needed of how change operated and what the forces for that change involved. Not surprisingly, respondents differ over which factors were seen as most significant in shaping the new corporacy of ACPO. To an extent, this reflects the various timescales involved and indicates that the process of change was an incremental one. For example, current members tended to focus on the role of political initiatives, such as the Sheehy Inquiry on pay and conditions (Home Office, 1993a), as important stimuli, whereas past Presidents stressed such factors as controversies over public order as key influences. However the views expressed by all respondents are not overly divergent; indeed three names appear to dominate the discourse of change within ACPO, some less well known than others and constituting somewhat strange bedfellows! Kenneth Clarke, Peter Wright and Arthur Scargill. The forces for change within ACPO are grouped under four headings: 'political factors', 'environmental factors', 'people factors' and 'formative events'.

Political Factors

All of the respondents cited political pressures or political influences of some sort as motive factors in the shaping of ACPO. These have taken the form of both central and local political influences. They can also be distinguished as political *inducements* to which ACPO was to respond on the one hand, and political *threats* to which ACPO was seen to have been forced to react on the other. It is clearly difficult to separate the two, as failure to respond to encouragement can lead to more punitive sanctions. However, it will become apparent that there is a substantial difference between them.

Political encouragement and pressure on ACPO to operate on a more corporate or consistent basis has been documented by other commentators. Reiner's study of chief constables referred to the stance adopted by Douglas Hurd at the ACPO Autumn Conference of 1989 advising ACPO:

> ... to become the body for harmonising policies between forces. He [Hurd] called on them to 'deliver effectively coordinated operational action'. Failing this, he implied, the present structure of local policing might be replaced by either regional forces or a single national force (Reiner, 1991:31).

This 'inducement' is an example of when encouragement can quickly become a threat. Furthermore, the Home Affairs Select Committee, in its Fourth report for the Session 1988–89, stated that:

It is clear from the evidence that it is towards the Association of Chief Police Officers ... that the Home Office looks to provide a police view on such matters as common police services' (Home Affairs Select Committee, 1989:x).

Reference is also made in the Report to the fact that the Home Office 'appears to rely on ACPO in relation to a wide variety of matters over the whole field of police policy' (ibid.). Despite this, Hurd's frustration at not being able to discuss and decide on policing issues like some of his European counterparts was well known.

Although respondents from the sample of ACPO members plus past Presidents did not adhere to the straightforward explanation provided above as to the motives of the Home Office, there was broad agreement in principle, with some caveats, that the Home Office did want more consistency and coherency within ACPO:

... the Home Office is interested in improving the ACPO because it thinks that the advice that it gets will be better, the ACPO will be more cohesive ... but I do sometimes wonder whether they feel that ACPO has a certain independent stance that isn't attractive to one or two senior people in the Home Office ... (P04).

A number of the members also cited Hurd's steer as an important factor:

Douglas Hurd started it all off, 'come on you're going to have to change yourselves, you're going to have to get cracking' (P06).

The Home Secretary, Douglas Hurd, was very keen to be able to pick the phone up and know what the police views of X was ... now that implies that chief constables could generally say that 'yes' we all agree that must be the answer (P01).

This was seen as a positive inducement for ACPO to organise itself and attempt to act in a more cohesive fashion. This encouragement to develop corporacy was to have a very direct impact on the organisation of ACPO. It underpinned the decision by the Home Office in 1990 to respond to ACPO's requests for financial support (see below). The strengthening of ACPO was thus, at that point at least, consistent with the political will of central government.

Less positively, respondents identified a number of formative political threats which, at various points since the early 1980s, were held to have played a crucial role in forcing ACPO to become more cohesive as a reaction to them. Initially these were seen to emanate from local government. In particular, the clashes between certain chief constables and their local police authorities in some of the larger metropolitan authorities in the early- to mid-1980s (as mentioned in chapter 2) over the independence of chief constables were seen as important spurs by some respondents for ACPO to strengthen its own resolve. One past President stated that:

> ... so many issues were now cropping up affecting police forces and the position and independence and autonomy of chief constables ... it seemed ... that we should be having a similar dialogue within ACPO at national level to make sure our responses were coordinated and that we were not creating trouble for each other ... we wanted to be sure that the advice that was being sought from us as ACPO members ... was unified, that we were speaking with one voice (P10).

However, of greater apparent significance were the perceived threats coming from central government and from dramatically different agendas during the early 1990s. The Conservative Government's plans for the reform of police authorities and the Sheehy Inquiry (discussed in chapter 6), together with the particular propensities of certain Home Secretaries were identified as vital stimuli for the adoption not just of a concerted response, but also a more proactive response. Just as the individual characters of Presidents of ACPO led to changes within the organisation so the particular characteristics of Home Secretaries also brought about different organisational changes. It is clear from the responses that although Hurd and Baker encouraged the reform of ACPO, ACPO did not necessarily respond well to encouragement. Given the structural and individual difficulties within the organisation (for example, strong, independent chief constables and a constricted administrative centre) ACPO were more likely to be kick started with slightly more threatening overtones. Kenneth Clarke did just that. One past President referred to Hurd as 'lovely', Baker as easily challenged ('I remember at that time saying to Kenneth Baker, well if you have a go at us, we'll have a go at you') but Clarke as someone who 'frightened' them (P06). Others have reiterated the sentiments or reaction to threats:

> ... we must stand together, if we are divided in opposition to the Government's reform programme we'll lose (P05).

> ... the big changes we've seen ... in recent years ... have come about to some extent by Kenneth Clarke putting his suede shoes under the desk ... when he started his police reform we all awakened from a deep sleep and realised that we had to get our act together. I think we had our act together generally ... but it was then realised that we had to get down to things (P06).

> ... the more powerful the enemies that you confront, the greater the need for corporacy, and ... Sheehy, the Police and Magistrates' Courts Act, probably have been the most significant developments which have caused the police service and the upper echelons of the police service to really become cohesive (P04).

> ... we have reacted to perceived threats from outside, the primary one being government ... particularly during the brief but painful Home Secretaryship of Kenneth Clarke, where he tried to bulldoze and bludgeon the service in the way he wanted it to go and using Sheehy and so on ... that was a turning point ... people were more willing to work corporately than ever before because they perceived that there was a need to do that because we were stronger as a service if we did. We could be picked off by somebody saying in the Home Office, 'oh yes, we have these 43 independent chief constables, they never agree on anything' and that was a weakness we had to address (P01).

One past President could not believe that ACPO could act in such a cohesive manner. He stated that chief constables would agree to ACPO policy 'without debate ... because of the threat imposed from outside' (P04). This is a tremendous development from the ACPO that was described at the beginning of this chapter, one which would not agree on ACPO policy either before or after debate.

Ironically, given the points about the threat presented by the local authorities referred to above, one response to this perceived threat from central government in the early 1990s was to move more closely to the local authority associations, (then the Association of Metropolitan Authorities and the Association of County Councils, which became the Committee of Local Police Authorities, now the Association of Police Authorities) viewed in the past by some chiefs as a bastion of anti-police sentiment:

> ... the relationship ... between ACPO and these associations which are represented by police authorities ... was made very much better as a consequence of this threat, this threat of government to make those changes, and I think it will continue to be good (P04).

This seemingly (at the time) unlikely union is a relationship that still survives. Strategic alliances such as this one will be discussed in more detail in chapter 6. At this point it is important to acknowledge the effects of the political environment on the shaping of ACPO. Another source of influence is the policing *environment*.

Environmental Factors

A more gradual, incremental and longer term source of the growing corporacy and consensuality of ACPO identified by respondents related to the policing environment, and in particular the increasing complexity of policing and its consequent impact on policy-making. The view expressed tends to be that as the volume of policing issues on which a policy needs to be formed has increased, along with the gathering of information and analysis this entails, the tendency of ACPO members to rely on specialist committees and subcommittees for a steer on any particular matter has grown. This problem was discussed earlier in relation to ACPO's response to requests for information from the media. This technique of allowing specialists to speak on certain matters no matter where in the country the incident arises has also significantly professionalised ACPO's media relations, which will be discussed in more detail in chapter 6. Comments include:

> There are so many issues which are so complex that what you're seeing now is a trend towards specialisation by chief officers of ACPO (P02).

... the service itself has moved so quickly and has had so much change upon it since the early 1980s that nobody can afford the time and energy to maintain individualists.... I couldn't begin to understand the deep intricacies of traffic committee ... there are too many issues on the agenda. I have to rely on my colleagues who look after traffic to say ... we at traffic think the best way to police a motorway is this way; I am much more inclined now to presume that to be the case until someone shows me that it is not (P03).

This overlaps with what will be referred to later as '*the presumption in favour of compliance*'. As ACPO has developed, there has been an increasing assumption that individual members will accept the policies recommended by the Association on any particular aspect of policing. That is predicated on the general acceptance that the work and policies developed by the specialist committees (Crime, Traffic, etc.) can be taken as appropriate for the service as a whole — with the proviso that individual chiefs can in the final analysis still withhold compliance. The demands on the police workload and the complexity of the processes and organisations related to the policing function, have meant that the reliance on specialist committees within ACPO has grown. This in turn has facilitated the overall strengthening of the influence of the Association at force level.

At this point a note of qualification is necessary. There is a danger of assuming that political pressures and environmental factors have simply forced the membership to accept the need for corporate action. This ignores the issue of the increasing *propensity* of members to accept a collective approach, not simply because it is seen as necessary but because, as was noted earlier, it is held to be desirable. This relates to the attitudes of chief officers and the ways in which those attitudes have been shaped by training, events and interaction with one another. The changing environment of policing is seen to require a different type of chief officer:

The whole complexity of the challenge has changed ... so you actually produced a much more thoughtful cross section of management, from middle management upwards ... the old days of the sort of 'follow me chaps' type of leadership has had to change (P02).

This raises the issue of 'people' factors.

People Factors

Reiner (1991) has documented changes in the social profiles of chief police officers and the relationship between such profiles and officers' attitudes and world views and in turn their approach to policing and police management. A number of respondents in our study referred to such 'people' questions as also important factors in the shaping of ACPO:

> ... another factor is a change in character of senior police officers ... the individualism of chief officers and their deputies and assistants has markedly gone. We can all be accused of acting as feudal barons sometimes ... but the characters have changed enormously. I've known chief constables who if his neighbouring colleague painted his cars white [he] ... would paint his blue. Those characters have, not gone, but almost gone. I like to think ... that there is a generation who want to do much the same in [force named] as they do in [force named] (P03).

This growing consensuality is attributed to the awareness gained from both increased mobility of officers between forces (not as common in the past) and regular and increased contact with other senior officers:

> You are getting people who are more aware of things beyond their own domain ... nobody gets to the rank of chief constable without having been in a number of forces ... they are aware that nobody has all of the knowledge on any particular topic, there is an advantage to be gained in tapping into knowledge and experience elsewhere (P04)

> ... most of us have trained together, gained managerial experience together, progressed through the service together and developed similar attitudes (P02).

> We've grown up together ... we know each other pretty well, perhaps we've come through the life of Bramshill [the senior police college], to a greater or lesser extent we've perhaps served together, we've moved around a lot more so that we've served in different cultures, different forces, I think our approach is more broadly based. ... I think we're more receptive to new ideas as well, I think some of our predecessors had convinced themselves that there was only one way to do something (P01).

The movement away from the idea that each police force could be run as a completely independent and isolated kingdom was a significant move given that the practice had remained with the police service for so many years. Historically, the relative lack of mobility of citizens, in addition to offenders, meant that each area could, to a certain extent, run alone. Increasing mobility coupled with the use of national training and development programmes for police officers has meant that increased communication between forces was inevitable. However, these developments took place many years before chief constables finally began to relinquish some control over the force reins of every aspect of policing. The regionalisation and nationalisation of certain aspects of policing, most notably in training and education, has then played a part in the growing corporacy of ACPO. Ironically, therefore, the creation of regional and national structures of police education could be argued to have assisted ACPO in its development, the very development that to some observers prevents increasing centralisation of policing.

The Bramshill College, (where all ACPO ranks are required to have undertaken the Senior Command Course), appears to have made a significant impact on the increased and improved communication between senior officers, if not quite so successful in its primary focus of creating future managers of the police service (see chapter 4). Programmes such as this and the Special course, offered at an early point in the career of identified high-fliers, could well have played their part in generating greater consensuality amongst senior officers.

However, change did not always emerge because of something outside of the organisation, whether outside the police service in terms of political pressure or outside ACPO itself through evolutionary changes to the police service. As mentioned earlier, pressure for change also came from within the Association based on a desire to change. Although it was sometimes difficult for ACPO members to foresee how change would materialise, and there were clearly identifiable obstacles in the way of that development, the desire was apparent.

Formative Events

Just as particular events, such as the inner city disorders of the early 1980s, have shaped policing in general, incidents and events have also been seen to have contributed to the shaping of ACPO. Paramount in this respect have been public order incidents. The problems of coordinating the policing response to public disorder were particularly pertinent to ACPO, as discussed in chapter 2. Linked to these events was the impact of the Scarman Report which recommended far reaching reforms of policing and police management (Scarman, 1981). The Report was seminal as a review of the appropriateness of policing methods and policing philosophies in modern Britain (Reiner, 1992), and its effects on ACPO would seem to have been significant:

> The Scarman Report was the shot in the arm that ACPO really needed ... [it was an] injection that ACPO needed to make them say to themselves ... we've got to start to mould public opinion if nothing else and I think that that's when we started becoming more proactive rather than reactive (P13).

Even more controversially, the events surrounding the policing of the National Union of Mineworkers' strike in 1984–85, were cited by some respondents as important influences. Arthur Scargill, as leader of the NUM, is the second character to have played (in this case indirectly) a role in the development of corporacy within ACPO. Of the three names that in some way or another played a role in the development of ACPO, each would have very different reactions to having played a significant role. Whilst Kenneth Clarke felt the need for increasing cooperation between senior police officers, but had some reservations about too strong an ACPO, Peter Wright (as we shall see) was committed to developing a more corporate organisation. However, one of the least intended outcomes of the miners' strike for Arthur Scargill would have been a role in the development of ACPO as a corporate, consensual and professional policing body. Despite this, a number of respondents nevertheless alluded to the significance of this experience to the shaping of ACPO:

> ... another watershed would have been the miners' dispute and the first time we sort of banded together, chief constables who before hadn't seen the desirability of being corporate realised that the only way in which they could exist and manage their affairs was to rely upon their colleagues ... (P04).

> The miners' dispute was a watershed ... because it was seen that we could act collectively together without undermining our independence (P05).

This latter observation is very interesting, as it contradicts the view of some outside commentators (referred to in chapter 2) that the collective action of the police under the National Reporting Centre was evidence of the political utilisation of the police by the Conservative Government. It raises a thesis presented by a number of respondents, which is that a strong ACPO can be a means of withstanding demands for a national police force and the political controls over policing that might engender. Another past President expressed it thus:

> ... a uniform approach [through ACPO] towards the delivery of policing ... prevents there being a great public or government clamour for larger police organisations, perhaps even a national police force (P04).

Such readings of the relationship between police and government complicate the association which has often been drawn between centralisation of policing and politicisation (both discussed in chapter 2). In this respect the centralising influence of ACPO is held up as the countervailing force to increased political interference with policing policy. This is consistent with the view raised earlier, that one of the formative influences on ACPO has been the perception that government has sought to increase its controls over the police service and that therefore a concerted response by ACPO is a means of resisting such a development.

It should also be stressed that not all respondents were of the view that the policing of the miners' strike was a watershed in this way; one referred to it as an 'exceptional' (P03) case from which little of longer term relevance in terms of the shaping of ACPO can be drawn. Nevertheless, although the cohesiveness and deliberateness of purpose in such areas of mutual aid provision may have been exaggerated by some external commentators, experiences of major incidents of public order policing (more recently the events at Wapping and the poll tax demonstrations) do seem, as far as some respondents are concerned, to have played a part in the development of ACPO.

What each of these points addresses is the extent to which, over time, ACPO has responded to the pressures, inducements and calls from within, by developing into a more concerted, cohesive and corporate body, particularly in recent years. The evidence from the research is that the days of the individualistic (or 'maverick' (M39)) chief constable have gone, and given way to a more consensual style:

> If you go back ... [there were] ... a lot of idiosyncratic, more powerful [chief constables] ... we're much more apparatchiks now I think than we were in the past ... there has been a developing uniformity and an acquiescence in the willingness ... for all of us to adopt common standards (P02).

The forces for change within ACPO are now apparent but those developments needed to be supported and underpinned by an organisational structure which facilitated a more streamlined and cohesive policy making machine. The will was emerging; what needs to be analysed now are the mechanisms and dimensions of achieving that cultural change.

MECHANISMS FOR CHANGE

Organisational

Organisationally, ACPO has developed and restructured to a considerable extent over the past decade. ACPO has an executive committee made up of key members of the Association including the Presidential Team consisting of the President, First and Second Vice-President and immediate past President (see appendix 1 for full membership of the committee). This is complemented by the Chief Constables' Council through which all policy decisions are ratified. One of the major changes within ACPO has been the establishment of the full time Secretariat, based in London, which coordinates the main work of the Association, services the main committees and runs the information and press office. Established in 1989 on the recommendations of a Home Affairs Select Committee, the Secretariat has contributed significantly to the growing internal professionalisation of ACPO and now employs 17 staff. The Home Affairs Select Committee stressed the importance of ACPO to the Home Office and the value that it placed on its work. The Home Secretary agreed that in national interests the ACPO Secretariat should be strengthened. The Select Committee believed that the costs incurred by the changes were extremely low, '... given the importance attached to the views and advice of ACPO by the Home Office, which appear to rely on ACPO in relation to a wide variety of matters over the whole field of police policy ...' (Home Affairs Select Committee, 1989:x).

The Secretariat has been continually strengthened during its existence and now services all the main committees, which have been
streamlined into a matrix model with cross functional representation
(see appendix 1 for fuller details). In the past ACPO has been funded
through Common Police Services, a top slice from each force at source
which includes the funding of police training and the National Criminal
Intelligence Service. In addition to this funding provision, ACPO now
receives money from each force based on the Standard Spending
Assessment, the formula by which central grants to local authorities are
estimated. ACPO receives a Home Office grant (£458,000 in 1998–99)
and has in the last few years been able to raise revenue through its
conferences, most especially the exhibition held in the summer
(£77,987 in 1998–99). There is also an issue of the *hidden* costs of
ACPO. Much time is spent by police officers of all ranks on ACPO
business within force areas, especially if a key role within the
Association is held (e.g., President of ACPO or Chair of the Crime
Committee). This time is effectively sponsored by local police authorities who are funding police salaries. ACPO estimate that hidden cost to
be £1.3 million, but it is virtually impossible to make any definitive
estimate. This will be considered later in this study (see appendix 2 for
more details of the funding of ACPO). The benefits of a professional
Secretariat are outlined by one past President of the Association:

If we have a really good structure we would grasp some of those
issues and pursue them rather better if we had a more effective
committee structure rather than hoping that some poor ... inspector,
sat in whichever police force is going to volunteer to do the job next,
has the time, energy, skills to come and put into it so the professional
Secretariat is more likely to give us that cohesion and direction that
we would need (P03).

The increase in funds to the information and press office has furthered
the public profile of ACPO, which has grown from a relatively
haphasard to a more coordinated and proactive outfit in its dealings with
the media. The information office coordinates responses to requests
from the media for information and comment and also maintains close
links with information offices around the forces. This has enabled ACPO
to 'compete' with the Police Federation, whose media and public
relations machinery were already firmly in place. In the past the media

would tend to go directly to the Police Federation for comment, as there was always a spokesperson present and always, if not a consensus view, a view from the Executive of the Federation available. However, with an increasingly effective ACPO publicity machine, the media are more willing to take the views of the senior management of the police service, a view which although perhaps slower in formulation than that of the Police Federation is likely to be more widely agreed with within the organisation. The tendency for Federation spokespeople to put forward a view not widely supported within the organisation tends not to happen as much within ACPO, due in part to the ease of communicating with some 240 members rather than 125,000, but also due to ACPO's increasingly professional methods of consultation and the more delib- erate use in the media of ACPO officers with specialism in certain areas of policing and criminal justice (discussed further in chapter 6).

At approximately the same time as the development of the Secre- tariat, a further internal development emerged within ACPO. Mention should be made of the role played by key individuals who, during their Presidential term, have made specific and significant contributions to the development of corporacy within ACPO. Undoubtedly each President has made a particular mark on the Association. However, some have played a notably formative role, linked no doubt to the conditions facing the police service at the time. This brings us to the third name in the list of the three men that played an important role, one way or another, in the development of ACPO. Peter Wright, who was President of ACPO from 1987–88, is said by a large number of respondents to have brought about a qualitative shift in the business of ACPO:

He first of all marked up to the service that there are some things about which it makes absolutely no sense to have 42 different policies or, to put it another way, if ACPO is to have a view, then that view has to be established across the country ... [he] said to us there are some things about which we should have common policy and practice (P03).

... during Peter Wright's Presidency, having debated and agreed a policy at Chief Constables' Council ... it was decided that chief constables would sign up to that particular policy. In the event that they couldn't sign up to it they would have argued their corner at

ACPO Council and they would express their contrary view in writing
to the President of the day ... that was a significant watershed that
caused people to think about not conforming with ACPO policy
(P04).

... if a chief wishes to dissent from some established policy he [sic]
has now to formally indicate that in writing (P02).

In other words, it was from this point onwards that the principle of what
we have called *'presumption in favour of compliance'* gained a footing
within the Association. This step introduced the procedure whereby
individual members who had decided to depart from the accepted policy
of ACPO, agreed at Chief Constables' Council, would be expected to
cite the reasons for doing so to the President, and not simply fail to
conform. Many respondents referred to this development as an
important divergence from previous practice, and a significant moment
in the development of the Association. Action had to be taken in order
not to follow ACPO policy as opposed to inaction following the
agreement of ACPO policy.

No ACPO member interviewed was aware of any such formal breach
of ACPO policy having occurred (but see chapter 5). It is not clear
whether this seemingly successful record of compliance in implementing ACPO policy is either because any problems in agreeing policy
were ironed out in the negotiating stages, or because chief constables
simply act locally without complying with this procedure. Nevertheless,
the adoption of this principle represented an increase in the mechanisms
for the development of corporacy. However, the principle of independence is also stated and chief constables at no stage have to comply with
ACPO policy. This was exhibited publicly after the completion of
interviews with ACPO members when the chief constable of Greater
Manchester Police decided not to adopt a register of freemasons within
his force, a policy adopted by ACPO and ratified in the Chief
Constables' Council. In the words of the *Guardian*, he has 'defied his
professional body' (10 April 1997). Nevertheless, the very fact that the
views of a chief constable about a matter concerning his force should be
seen as defying anybody still remains significant.

However, the most important internal change within the Association
has to be the recent split of ACPO into two distinct bodies, a staff
association and a professional body. Pressure for change within the

organisation had been apparent for a considerable amount of time, but it was only in late 1993 that a paper was submitted to the ACPO Autumn Conference with firm recommendations and agendas for reform. The thrust of the paper, and indeed the rationale behind the move, was that better coordination was needed of the work of the Association and that the professional appearance of ACPO to outsiders needed to be improved, especially with regard to the Home Office. There was a perceived need to improve the role and status of ACPO as a professional body and the need for a clearer distinction between the professional and staff association; a better way of doing business with the Home Office and the need for funding arrangements to enable both functions to be carried out adequately. The initial proposal was for the professional side of the organisation to be called the Royal Institute of Policing, but the acronym RIP was considered inappropriate!

The split occurred in April 1996 with the name of ACPO being retained for the professional side and the name CPOSA (Chief Police Officers' Staff Association) being given to the staff association side. CPOSA has its own constitution, identity and funding base (consisting of membership subscriptions). CPOSA is headed by a Chair who is a separately elected member of the Association. The Chair negotiates at the Police Negotiating Board on members' salaries and conditions of service. However it emerged through a written answer in the House of Lords to a question from the Earl of Haddington that in addition to the revenue gathered from subscription, the Home Office made a £2,000 contribution to CPOSA in 1998–99 (Hansard, 1998). An answer was not provided to a further question concerning which other 'unions' received Home Office funding!

At about the same time as this debate there were discussions taking place on the possible establishment of a professional 'policing institute', a body contributing to the development of policing policy. It was envisaged that the professional side of ACPO would form this institute within a few years of its inception although this idea remained dormant for some time. It has recently been resurrected and discussions between the Association of Police Authorities, ACPO and the Police Federation are progressing. ACPO were keen to have the support of the two police representative bodies (the Superintendents' Association and the Police Federation). The role of the Institute would be to 'disseminate and collate best practice and provide a discussion forum' (*Policing Today*, 1999:8).

From interviews with ACPO members two types of rationale in favour of the split emerged. First, that in separating the two functions it would be easier for ACPO to be seen to be speaking 'on behalf of the whole service' rather than according to their own occupational interests:

> It's overdue ... it's certainly timely because there was a real danger we were going to become isolated and the roles confused ... there was a danger ... that it would divert perhaps the value that was put on the consultative and professional responsibilities of the organisation (M44).

The second, complementary rationale was that the split would strengthen the capacity to defend and promote members' conditions of service and pay:

> ... dividing the Association into two [is a recognition that] the staff side of ACPO has perhaps got to become more robust than it's been in the past because for the first time now we're being subjected to quite stringent conditions of service in terms of fixed term appointments ... it's going to get harder and that's the way of the world and that's how things are changing ... (M44).

Some members were very much opposed to the split, no doubt echoing arguments which were advanced during the debate within the Association before the split:

> I don't know why and what it is that was the major problem that wanted us to split the staff association ... I don't think anybody in the country ever regarded [ACPO] as a union, I think it's been regarded as a professional body and so I voted against it (M01).

The implications of the split are that ACPO can take a more public stance on policing policy, and arguably, a more professional stance (this is discussed further in chapter 6). Increased funding for the Secretariat has provided a more efficient and effective committee structure and with the appointment of an additional press officer the public profile of the Association has been raised. More recent changes that have taken place since the completion of interviews with ACPO members will be discussed at the end of this chapter.

Cultural/Educational

There is no doubt that there has been a cultural shift in attitude within senior management in the police service, reflected by changes in the social profiles of chief police officers and their approach to policing and police management. Reiner produced a typology of chief constables categorising them into 'barons', 'bobbies', 'bosses' and 'bureaucrats' (Reiner, 1991). Whilst adding that each chief constable was somewhat unique, he offered the typology as an example of how chief constables have changed over time. He described the bureaucrat as the 'wave of the future' (ibid:340), a chief constable who has:

> an upwardly mobile working-class background, and he will have a degree and probably extensive experience of research and training. He is very much a believer in, indeed a propagator of, the *Zeitgeist* of the period, the post-Scarman philosophy. He developed this through his immersion in the central institutions of the police world. Paradoxically this attachment to the values of the centre makes him a fervent advocate of the virtues of local consultation. (ibid:308).

Reiner was accurate in his analysis of the bureaucrat, which perhaps could now be replaced by 'business manager', as increasingly displacing the other types of officer and our research has confirmed this. One of the striking developments that has been observed in senior police officers, which was mentioned earlier, is this change in character from the dominant, rather autocratic figure of the 1980s to the new modern manager willing to work more closely with colleagues within the force and, perhaps more interestingly, to work with other forces around the country via ACPO.

Educational background may also be a key 'people factor'. Arguably, more educated chief officers are more likely to appreciate the value of working collectively. The educational profile of both senior officers specifically and throughout the ranks generally has changed considerably in the past decade. A study by Halsey *et al.*, (1980) found that although 25 per cent of chief constables held degrees, none had been obtained prior to their entry into the police service. Robert Reiner's study of chief constables was published in 1991 with the research carried out in the late 1980s (Reiner, 1991). Reiner considered the educational achievements of chief constables and found them to be much higher than from people from similar class backgrounds with 77.5 per cent attending grammar school and 25 per cent attaining a degree (note there were no graduates prior to joining the police). It must be borne in mind that it is not possible to draw direct comparisons with the work of Reiner as he interviewed only chief constables but some interesting patterns do emerge. As can be seen, the increase in higher educational achievements is remarkable and shows an increased awareness of the value of higher education and qualifications in addition to policing experience.

Figure 1: Higher Education Achievement within ACPO Ranks

PERCENTAGE OF SAMPLE HOLDING A FIRST DEGREE	
Reiner's research (conducted mid-1980s)	25%
Our research (conducted mid-1990s)	71%

If we considered only chief constables as Reiner did (although the sample of chief constables used for this study was much smaller) the figure increases to 80 per cent, and with the omission of the Metropolitan Police rises again to 86 per cent. This trend is also demonstrated in the increase in the number of deputy chief constables holding a degree, a rise from 43 per cent in Reiner's research to our findings of 75 per cent. As mentioned, Reiner's 25 per cent gained their qualifications in service, half of them through sponsorship via the Bramshill Scholarship scheme (sending potential high-fliers to University to study full-time, on secondment, for an undergraduate degree, since stopped; fuller details in chapter 4). Of the 71 per cent from this research, a quarter had gained their qualifications before entry into the police service and 48 per cent were part of the Bramshill Scholarship scheme.

These figures indicate two factors, first that the non-graduate ACPO member is becoming something of a rarity, a process that has accelerated quite dramatically in a relatively short space of time and second, that the Bramshill Scholarship scheme continues to figure as an important feature in the profile of the modern police manager, although it will inevitably decline as the system unwinds and the numbers of graduate recruits increases.

As a reflection of the population generally there are also growing numbers of police officers with or taking a higher degree, 17 per cent of our sample with postgraduate degrees including three with doctorates. Before very long the number of ACPO officers with a *higher* degree will be the same as was the number of graduates only 10 years ago. In a very short period of time the educational qualifications of senior police officers have improved fairly dramatically.

In addition to this increase in graduates, there has also been a shift in subject type. Under the Bramshill Scholarship scheme, the most popular subject choice was law although choice of degree was entirely the decision of the student. Half of Reiner's sample took law degrees but our research found a drop to 33 per cent. This can in part be explained by the rise in the availability of other types of degrees, namely the rise in social and political science degrees but also due to the realisation that law was perhaps not the most relevant subject for policing and that a much broader grounding could be gained by a social and political science degree. Funders of degrees, now almost exclusively part-time, also favour the social sciences and some even go so far as to specify police studies.

Figure 2: Degree Disciplines

TYPES OF DEGREE	
ARTS	4
SOCIAL AND POLITICAL SCIENCE	12
LAW	10
MANAGEMENT	1
PSYCHOLOGY	3

There may also be a trend away from Oxbridge towards the red brick universities and we may see in the future the rise of the 'new' universities, particularly in the light of the rise in part-time/in-service and self-funded higher education, coupled with the emergence of schemes for the accreditation of police training programmes within higher educational courses. If this is the case then it is possible to anticipate a continuing change in the cultural profile of the most senior ranks in the police service.

A former Home Secretary talked positively of the increasing educational qualifications within senior police management:

... they've become more graduate oriented ... (E01).

Another, perhaps related, dimension of the professionalisation of ACPO is a greater acceptance of research as a basis for policy development. They have made far more use of focused seminars, one day conferences on specific areas of interest, workshops and are far more proactive in areas such as research. ACPO have also set up various task forces where topics will be examined for a stated period, for example in 1998 ACPO considered two topics, police/race relations and corruption in the police service. The Audit Commission has completed over 15 papers on the police and have commented on how the police service are the most receptive of public bodies to both examination and change.

The Chairman of the Audit Commission wrote:

The police have always been among the Commission's most enthusiastic partners, showing a great willingness to analyse what they do and a readiness to change. They have achieved a great deal ... (Audit Commission, 1995:6).

However, it should be noted that this position could be explained by the fact that the Audit Commission may be pursuing an ACPO-shaped agenda so chief constables are using the Audit Commission for reforms. The relationship between the Audit Commission and ACPO has been discussed in chapter 1 and will be discussed further in chapter 5.

'HOW WE ARE'

Internal organisational developments within ACPO in the form of structural and cultural changes have shown a marked shift from a 'club' approach to a more professional, coherent and proactive organisation. Members of ACPO were asked to comment generally on their perceptions of ACPO as an organisation and specifically if their views had changed over time. This can be used in comparison with the comments made by past Presidents and considered earlier in this chapter. A large majority of respondents (83 per cent of the sample) were of the view that ACPO had become a more cohesive, corporate and consensual body, particularly in recent years. This is discussed at length in chapter 5, but in this context typical sentiments were:

> ... I think they [ACPO] are consensual, it's happened in the last five years and it's extremely powerful (M18).

> I think it's [ACPO] started to become much more cohesive, much more led by the Presidency ... (M03).

> ... the police service in my view is in good hands, with the young people coming through and I'm tremendously optimistic, which then leads me to be tremendously optimistic about the ACPO because I think they caused that to happen. They facilitated that confidence and togetherness of policing in a way that I never thought the ACPO could achieve. They've done a remarkable job, remarkable job ... (M18).

What seems clear is that, at least according to this particular sample, the vast majority of members consider that the organisation has become significantly more corporate in recent years and that this development is widely welcomed — indeed, one respondent referred to adherence to ACPO policy as nothing less than 'a matter of professionalism' (M02). There are important qualifications to such sentiments. As we argue in chapter 5, ACPO is by no means as corporate as it could be, or that it sometimes would claim to be. Nevertheless it is the case that the membership are broadly of the view that, at least as far as they are concerned, ACPO has indeed become a more corporate and internally cohesive organisation. This is also the view of many of those we interviewed from *outside of ACPO*.

Most of those from organisations with whom ACPO in various ways 'does business' tended to take the view, that from their own perspective ACPO had become a generally more cohesive body than had been the case in the past. For example, a former Home Secretary when asked whether in his opinion ACPO had become more corporate over time stated that, 'I think that's probably true' (E01). He went on to say:

> I think that it's a natural development, I think they come together because they feel they want to exchange experience, they want to

have some sort of corporate togetherness, that was what drove them forward (E01).

A representative of the Audit Commission commented positively that ACPO:

... do ... in terms of developing policies and trying to get coherence about good practice ... an exceptionally good job given extremely limited resources which they have at their disposal (E04).

This interviewee went on to state that:

... even in the four years that I've been working with the police ... they are much more coherent, much more corporate. I remember people saying when I first came here that if you got four chief constables into this room, they wouldn't agree on the colour of the carpet ... I think even within the very short space of four years that attitude has just gone completely (E04).

In a similar vein, a very senior member of the Home Office, who was better placed than most to judge any changes in the approach adopted by ACPO to policy making, argued that:

... just looking back over recent years ... I was very, very struck with the way in which they [ACPO] had got their act together over that period and ... they now seem to me to be acting as an effective, cohesive kind of organisation in terms of their dealings with us ... (E37).

However, we would not wish to imply that the views of these representatives are absolutely typical. As we shall see elsewhere in this study, there are many qualifications to the thesis that ACPO has become a more corporate body. For example, another member of the Home Office staff who in different ways has had close dealings with ACPO took a very different view of the organisation in this context. In response to the same line of questioning this individual described the way ACPO does its business, in terms of its committee work as follows:

I think it's a mess, absolute mess ... Why? I think there are two main reasons: one is the turnover of staff ... [ACPO committee named] have had three different chairs and two different secretaries and almost the whole of the membership's different. That's one problem, the other one is they've got no resources. So anything they do is beg, borrowing and stealing each other from somebody ... (E38).

We shall have more to say about such qualifications regarding the corporate status of ACPO later in this study.

CONTINUING TRENDS

Although the period of ACPO's development that is most interesting and contained the most dramatic change was the first half of the 1990s, it is important to consider more recent changes within the organisation in order to later assess the current position of ACPO as a professional association. Probably the most significant recent development within ACPO was its move to company status in 1997. This is in line with other professional associations and places ACPO on a firmer and less *ad hoc* basis than could have been argued to have been the case before. ACPO has retained its name but was incorporated under the Companies Act 1985 as a private company which is limited by guarantee. The nature of its business is according to the registration details at Companies House, a 'professional organisation'. This initiative was driven, according to the Secretariat, by the recognition that ACPO would be handling far bigger sums of money, especially through the relationship with Labelex, the company that presently runs ACPO's summer conference. Gaining charity status or 'plc' status was considered but the former precluded lobbying and the latter was too expensive. As we shall see in chapter 5, lobbying now plays a significant part in the activities of ACPO so the reluctance to part with their new weapon is understandable.

The Memorandum and Articles of the Association have altered and are publicly available via Companies House. The objects of the company, as stated earlier, are to 'promote the effectiveness, efficiency and professional interests' of the police service and it can now do various things in order to realise this aim. These include raising money, accepting gifts, issuing appeals and holding public meetings in order to achieve their objectives. However, it goes on to add that members of the company can 'do all such lawful things as shall further the attainment of the object of the company'. Given that the object of the company is rather vague and involves furthering the 'professional interests' of the police service, this effectively means that any legal activity is permitted in order to promote ACPO and its activities. By formalising and providing legal status to ACPO's existence, ACPO appears to have formalised an increase in its powers. Members of the Executive Committee are now Directors of the company which has, amongst other matters, caused concern in the House of Lords. The Earl of Haddington questioned the appointment of these Directors on a number of fronts and was concerned that procedure may not have been followed. His questions included whether local police authorities had given their consent to senior police officers from their forces becoming directors of ACPO; whether the directors had submitted their names for nomination to be directors; and why the directors had not notified Companies House of their appointment (Hansard, 1998). Unfortunately these and other questions were not answered as ACPO is not part of the Home Office or accountable to the Secretary of State. It was argued that these were matters only for the internal management of ACPO. When accountability is considered later in this study (chapter 7) we shall see that ACPO members use accountability through the tripartite structure of policing (which includes both the local police authorities and the Home Secretary) as justification for a sufficient structure of accountability for ACPO.

As part of the professionalisation of ACPO, the organisation has widened its membership base. Although the 230 full members make up the significant part of the Association, there are now 31 senior civilians who may apply to join ACPO. This is in addition to 15 senior police officers from non-Home Office forces (e.g., British Transport Police, States of Jersey Police; see appendix 1 for the full list) who are invited to join. Neither group are full voting members but have limited voting rights. However, since 1998 full voting rights have been given to senior police officers from some of the national policing organisations: the National Crime Squad (NCS), the National Criminal Intelligence Service (NCIS) and the Police Information Technology Organisation (PITO). There is also a category for non-voting honorary members who have, in some way or another, made an outstanding contribution to policing. These categories will be helpful in establishing the membership of a Policing Institute should it emerge.

One other strand of the organisational professionalisation of ACPO comes in its voting system for President, or 'head of the Company' under the new arrangements. This has changed considerably over the years and has moved from 'Buggins' turn' (p. 11) to 'something like the selection of the Pope' waiting for the 'white smoke to come out' (p. 12) to a simple majority system and now to the system of the single transferable vote. The electorate is asked to list the candidates on the ballot form in descending order of preference; if on the first count no candidate receives an absolute majority, the bottom one falls out and the second preference votes of their supporters are distributed. The votes are recounted and the process repeated until one candidate achieves an absolute majority. A clause has been added that the President can hold office for more than a year should the Executive Committee require the time period of one year in office to be changed. This situation has not yet arisen although discussion is underway concerning the issue of a full-time President for the Association. Jack Straw, the Home Secretary, has apparently been very keen on the idea of a full-time President and the further development of ACPO.

Organisationally and culturally there have been enormous changes within ACPO over a relatively short period of time. Using Bourdieu's 'field' and 'habitus' analysis we can see in the context of ACPO that both the organisational and structural conditions ('field') have changed allowing change within the cultural knowledge ('habitus') of senior police officers (Bourdieu, 1977). The two processes have interacted and developed together. Changing senior police culture has therefore taken on both changes to the 'field' and the 'habitus' of senior police officers.

These organisational and cultural changes have been a process of development and in that sense there has to be agreement with those cultural analysts, particularly anthropologists, who argue that organisational culture is not something which can be 'created', rather it emerges through social interaction and the transference of ideas, values and norms over time — the 'social emergent' approach to culture (Lynn-Meek, 1994:274). The changes in attitudes and opinions of ACPO from past Presidents to current members have exhibited this process of development and show significantly different cultural ideas. The theme of corporacy and professionalism is strong within ACPO, emanating from pressures outside the organisation coupled with an internal desire for change. The result is that, organisationally at least, ACPO and CPOSA have all the machinery in place for a highly effective professional association and staff organisation. As a former Home Secretary commented:

> ... any sensible Home Secretary pays a lot of attention to them [ACPO] because they speak out of experience ... (E32).

The professionalisation of ACPO is part of a more general 'professionalisation' of the police service. It is driven by that 'professionalisation' but also contributes to it in terms of the development of policies that have been researched and debated and which will thus lead to more consistency in policing as a service. There is no doubt of the changes that have taken place within the Association over the past decade. This is related to a total sea-change in management in all areas of the public sector with a continued pressure to professionalise. With competition for the voice of the service between ACPO and the representative organisation of the lower ranks, the Police Federation, (as strong as ever see chapter 6), this could mean a growing divide between those who represent the management view and those who represent the workforce. However, despite the possible friction between the organisations, the Police Federation are themselves aware of the transformation in ACPO:

> Something remarkable has taken place in ACPO over a very short period, and it is time for the rest of the service to take note (*Police*, 1996:5).

What is now important to examine is exactly how these cultural and organisational developments have led to internal and external developments, both within ACPO and within policing itself. This will be analysed by a continuation of the consideration of the cultural formation of ACPO and in terms of the processes which together determine how a police officer becomes an ACPO officer.

Chapter 4
Becoming an ACPO Member: Selection and Training for Senior Managers in the Police Service

INTRODUCTION

In this chapter we shall examine the processes by which certain police officers come to join the police elite that is ACPO. If we are to understand how ACPO as an organisation operates, it is necessary to have an appreciation of its internal culture and profile. The internal culture of an organisation is fashioned in part by the mechanisms by which those who comprise it are selected and prepared for their role within it. In the case of ACPO, we need to understand the processes which enable the 200 or so men and women who make up ACPO to rise from the ranks and take on the most senior positions the police service can offer.

The processes which govern who is selected and prepared for the ranks of ACPO is an area frequently exposed to attack. Periodically, often in response to particular incidents or series of incidents, concerns are raised about the qualities of 'police leadership'. This was evident for example in the wake of the conflicts between certain chief constables and their (mainly Labour) police authorities in the early- to mid-1980s (see McClaughlin, 1994). Attacks came in this case from the left and from civil liberties bodies (ibid). Later on in the 1980s, Margaret Thatcher and some of her colleagues let it be known that they were less than happy with the performance of police leaders in the fight against crime — despite increasing levels of expenditure on the police they were 'failing to deliver' on crime reduction. There were murmurings of the need to introduce an 'officer class' into the upper echelons of policing, drawn from the military services — admittedly stimulated in part by the end of the Cold War and the subsequent release of numbers of senior armed service officers into the community! More recently, now under a Labour Government, a 'whispering campaign' which questioned once again the quality of police leadership emerged, in this case as a response to the questionable conduct of certain chief constables but also fuelled by the criticisms made of police conduct in the 'Stephen Lawrence' controversy, which exposed widescale deficiencies in police management regarding the police response to the killing of a black youth in London.

Whenever concerns are raised about the qualities of police leadership, the spotlight turns onto the system of police recruitment, training and selection. This system, after all, is responsible for determining who gets into, and alternatively who is kept out of, the upper ranks of the police service. Attacks on police leadership are, however, not the only reason why recruitment, training and selection have been put under scrutiny. The world of the police manager has been transformed in recent years by what has been called 'new public management' (NPM; see chapter 1). The police service, like all other areas of the public sector, has been forced to orient its activities more and more towards the pursuit of the '3 Es' — efficiency, economy and effectiveness. Initially driven under the agenda of 'Thatcherism' (Savage and Robins, 1990), the doctrine of the 3 Es has continued to occupy centre stage in British governments' strategies for the public sector. Under this rubric, the whole British public sector has had to rethink its structures, machineries and cultures in order to meet its requirements. This has meant that senior management in particular has had to rethink its approach to managing in the public sector; it has had to embrace the 'cultural revolution' that is new public management. In short, it entails the introduction of business management into the public sector. As these developments have unfolded across the public sector, new types of challenges have confronted public sector managers. Processes such as business planning and strategic management, financial management, marketing and information management, have become increasingly central concerns of managers in the public sector, demanding skills not previously critical to the day-to-day management of the public services (Farnham and Horton, 1996). In turn, this places increasing emphasis on the mechanisms for the selection and training of managers as a means of ensuring that those appointed to senior positions within the public sector organisations are equipped to the tasks that confront them.

Although the full blast of NPM reached the police service relatively later than was the case for other public sector bodies (Savage and Charman, 1996), there is no doubt that major transformations along the lines of NPM have since taken place within the police organisation and across police management. A service that had maintained many of the traditions laid down in the nineteenth century has, in a short space of time, undergone fundamental change. Growing demands on police resources, expenditure constraints, pressures from the Home Office and value-for-money reviews by Her Majesty's Inspectorate of Constabulary and the Audit Commission, have all had an effect (Savage and Leishman, 1996; Savage et al., 1997). Internally driven pressures for change have also played a part as senior police managers have exchanged views and best practice on police management within their own professional association, the Association of Chief Police Officers (ACPO) (Savage and Charman, 1996). As a result of all of these influences, one might now even talk of 'new police management' as a variant of NPM (Leishman et al., 1995).

Any consideration of the processes leading to the appointment of senior police managers should acknowledge what is to a great extent a distinctive feature of the police vis-à-vis other areas of the public sector. The police in Britain, unlike their counterparts elsewhere in Europe, operate a 'single-entry' system of recruitment (Leishman and Savage, 1993a). All senior police officers, without exception, began as police constables and have in virtually every case proceeded through every tier of the rank structure before attaining ACPO rank. The single-entry system places particular pressures on selection and training processes. In dual- or multiple-entry systems, where candidates, subject to completion of training and education, can begin at inspector or even superintendent level, police staff can be recruited from the outset on the basis of their possessing management potential, and all subsequent training can be oriented in that direction (ibid). Single-entry systems, on the other hand, entail recruitment at the same points of both those with management and supervisory potential and those better suited to work as a constable, a position in which the vast majority of those who join the British police remain. This then necessitates a range of special provisions for the identification of 'high-fliers' amongst the rank and file and training/educational programmes to match. Thus whereas, for example, the Dutch police manager is recruited with managerial potential in mind and given the vast bulk of management training at the beginning of his/her police career, normally on the basis of a four-year course at the Police Academy (ibid), the British police manager is identified as such at a variety of career points and is provided with management training much later in his/her career. The effectiveness of the machinery for in-service selection and senior management training thus becomes an acute concern.

The approach taken in this chapter is not to seek a full assessment of the selection and training of senior police managers as such, but to examine ACPO members' own views of the processes by which they were selected, trained and appointed. Clearly in this sense this discussion does involve a degree of evaluation of those same processes, but one which draws very much on the particular perspectives of those at the 'receiving end'. We are interested in members' assessments of the mechanisms which they have had to pass through as they have attained senior positions within the police hierarchy. In this respect a note of caution should be made. The processes we examine here have themselves been very much a 'moving target'. They have been subject to continuing review and adaptation. The experiences documented here in terms of selection, training and appointment are not necessarily a reflection of current practice, and in a small number of cases involve procedures endured some considerable time ago. Some qualifications are therefore required in deriving from these experiences broader interpretations of the standing of the processes of 'getting to the top' in police management; we make these qualifications accordingly as we proceed. Nevertheless, we are satisfied that what is examined in this study does reveal some important features of the basis on which the current crop of senior police officers have become what they are: the leaders of the modern police service in England and Wales.

The chapter focuses on the three primary stages of the process of 'becoming an ACPO member': first, the mechanism of *selection* from middle-ranking officers of those deemed to have 'ACPO potential'; secondly, the programme of senior management *training* provided to all those thus selected and without which no officer can be appointed to ACPO rank; thirdly, the process of *appointment* of officers to specific ACPO positions within police forces, a process formally undertaken by local police authorities. After a descriptive outline of the mechanisms involved at each stage, the study goes on to present ACPO members' own assessments and experiences of selection, training and appointment. In considering these processes we shall also identify on-going and likely future changes in the arrangements for the selection, training and appointment for senior police managers.

In advance of all of this, however, we need to discuss measures taken by the police service to begin the process of selection to ACPO or other senior positions at very early stages of a police officer's career. Given the points made earlier about single-entry recruitment of the police service, mechanisms were devised many years ago to identify potential 'high-fliers', either at the point of the candidate's initial application to the police service or early on in the officer's career as a police constable. Many of those who eventually attain ACPO rank were identified in this way. We shall now consider the processes which were triggered accordingly.

DESTINED FOR THE TOP?: IDENTIFYING POTENTIAL 'HIGH-FLIERS'

As has been noted, the British system of 'single-entry' recruitment to the police service presents particular difficulties with regard to the development of high quality senior management. The long career path to ACPO rank can mean that officers do not attain higher office until late in their police career, thus 'wasting', or at least delaying the impact of, managerial skills which could have been put to good effect while they were younger. A related problem, certainly in the past, has been a shortage of highly educated candidates for top management positions. As a consequence, various schemes were created in the 1960s either to identify potential 'high-fliers' at an early stage in order to allow for forms of 'fast tracking' of officers, or to increase the overall education levels of officers showing promise (Hill and Smithers, 1991). The primary schemes in question are the 'Graduate Entry Scheme' (GES), the 'Bramshill Scholarship Scheme', the 'Special Course' and the 'Accelerated Promotion Scheme' (APS). The Special Course was in fact a forerunner of the APS. All of these schemes were established at a time when the number of graduates in the police service was remarkably low — less than 200 out of a force of almost 100,000 in England and Wales in 1968 (ibid:299).

The GES was set up both as a means of increasing the attractiveness of a police career amongst graduates but also as a means of streamlining the promotion system in such a way that candidates selected could proceed more rapidly through the ranks than the non-GES officer, and thus attain seniority at a younger age. The latter objective has met with some success, as GES officers have on average reached upper-middle ranks some five years earlier than officers promoted through the standard channels (ibid:308). A question is whether this scheme is as necessary as it was given the dramatic increases in the numbers of graduate entrants into the police service since the 1970s (ibid). It could be argued, however, that even with the increase in the ratio of graduates entering the service the police still need to compete with other employers in attracting the best graduates, hence the need to continue to offer an appealing package of incentives in the form of the GES.

The Bramshill Scholarship scheme (named after the college in Hampshire responsible for advanced police training — to be examined later) was established as another means of increasing the numbers of graduates in the police service, by providing for secondments of officers to undertake sponsored full-time degrees at specified universities early in their career (normally at sergeant or inspector ranks). Those chosen for scholarships were often those already identified as potential high-fliers, having been through the 'Special Course', to be examined shortly. The most popular degree programme chosen by Bramshill scholars has been a law degree, although it should be noted that, once selected for a scholarship, the choice of course was very much at the discretion of the officer concerned. While the scheme was abandoned in the early 1990s (although some forces opted to run a scholarship scheme of their own), its effects will continue to be felt within the service for some time into the future as scholars move on through the rank structure. It should also be noted that a related scheme, the 'Bramshill Fellowship Scheme', which sponsors officers to undertake *research* degrees, still operates.

As discussed in the previous chapter and referred to briefly here, our research on the current cohort of ACPO members considered the question of higher educational qualifications amongst senior officers. In comparison with Reiner's (1991) research some interesting patterns emerge — although it should be emphasised that Reiner studied only chief constables, while our research considered a sample of all ACPO ranks, and as such some caution is necessary. Based on interviews conducted in the late 1980s, Reiner found that only 20 per cent of chief constables possessed a degree (although by the time the research was published that had reached nearly 50 per cent). All of the 20 per cent of chiefs possessing a degree had gained the qualification while serving as a police officer, half of them through the Bramshill Scholarship Scheme. Our research found that 71 per cent of the ACPO sample possessed a degree, a quarter of whom had joined the police service as graduates, although just under half of the graduates had still gained their degree in-service through the Bramshill Scheme. Of those officers in our sample entering the police service as graduates all but one had done so under the GES, some measure of the scheme's success in 'fast tracking' high potential graduates.

More broadly, these figures indicate two factors, first that the non-graduate ACPO officer is becoming something of a rarity, a process that has accelerated quite dramatically in a relatively short space of time; secondly that the Bramshill Scholarship Scheme continues to figure as an important feature in the profile of the modern police manager, although it will inevitably decline as the system unwinds and the numbers of incoming graduates increases. In that sense one could look upon the scheme as a success, in so far as the early investment in those identified as potential high-fliers would be seen to have paid off in eventual career attainment. We must of course be cautious in this area. To begin with, the high ratio of Bramshill scholars within ACPO may reflect a form of 'self-fulfilling prophecy' in which it is not so much a case of the scholarship experience itself leading to career enhancement, but rather a case of perceived talent being 'rewarded' both by a scholarship and by subsequent promotions. Furthermore, there is the question of those scholars who do not achieve ACPO rank — who of course can still make a valuable contribution to police management — but this is an area in need of further investigation.

As regards higher education, again an issue examined earlier, another interesting comparison between our findings and those of Reiner's relates to the *type* of degree officers have undertaken. Reiner found that half of the graduate chiefs had studied law at university. In our sample just over a quarter of ACPO members held law degrees; there was a much wider spread of subjects studied, including an emphasis on social and political science. Arguably, this indicates that ACPO members now exhibit a much wider and broadening higher educational experience than has been the case in the past, perhaps some sign of the new demands created by 'new public management'. The traditional preference for law appears to be giving way to one which sees some value in a greater appreciation of contextual and environmental study, seemingly more relevant to the modern police manager than legal technique.

While the GES and the Bramshill Scholarship Scheme have both been concerned directly or indirectly with increasing the numbers of graduates in the police service, the Special Course was set up in a way as a means of *compensating* for what was at the time of its formation the dearth of highly educated officers in the police service. The Special Course was established at Bramshill in 1962, and was designed for constables selected through a process of extended interview as showing high potential. It was initially a year-long programme (subsequently reduced) of both 'academic' and professional education which, on completion, would lead automatically to promotion to sergeant and rapidly on from that point to inspector. Therefore, the Special Course has been both a broadening educational experience and a mechanism for accelerated promotion (later to become the Accelerated Promotion Scheme itself), although as regards the former it should be noted that graduate officers have also been attached to the Course.

While the Special Course has had a mixed record of success (Hill and Smithers, 1991), our research at least found a high degree of approval from those ACPO members who had experienced it. In fact 41 per cent of our sample had taken the Special Course (admittedly some considerable time ago), which is some measure of success in itself. More significantly, members were generally positive about the Course and of the view that it had contributed in a valuable way to their career development. Typical comments were:

... having experienced a year on the Special Course, when I came out I was a much better, rounded person than when I went in ... the year on the Special Course I thought for me was superb (M01).

[the] Special Course, [was] generally very useful, it opened my eyes to a lot of things that I didn't really know about ... exposed me to wider people, wider forces, wider issues ... (M15).

It is interesting that a number of members valued the Special Course experience because of its broader *educational* rather than specifically *professional* grounding, interesting because, as we shall see, the tension between 'education' and 'training' is one that frequents the debate on the proper role of higher police training. One member expressed it thus:

> The content of the courses I found largely relevant, and certainly the Special Course [had] a heavy emphasis on the education and learning side, rather than a professional course, and I enjoyed that aspect of it very much (M02).

Again, we must use caution in assessing the effectiveness of the Special Course as a mechanism for selecting and supporting potential high-fliers. A fuller picture would be gained by examining not just those Special Course graduates who have succeeded in reaching senior office but also those who have not, either through failure to gain promotions or through wastage to the service. That consideration was outside of the scope of this particular research project. Furthermore, as with the GES, there may be a self-fulfilling prophecy at work so that *selection* for the Special Course is equally if not more important than the Course experience itself. Nevertheless, on balance there is sufficient evidence to support the view that this particular mechanism behind 'becoming an ACPO member' has had a degree of success.

SUITED FOR THE TOP?: SELECTING 'ACPO MATERIAL'

The identification of potential high-fliers is a long game; it can be many years before that potential is realised, if at all, in senior appointment. ACPO members must survive a more immediate and direct hurdle before attaining high office: the Extended Interview (EI). It is effectively a requirement that all officers eligible for ACPO rank must undertake the Strategic Command Course (SCC), the most senior of the police management courses run at Bramshill Staff College (discussed below). In order to be offered a place on the SCC candidates must first of all be selected through the EI, an annual round of selections for suitably qualified superintendents (formerly chief superintendents before the rank was abolished in the wake of the Sheehy Inquiry (Home Office,

1993a). In that sense the EI occupies an extremely crucial position in the process of becoming an ACPO member.

The EI method has been used in the police service since 1962 and descends from practice elsewhere such as civil service and military selection procedures (Evans, 1990). It has been used for the GES and Special Course schemes, although it is its role in selection for the SCC which is of significance in this context. The EI is held at residential assessment centres and involves three days of written exercises, 'objective' tests of ability and a variety of group discussions and simulations. The assessors are serving ACPO officers and external specialists who grade the candidates in three categories: those recommended for the next SCC, those recommended to a later SCC and those not recommended for the SCC.

Given that so much rests upon the EI in career advancement it is not surprising that the process has been the subject of close scrutiny. Criticism has been made of the lack of 'openness' of assessors' reports and the shortage of feedback in the system (Tomkins and Brunstrom, 1995; Evans, 1990), and the process has been the subject of continuing review. However, our research found a high level of support for the EI method of selection amongst ACPO members. Of course we must be careful in this respect: we solicited the views of those who had been *successful* in the EI, and therefore might not view the process as critically as those who had failed to gain the positive rating. Nevertheless, the breadth of positive views on the EI across our sample does indicate a highly regarded selection machinery, an assessment which, as we shall see, contrasts sharply with members' views of other dimensions of the process of becoming an ACPO member. Members were asked to state their assessments of the EI as an effective selection mechanism. There were few negative comments overall. Typical comments were as follows:

Very demanding, very draining, it was everything that I had been led to believe it would be in terms of its ability to get to the real you ... having seen it from both sides now, it's an exceptionally fair process and they bend over backwards to make sure it is and the commitment from the assessors, again I think, sells the system to me (M06).

It is probably the most thorough and vigorous selection process in any profession ... (M09).

I approve of EI, it's not easy but then it shouldn't be easy, I think actually it should be a minimum test to get to a certain level in the police service. I actually think the EI test should be applied to get to Superintendent, because there are a significant number of underemployed Superintendent ranks around the country that will start to erode and wither now, there's so many less of them, the competition will excise some of the less able (M31).

There were however a number of critical comments which, while not dismissive of the EI, raised some reservations about its contribution to senior selection. One view was that it tends towards uniformity in selection and inhibits those who do not fit easily into the 'mould'. Contentiously, one respondent claimed:

... the only difficulty I have with EI is that I am concerned that it is not very easily capable of dealing with the individual who doesn't fit into a mould. I do believe it rejects some of our most talented people because they are irregular in their thought patterns or whatever. I'm concerned that it does tend to bring people along who fit whatever the preconception is of what senior police officers are like (M04).

One respondent raised concerns about the dangers of a 'cultural bias' in the tasks set for the candidates, at least in the past:

... the tests that I did which would have been about two years ago and which I understand are in the process of being changed, include some tests which I feel are very unfair, for me the general knowledge test was fine if you were a white middle-class person who'd probably been to a red brick or Oxford University, lots of mythology type questions and lots of who wrote Tin-Tin type things and I really had some problems with the ethos of the general knowledge test, maybe that reflects that my general knowledge was poor, but I just felt I didn't like where it was coming from. The test I did included a written exercise that involved shipping tractors and big items of vehicles to Russia so we had nice crunchy male objects, tractors going, various vehicle bits and pieces where I didn't understand the words, what the different parts of the tractor were, then the letter of complaint we had to deal with concerned yet again a garage with a noisy set of lorries and they used words in the letter that I didn't know what they meant, now I'm not saying that all men would know them either but it was just this, where were these people coming from in terms of issues that they were presenting to a wide range of candidates, some of whom were not brought up in an environment playing with tractors or cars or whatever (M42).

Having cited these criticisms it should be noted that those concerned remained, overall, in favour of the EI system as better than the alternatives. As such, this component of the process of becoming an ACPO member remains one which ACPO officers themselves are generally supportive of as an effective means of assessing those who are made of 'ACPO material'.

TRAINING FOR THE TOP: SENIOR POLICE TRAINING AND EDUCATION

Selection through the EI leads automatically to a place on the Strategic Command Course. The Strategic Command Course (SCC), so-named, began in 1996; it was formerly entitled the Senior Command Course, but was for a brief period (1994–96) called the Strategic Leadership Development Programme. The SCC is, as mentioned, the most senior of the police management courses run at the police staff college at Bramshill. It is, along with the Special Course, the only course to be entered via the EI selection process. Attendance and completion of the SCC however, unlike the Special Course, is effectively a compulsory stage of the career path of officers seeking ACPO rank. This follows the recommendations of the Home Affairs Select Committee (Home Office, 1989). The Committee was concerned with improving the quality of senior management in the police and considered completion of the SCC to be a necessary precondition of progression to ACPO rank. ACPO officers on that date who had not attended the then Senior Command Course were required to attend a chief police officers' course, a one-off arrangement in 1991 which acted as a 'catch-up' programme.

The SCC was a six month residential course, although it has since been reduced to 14 weeks. It is for those officers who are seen as having the potential to reach the highest ranks of the police service. It is also open to overseas officers, civilian equivalents in the police service and members of the armed services. The course is assessed through written work, exercises, participation, a placement in industry with an external association and general abilities that are demonstrated throughout the course. The assessment process is also based on the core competencies identified as essential for ACPO rank. These are strategic thinking, analytical skills, interpersonal skills, flexibility, influence, communication skills, decision-making and resilience. The assessment system is, according to the College, fairly open and at the end of the course the Director of the SCC grades the officer and comments on the comparative abilities of the people on the course and their potential for future ACPO rank. A copy of this report is sent to the officer's chief constable, to the Home Office and, after comments have been included by Her Majesty's Inspectors of Constabulary (HMIC), accompanies applications made for a chief officer's post.

The focus of the SCC shifted in 1989 away from the role of assistant chief constables to also include the roles of chief constables (Barnes *et al.*, 1990). By doing this it was hoped to train officers in the environment in which they would be working, that is the environment of the top team in an increasingly political arena and in a period of increasing economic control. It indicated an important shift towards long term strategic thinking, (apparent in the change of course title) towards policy and philosophy and a move away from tactics and detail (ibid).

The aims of the SCC as outlined in the Bramshill portfolio (1996–7) are:

> not just concern with the development of strategic plans, but rather with the exercise of strategic leadership ... the course concentrates on the personal and interpersonal qualities required by a senior, influential member of a senior management team as well as on techniques of setting policy and strategy.

A further change in the SCC has been the accreditation of the course since 1996 by the Institute of Criminology at Cambridge. An additional four weeks of study after the course can result in a Postgraduate Diploma in Advanced Criminology. Take up of this option might be seen from one angle as modest (latest figures indicate that around one half of students opt to enrol on this programme), although this may be due to the high numbers of officers who already possess degrees, in some cases two.

Reservations about the SCC have been apparent for a considerable amount of time and unlike the EI where there was a high degree of support from officers, the SCC suffers from a high degree of criticism. Members of the 1994 Strategic Leadership Development Programme conducted some research into the selection process, in part due to a lack of clarity and shared understanding at key stages. They argued that the course was too long, and far longer than the majority of private sector courses which were run on a modular basis as and when required. Training, they felt, should be focused on individual needs rather than the 'scatter-gun' approach (Bramshill Police Staff College, 1994). This it seems is especially important when considering the needs of senior managers, many of whom will have experienced very different career paths and will have very different training needs. Criticism was also levelled at the secret nature of grading, assessment and final report. There was also a suggestion of the SCC following selection to ACPO rank rather than the other way round, 'human resources should be trained for a job they are required to do, not one they might be required to do' (ibid). Of course, this view can be challenged; there is a case for training to precede selection, in the sense that the training process may itself actualise potential not previously apparent.

In our research we invited ACPO members to comment on their experience of senior police training via the SCC and more generally their views on Bramshill as a senior police institution. In representing these views however two qualifications must be borne in mind. First, our research did not involve a full evaluation of the SCC as such, only participants' assessments of the SCC, valuable as that may be. Secondly, our sample was a representative one, stratified by age amongst other factors and therefore reflects the views both of those who may have taken the course many years ago and some who may have taken the course very recently. However, what we can provide is a cross section of views from the current crop of chief officers of their experience of senior police training just prior to them being appointed to ACPO rank.

Members' views on the SCC were interlaced with their broader assessments of Bramshill as an institution in terms of the 'philosophy' of the college and the direction in which it is going (or should be going in their opinion). In this respect a majority of our sample, 68 per cent (28), expressed negative views on Bramshill and senior training, 27 per cent (11) expressed views which can at best be called 'mixed'; only 5 per cent (2) were clearly positive about the Bramshill experience.

Criticism of the SCC took a variety of forms. Some thought that there was a weak relationship between what training senior police officers need and what the course itself provided. For example:

> There had been no kind of training needs analysis done, you know, 'what do we need to train these people with if they are going to become ACPO and therefore they must learn this, they must learn that' and build the course around the training need (M01).

Another form of criticism related to the teaching and learning strategies employed by the College, which had become increasingly 'facilitative' over the years:

> I had some concerns about the Senior Command Course . . . there was much too heavy an emphasis on self analysis and on self development . . . the thrust of the course was to be about being a team member, it was to prepare people for membership of a police top team. I'm not sure that it actually adequately fulfilled that function (M13).

Related to this was the concern that the course did not contain clear performance measurement or assessment:

> There was very little pressure, no sense of graduating from it and no testing whatsoever of the various people who were on it (M26).

We should perhaps reiterate in the light of these views that a change of process is under way within senior police training and that some of these concerns are being addressed.

A number of members (15 per cent) referred to the course as being 'too long' and in this respect the SCC was compared unfavourably by some with senior executive training in other sectors, such as civil service training — indeed, a view was expressed that senior police officers could be trained alongside their fellow executive trainees in other organisations, an interesting view in the light of the traditional belief that policing is somehow 'unique' as a public service.

What appeared to underpin these specific criticisms of the SCC, however, was a more fundamental concern about the role and direction of Bramshill as an *institution*. Members themselves differed over whether Bramshill should adopt a specifically 'training' philosophy in

which courses are geared to specific competencies, or whether it should
be based upon a broader 'educational' philosophy parallel to university-
type programmes of study. Linked to this is the question of whether
Bramshill should aspire to be a 'police university', a centre of
excellence with a framework of courses built around a research culture.
Whichever way, a significant number of members considered that there
was confusion over what role and direction the College itself does or
should adopt. Thirty per cent of our sample considered Bramshill to be
an institution suffering a form of 'identity crisis'. For example:

> ... it is in danger of losing its way ... it is not the university of the
> service, it's not the staff college of the service and I'm not quite sure
> what it is, it's drifting and it's drifting quite badly (M26).

> I have watched it go through fashions, it doesn't know what it wants
> to be and still doesn't know what it wants to be, it wants to be an open
> school of experience and learning as a university but it wants to do it
> with the discipline of a training school (M01).

What is perceived to be a lack of direction and clarity of role with the
College is also associated with the belief that Bramshill suffers from a
low 'academic base' — 20 per cent of members commented critically
on the academic standing of the College — and a neglect of a research
orientation which makes it difficult for it to lay claim to be a centre of
excellence. Part of the reason for this may have lain with formal
restrictions on Bramshill staff to publish research papers without Home
Office approval, hardly a framework for an active research culture.
Indeed two prominent academic specialists in police studies had given
evidence to a Home Affairs Select Committee in 1989 that they
personally had withdrawn from applications for academic posts at
Bramshill because of the constraints on the dissemination of research
(Home Office, 1989).

These criticisms, however, should be taken in the context of on-going
developments at the College and in particular the creation of units such
as the 'National Crime Faculty' which, while still in its infancy, does
seem to offer the potential of a 'research arm' for the College. The Crime
Faculty is concerned with both the provision of advanced investigative
training and with the establishment of a database of serious crimes and
crime pattern analysis, practically oriented but research-based neverthe-

less. The importance of a research dimension within Bramshill is clearly acknowledged internally. A senior member of the College interviewed as part of our research put it this way:

> I think we are beginning to make people understand that you actually can't be a training establishment or any kind of learning institution which is trying to keep people at the forefront of developments in a field without actually having some sort of research capabilities ... (E14).

It is also important to acknowledge that in other respects the SCC and Bramshill were regarded by some members to have made some very positive contributions to their own career development. One ACPO member expressed it this way:

> I think on balance the whole experience actually did I feel prepare me for what was coming my way in terms of the whole ACPO thing, and I think as the years have moved on in the ACPO position I found it beneficial to reflect back on it (M41).

Even many of those critical of the SCC overall referred to positive aspects of the experience, above all the opportunity to form 'networks' with others who were, like them, to move on to senior ranks. Twenty per cent of members cited networking as a useful outcome of the Bramshill experience. While the SCC might be an expensive way to facilitate networking, its contribution in this respect is not to be dismissed too lightly.

In concluding this section it must be emphasised again that the views represented do relate in some cases to experiences gained some time ago and should not necessarily be taken as part of an assessment of the current provision of senior training at Bramshill. Furthermore, the whole police training establishment is at the time of writing in the throes of a fundamental review, with radical changes likely in the future. Nevertheless, the issues raised by those interviewed as part of our research are relevant to an appreciation of the processes by which police officers 'get to the top'. This takes us naturally to the next and final stage in that respect: appointment to ACPO rank.

GETTING TO THE TOP: APPOINTMENT AT FORCE LEVEL

Each of the police forces in England and Wales, with the exception of the Metropolitan Police Service, is attached, constitutionally under the 'tripartite system', to a local police authority (LPA), the other two legs being the chief officer and the Home Office. There have been significant changes in recent years to the constitution and membership of the LPAs as a result of the Police and Magistrates' Courts Act 1994 (Jones and Newburn, 1997), but one constitutional function of the LPAs has remained untouched: the responsibility to make all appointments of police officers to ACPO rank. Thus while all appointments to ranks below the level of assistant chief constable are made internally, appointments above that rank are made by the external committee of the LPA — although typically such committees are chaired by the chief constable.

The ACPO appointments process has been the subject of heated criticism in the past. To put it mildly, the whole system has been described as an 'unprofessional lottery' (Tomkins and Brunstrom, 1995). A number of facets of the process have been singled out for criticism. First, concerns have been raised about the role of Her Majesty's Inspectors of Constabulary (HMIC) in the appointments process. Once an application has been made by a candidate for an ACPO post the HMI attached to the region in which that force is based prepares a report of his or her suitability. This report is based on a personal assessment made by the candidate's current chief constable, and of course reports from the SCC and any other information the regional HMI may have picked up over time. The report is then presented to the Home Office, who maintain a list of 'suitable' candidates for senior appointment which can be used to approve or not approve shortlists of applicants put together by the police authority prior to interview (it should be noted that the police authority's actual choice must be approved after interview by the Home Secretary). One concern is that the report contains a grading of candidates by HMIC according to a scale of three grades presenting levels of 'readiness' for an ACPO position. This grading is not disclosed to candidates or the selecting police authorities. The secrecy surrounding this process and the potential for central, Home Office, influence over local appointments has as a consequence drawn criticism (ibid). A second area of concern has been the wide variety of procedures adopted by police authorities for interviews of shortlisted candidates. Some of these border on the bizarre, as we shall make clear shortly. More generally, questions of fairness, equity and objectivity have been raised in the light of equal opportunities controversies, issues which have recently led to the Home Office drawing up detailed guidelines on selection procedures for chief officer appointments (Home Office, 1995b).

Our research would certainly add weight to this chorus of criticism. In fact, of all the stages of 'becoming an ACPO member' considered in this study it is the process of appointment at force level around which there is most consensus — and it is very much a negative consensus. A number of features of the appointments process were raised by ACPO members in our sample. First, there was concern that senior appointments could be made by people outside of the policing profession:

It's absolutely daft to involve well meaning amateurs in the selection process and the involvement of the police authority is just an antiquated old fashioned idea and I would do away with it. The person I am going to work for and to is the Chief Constable and is there a Chief Executive in the world who is going to allow somebody else to pick the people who are going to work for him and I would suggest that the answer is no and so the selection of the Assistant Chief Constable I think should be entirely within the service, there is no role for the amateur to play (M01).

Some outlined what seemed to be, by any standards, questionable practices by police authorities:

I can think of one authority in particular where once they'd asked the question and you gave the answer nothing happened after that, because (a) the interviewer didn't understand the question he or she was asking, and this is quite serious and (b) they didn't understand the answer that was coming back again ... (M07).

... the worst interview I had was actually going into a room where there were 28 people and you're sat on a chair with a big horseshoe around you in a massive room and you could hardly see the person who was actually speaking to you, in terms of spotting who it was amongst the crowd. I mean it was literally a scan round when somebody started talking hoping you were going to latch onto the right person (M44).

... they [candidates] had one minute to read the questions, and they would then be required to follow him into the room, where the full Police Authority is assembled and he would have to speak for five minutes on each question. As I say, addressing the full authority. That was the selection mechanism. When it came to my turn to go in, 42 members of the Police Authority were in various states of, I think it fair to say, disinterest, two were certainly reading newspapers, one was asleep, several were smoking and seemed to be in a very relaxed state, more anxious about where the next pot of peppermints was coming from, than probably the next candidate (M27).

In fact, as mentioned, members relayed to us some quite amusing stories about the interview experience, including 'trial by dinner':

Somebody rang a bell or whatever and half way through the meal you got up and took your plate with you wherever and moved seats and I didn't really believe it but it happened just like that, they did try their best to make it a reasonable time, you know, so when you'd finished the soup, you changed over but you'd have to get up half way through the main course and take your plate with you and then move on to the next seat and sit between two new people (M10).

In this respect it is interesting to note that the new Home Office guidelines refer specifically to the dangers of 'informal contacts' between interviewees and members of the interview panel through 'social functions' (Home Office, 1995b:9). As regards current ACPO members however it is not surprising in all of these circumstances that candidates often expected that the actual appointment was in effect a *fait accompli*:

I have a deep suspicion that outside London it is carved up, it's who you know, there's no sour grapes here at all but I have this deep suspicion, anecdotes, everyone knows that I think it's basically done on phone calls because in the absence of feedback and what's said about you being revealed makes me deeply suspicious you know, why can't it be as an open system? It's not stopped me from applying for things, simply that I have no real confidence that it's on merit, it's on who you know (M17).

It is interesting to note in this latter statement that reference is made to appointments in London. Perhaps ironically, the force with by far the largest number of ACPO officers, the Metropolitan Police Service, appoints officers through a panel made up largely of senior police officers (the commissioner and assistant commissioners). There is therefore a major discrepancy between the machineries for appointing ACPO officers inside and outside of London, one largely internal to the profession, one mainly external. However, with the creation of the new Police Authority for London, an idea long supported by the Labour Party (and now, it should be noted, very much favoured by senior Metropolitan Police Officers), it is inevitable that this situation will change in the future.

Having made this point, it has to be stated that according to some of those interviewed, appointments in the 'provincial' forces, despite the role played by police authority members, were largely at the behest of the chief. Commenting on one experience, an ACPO member read the situation in this way:

> I think the panel without exception would have acquiesced to the chief constable (M06).

Indeed, one chief interviewed was quite clear about the role his preferences played in appointing staff to his team:

> ... yet I'm not allowed to choose my own senior staff, which is obviously a nonsense. Except of course that I do choose, or powerfully advise ... My authority here wouldn't dream of appointing anybody without a great deal of advice and work with me (E02).

In relation to this issue it should be stressed that a sizeable number of those interviewed in our sample did state support for the *principle* of local police authority participation in the appointments process.

It is clear from such statements that what is at issue is more to do with the quality of the process than the fact of local/external involvement in that process. All of these point at the very least to problems of inconsistency and arbitrariness in the appointments process, issues which may or may not be resolved with the production of Home Office guidelines referred to earlier. Of more relevance, however, are the potential changes to the process which might take place with the changes to the police authorities inaugurated through the Police and Magistrates' Courts Act 1994. This has meant that police authorities now have many fewer members (normally only 17), and that this includes new 'independent members' (Jones and Newburn, 1997). It will be interesting to see whether these new members will contribute to the 'professionalisation' of the appointments process given that many come from business backgrounds. As yet this is not possible to gauge, but given their role in other areas of police authority business, particularly in relation to financial management (ibid), the signs are that the whole exercise could be a more challenging one than was the case when the ACPO members in our sample were appointed.

Having made these points it is important to clarify that despite the problems identified above this was not taken by most members to be an indication that those appointed by these means were somehow unworthy of ACPO rank. In fact many members expressed the view that the processes which preceded formal interview, and in particular the EI, ensured that those who were eventually to make the appointments shortlist had already established their merit as people who qualify for an ACPO position.

> ... it's a local decision basically; they're picking ... from a group of people, all of whose professional conduct and professional performance has been certified by the Inspectorate, therefore it's a matter of preference, in terms of personal qualities (M27).

This view would be consistent with one expressed by a number of respondents, that one means of professionalising the appointments process for senior officers is for this to involve a central appointing body to undertake the initial stages of appointing to ACPO rank. Such a body would select a 'pool' of officers as confirmed ACPO ranks from which the LPAs could take their pick according to their particular requirements. In such a system, it would not be for the LPAs to identify ACPO potential, that would be a decision already made for them by the central professional body. However, while such an approach might have attractions in terms of professionalising the process, it would entail the diminution of the role played by the LPAs in ACPO appointments, on the top of what some would argue to be the already weakened status of the LPAs and the growth of centralisation under the new legislation for the governance of the police (Loveday, 1995).

CONCLUSION

In this chapter we have sought to examine the processes by which one 'becomes' a member of ACPO. Adopting primarily a 'users' perspective, i.e., the views of those who have experienced the various stages involved in 'getting to the top' in police management, we have provided one means by which each stage can be assessed, particularly in the light of current debates on the future mechanisms of recruiting and training officers for senior management.

In addition to the specific questions raised here about the mechanics of selection and training of senior police officers, there are questions of wider significance. First, is it necessary to continue with the 'single-entry' system of police appointments whereby each officer appointed to ACPO rank has in each and every case started his or her career as a uniformed constable? Is it not the case that many of the processes under examination here, in some cases processes criticised by those who have experienced them, stem from the absence of a 'direct-entry' system for police managers as found in most European countries, as discussed above? It has been argued that the adoption of more flexible career-entrance points within the police service could enhance both the process of appointing senior police managers and provision for the great majority of officers who will remain in the lower ranks, undertaking 'front-end' police work. We shall not rehearse this debate here as it has been discussed by one of the authors elsewhere (Leishman and Savage, 1993a), but it is a debate which tends to be rekindled periodically.

A second and even more radical question concerns the officer-status of senior police managers. Is it necessary for ACPO postholders to have been in every case a sworn-in police officer? We have already seen the emergence in recent years of the senior 'civilian' police manager appointed with professional expertise in areas such as personnel management, finance and administration. Such appointments are challenging the traditional boundaries between 'officers' and 'civilians'; ACPO as an organisation has recently recognised this with the creation of associate member status for certain senior non-police role-holders (Barton, 1996). The opening up of ACPO posts to non-sworn officers could provide a more flexible environment for the appointment of even the most senior police managers. More generally, as senior public sector managers across the public services increasingly find themselves confronting similar problems, requiring equivalent skills, is there not scope for cross-sector appointments and the wider circulation of senior managers throughout the public sector? This would not just be a case of opening up the police service to different types of senior personnel: it could be argued that other areas of the public sector would have as much to gain by employing those with police experience, or at least with a 'can-do' attitude often associated with police culture. The Chairman of the Audit Commission commented recently that:

> The police have always been among the Commission's most enthusiastic partners, showing a great willingness to analyse what they do and a readiness to change (Audit Commission, 1995:6).

Whilst we might have pointed to problems within the machinery for the selection and training of senior police officers, of how many senior professional groups in the public sector could one argue this?

We now know what procedures and mechanisms underpin the process of 'becoming an ACPO member'. In the next chapter we shall examine how those thus appointed operate on the policy-making and policy-shaping circuit.

Chapter 5
ACPO and Policy-shaping at the Local Level

INTRODUCTION

A central issue of police governance is the question of who or what shapes policing policy. This in turn is linked to the question of who *should* make or shape policing policy. These questions have been at the core of debates about British policing for many years, often overlapping, although not necessarily coterminous, with the issue of police account-ability. Yet with few exceptions (Jones *et al* 1994) there is little research evidence or even close analysis of the external and internal processes engaged in police policy-making. There is no shortage of what we might call 'tendential' analysis, which draws inferences from broader struc-tural or legal changes in the world of policing as to the general 'drift' of policing policy. As we have seen previously in this study, the best example of this is the 'centralisation thesis', much traded in the debate over the Police and Magistrates' Courts Act 1994 (PMCA), according to which the constitutional reforms embodied in the Act were seen to herald a new and more acute phase in the longer term 'centralisation' of British policing (Reiner, 1991 and 1992; Loveday, 1995). Important as such discourse has been (and we shall return to it later in this book), it has not always been accompanied by an empirical assessment of the extent to which *formal* changes in constitutional status of the police have impacted on the *substance* of policing policy. A full assessment of the policy process requires a 'grounded' analysis which takes cognisance of participants' 'reading' of sources of influence over policy as they have affected the decision-making process.

In this and the following chapter we shall address the basic question of '*who shapes policing policy?*'. In order to do this we will differentiate two levels of police policy and policy-making. On the one hand there is policing policy *at the local level*, policy which operates at the level of 'police forces' or 'police services', i.e., in terms of the 43 individual police organisations in England and Wales. Policing policies at the local level are the responsibility of chief police officers and their local police authorities (LPAs). On the other hand there is policing policy *at the national level*, policy and policies which relate to the police service as a whole. These may take the form of legislation, directives or 'guidelines' which are set by national bodies and agencies, such as the Home Office, Her Majesty's Inspectorate of Constabulary (HMIC), the Audit Commission, local authority associations and national police agencies (National Criminal Intelligence Service (NCIS), National Police Training (NPT) and so on) and, of course, ACPO. Policy-making at the local level cannot be separated from national police policy-making because, clearly, a major concern for local police policy-makers is the extent to which local policies should reflect national policies. Given the doctrine of constabulary independence (CI), the issue is the *extent* to which national policies influence, shape or govern local policing policy. It is this question which is the central concern of this chapter. In the following chapter we shall turn to the wider agenda of the shaping of national policy on policing and related areas. In both respects our focus will be on the role of ACPO in shaping policing policy and the ways in which that role has changed over time and why.

As we have seen in chapter 1, the term 'policy' is a contested concept; generally there are three competing and distinctive meanings of what constitutes policy. Policy can be seen as a set of goals to be pursued (Fischer, 1980:183); as a set of actions embracing its decisions (and 'non-decisions'), goals and effects (Dye, 1992:2); and as a set of constructed symbols (Edelman, 1985). Policy is thus all about what policy-makers want, what they do and/or what they appear to do. These multiple meanings are littered within the academic and, moreover, the so-called 'real-world' discourse of policy-making, including police policy-making, at both local and national levels.

No discussion of policing policy in the British context can ignore a central 'given' in the discourse of British policing, the principle of *constabulary independence*. Lurking around every corner of police governance, whether that be at local or national level, lies the 'untouchable' doctrine of the 'constitutional independence' of the police officer, whether that officer be an operational constable or a chief officer of police. The legal foundation for this still rests with what has become known as the 'Denning doctrine' (Lustgarten, 1986). This thesis stems from case law and has been embodied into a constitutional principle that chief police officers cannot be subject to any political authority in the determination of policing policies and operations and must remain fully independent of any such authority in the exercise of their duties. Lord Denning's original and infamous judgment, stated that, with reference to the powers of a chief constable:

Like every constable in the land, he [sic] should be, and is, independent of the executive ... he is not the servant of anyone, save of the law itself, no Minister of the Crown can tell him that he must, or must not, keep observation on the place or that he must, or must not, prosecute this man or that one. Nor can any police authority tell him so. The responsibility for law enforcement lies on him. He is answerable to law and to the law alone (*R* v *MPC, ex parte Blackburn* [1968] 1 All ER 763).

Much has been written on CI, most notably in relation to its legal foundations (Lustgarten, 1986; Marshall, 1965 and 1984) and its central role in the structures of police governance and accountability (Jefferson and Grimshaw, 1984; Reiner, 1992). The 'Denning doctrine' has been taken as an axiomatic foundation of the constitutional principle of CI. Its status has been the subject of much debate and indeed has been heavily challenged. Regarding the quote above Lustgarten (1986) has commented that:

Seldom have so many errors of law and logic been compressed into one paragraph (ibid:64).

Notwithstanding the legal propriety of the doctrine of CI, there is no doubting the discursive and political power of the principle, inside and outside of the police service. Most certainly the discourse of senior police officers is riddled with Denning-type interpretations of the role of the chief officer and his/her relationship with other authorities (Reiner, 1991; Savage *et al.*, 1999; see also chapter 7). Put simply the doctrine of CI presumes that chief police officers are fully independent from other bodies when it comes to a matter of police decisions or policing policies. Our own research on ACPO has exposed a deep seam within the discourse of chief officers which constellates around the construction of CI. For example, one former President of ACPO stated:

> the Chief Constable is autonomous in his [sic] command and that is a very important aspect of the constitution of this country . . . the chief constable's operational command . . . cannot be usurped by anybody apart from a court of law . . . this independence of the police service is unique to this country . . . and I think that is the strength of the British police service, that it is not politically directed or manipulated . . . it is a very sacred thing (P12).

The doctrine of CI has held sway despite the major structural changes in British policing over the past decade or so. Most notable in this respect are the reformed constitutions and responsibilities of the local police authorities and the Home Secretary contained in the PMCA (discussed in chapter 1) on the one hand, and the formation of the new national police agencies on the other. The development of national police agencies has inevitably shaken the old foundations of the essentially locally based nature of British policing. The creation of NPT, responsible for coordinating the core training of officers of all ranks, the NCIS, a body which coordinates criminal intelligence on serious crimes, and the National Crime Squad, a centralised criminal investigation unit, have compromised to an extent the local autonomy of the 43 separate police services of England and Wales. At the very least, local police services have had to accede a degree of policy-making power to those national agencies. However, despite these developments, the quintes-sentially *local* nature of British policing is still evident, whether in reality or rhetoric, amply shielded (or shrouded) by the doctrine of CI.

In the remainder of this chapter we shall examine the local police policy-making process as follows: first, we will consider the role of *policy-makers*, those actively charged with the formation of policing policy at the level of the police force/service; secondly, we will discuss the role of *policy-shapers* in terms of the respective roles of the national agencies which act as key 'players' in the policing policy world. This will allow us to focus more particularly on the role of ACPO and its relevance to local policing policy.

POLICE POLICY-MAKERS AT THE LOCAL LEVEL: THE 'ACPO TEAM' AND LOCAL AGENDA-SETTING

Determining exactly *who* governs policy at the level of local police forces or 'services' is not easy. To begin with, police research has long ago demonstrated that policing is an activity which is steeped in *ground level discretion*, in the sense that officers at the 'lowest' levels of the organisation have a very substantial degree of discretion over decision-making whatever the 'diktats' from supervisors and managers. In the famous words of Wilson, 'the police department has the special property ... That within it discretion increases as one moves down the hierarchy' (Wilson, 1968:7). Whatever the other implications of this 'special property' of the police (Reiner, 1997), from the point of view of policy analysis it means that there is the capacity within policing for a high degree of dissonance between *policy* as set from 'above' and what actually transpires in terms of the delivery of policing at ground level — an acute form of (potential) discrepancy between 'policy' and 'implementation'. This means that there is a danger that the *significance* of police policy-making can be overstated — to put it bluntly, it may not matter who makes, or who shapes, policing policy if that policy is ineffective in guiding or even affecting activity at ground level. Another complicating factor in determining who governs local policy-making in the police is that police governance, as has been made clear in chapter 1, is a moving show. The PMCA in particular has introduced a framework which allows a degree of local variation in the way that policing policy is formed in terms of the respective roles performed by the chief officer and the local police authority; those respective roles are also changing over time within police areas, as we shall see below. This makes it very difficult to draw up a standard or even typical model of local policy-formation within police services.

With these points in mind, some broad patterns can be identified. At centre stage of local police service policy-making is the 'ACPO team'. The ACPO team is made up of the ACPO-rank officers in each police service. In most services this involves the chief constable, deputy chief

constable and between two and four assistant chief constables — in the
Metropolitan Police Service, however, the ACPO team is vastly larger.
The numbers in each ACPO team has fallen since the mid-1990s as a
result of attempts to reduce management overheads and 'streamline'.
This has also involved the transfer of what were former ACPO staff
responsibilities to specialist senior civilian staff, including personnel,
training, finance and administration. In some areas the ACPO team itself
forms what is called the 'Policy Group' or 'Policy Team', responsible
for all major planning and policy formation for the organisation.
Increasingly, as a reflection of the 'civilianisation' of senior functions,
the Policy Team now includes figures such as Directors of Finance,
Personnel and Administration (or 'Corporate Services'). In other words,
the 'top team' is now not necessarily a 'police only' body as was the
case in the past. Nevertheless, within the police organisation it is still
the ACPO team which forms the nucleus of service policy-making,
hence its being often referred to throughout the organisation as the
'Command Team'. How such teams operate clearly varies substantially.
On matters of 'style' one respondent explained how he had experienced
two very different regimes:

> [Force named] where I've come from is very, very formal, you know
> almost the Assistant Chief Constables stand to attention for the Chief
> Constable ... here the Chief chairs it, but it is almost four friends
> sitting around saying 'right what's in the best interests of the force'
> with the Director of Finance (E23).

As the rigours of 'New Public Management' take a firmer grip on the
workings of the police service, there is little doubt that the militaristic
overtones of the 'Command Team' style of policy-making will give way
more and more to one closer to a 'Directorate' or 'Executive' model,
similar to that in other public sector organisations and, of course, the
private sector. However, CI, for the time being at least, ensures that
within this Directorate the ACPO team, and above all the chief officer,
will still hold sway. Nevertheless, the PMCA has brought about some
realignment of power in relation to service-level policy-making. The
Local Policing Plan process, as discussed in chapter 1, has created space
within which the local police authority can have a degree of influence
over annual policy-making/priority-setting for the service. The Local
Policing Plan is 'drafted' initially by the chief officer (and her/his ACPO

team) but then becomes the responsibility of the police authority. Research on the process of drawing up the policing plan (Jones and Newburn, 1997) indicates that the role played by LPAs differs from area to area, with some LPAs doing little more than 'rubber stamping' the chief's draft, whilst others have at least become 'junior partners' in developing the plan, in the sense of playing a relatively active role in the process. Since the time that research was undertaken it is highly likely that police authorities will have become *more* rather than less active partners.

Our 'case study' research certainly indicated that as far as the Policing Plan process is concerned there is most definitely a growing culture of *shared* responsibility between the ACPO team and the police authority, even if that may not yet be an equal share. The planning process in the case of this particular police service was outlined by one of the ACPO team:

The key meeting is a two-day planning seminar held in October where all the top managers from the force come together with a selected number from the Police Authority representing all the authority subcommittees and it's there that the current issues are debated and the Policing Plan for the following year begins to emerge and it's there that we are starting to think about what the financial consequences of any growth plans that we have will be. From then on in there is a very healthy day-to-day working relationship between officials within the force and within the Police Authority's office on the Policing Plan and also the five year Strategic Plan and that shapes all the policy development within the force (E20).

This view was reinforced by the Clerk to that Police Authority who stated that 'when the Chief takes the [authority] members away to do a Policing Plan you're there because its *our* Policing Plan' (E29). There is therefore evidence that, at least in terms of policy stemming from the Local Policing Plan, local policing policy can bear the mark not just of the ACPO team but also of the local police authority. Of course, much policing policy is determined outside of the Local Policing Plan process; nevertheless even those areas may, in the future, reflect the growing culture of shared responsibility for service-level policy-making.

Returning to the ACPO team, some comment should be made about their internal policy-making structures. There is no standard in this respect and most certainly, with the emergence of the senior civilian posts referred to earlier, there is constant change in the roles and responsibilities of the ACPO ranks. There are however certain typical service-level configurations. At the head of the organisation sits the chief constable, increasingly the 'chief executive' of the corporate body. The chief will have a deputy — a post which was to disappear at one stage but which, like some other ranks in the police service, has been reinvented — who will undertake many functions on behalf of the chief who will in most cases be away from the area, often on national ACPO business. The deputy also has statutory responsibility for complaints and discipline. There will then be the assistant chief constables, the number being dependent on force size but normally between two and four. The assistant chief constables (ACCs) are designated core responsibilities differently service-by-service, but some models, taken from actual police services, are as follows:

Police Service 'A':
assistant chief constable (Director of Operations); assistant chief constable (Support).

Police Service 'B':
assistant chief constable (Personnel and Training); assistant chief constable (Operations and Crime); assistant chief constable (Administration and Support).

Police Service 'C':
assistant chief constable (Crime and Support); assistant chief constable (Personnel and Training); assistant chief constable (Operations).

Police Service 'D':
assistant chief constable (Community and Internal Affairs); assistant chief constable (Crime Operations); assistant chief constable (Uniform Operations); assistant chief constable (Personnel and Training).

In our 'case study' the model was: assistant chief constable (Management and Training Services) and assistant chief constable (Operations). The assistant chief constable designations are important not only in terms of service-level policy-making but also in terms of ACPO as a *national* policy-making body. This is because it is common for ACPO members to 'pick up' national/regional ACPO committee and sub-committee work on the basis of their service-level responsibilities — the assistant chief constable responsible for Personnel and Training locally, for example, might be appointed to a subcommittee on foundation training. There is more than 'buggins turn' to this process. The work assistant chief constables do at national or regional ACPO levels is seen as an important part of their *career progression*. The chief constable in our case study was quite clear about the link between ACPO-organisational work and careers within ACPO: he saw it as one of his functions to encourage members of his ACPO team to work actively on the regional and national stages:

> ... it's good to be in the national scene, to be developing important policy and [to be involved in] working groups ... it's an important career development role ... (E22).

The work undertaken by the ACPO team on the national or regional ACPO front can assist in getting them 'known' around the other police services. This may be significant as ACPO officers must move around different services if they are to further their career; the rules governing ACPO appointments dictate that no officer can become a chief constable of a particular service without having served as an ACPO officer in a different police service.

The overlap between functions undertaken at the regional or national ACPO levels and the functional responsibilities of the ACPO team at local service-levels brings us to the wider issue of service policy-making. A central concern of this chapter is to discern the relative influence of the various national police policy-making bodies at the level of the local police service. One clear source of 'penetration' of ACPO national policy into service-level policy-making is through the activities of the ACPO team in national policy-making. Individuals within the ACPO team in virtually every local service will spend a great degree of their time on regional or national 'ACPO business'. Most chief officers view these activities as part and parcel of the ACPO role. In our research we found that in the majority of cases ACPO officers spend over 10 per cent of their time on committee or subcommittee work on behalf of ACPO. ACPO members are not therefore simply 'recipients' of ACPO policy from above but active participants in its formation. It should not be surprising, therefore, for ACPO as a body to be a major source of influence over service-level policy. It is the extent of such influence and the comparison between ACPO's influence and that of other national bodies which is the concern of the remainder of this chapter.

THE POLICY SHAPERS: NATIONAL AGENCIES AND
SERVICE-LEVEL POLICY-MAKING

In chapter 1 we identified a range of bodies as key players in the policing policy process and core shapers of policing policy: the Home Office/ Home Secretary, HMIC, the Audit Commission, the LPAs and, of course, ACPO. Each has differing degrees of influence over police policy- and decision-making and that influence has changed over time both absolutely and relatively. Assessing the extent and pattern of that influence is by no means a straightforward task. One research strategy is to take specific areas of policy and 'trace' or 'track' their origins and formation. This approach was adopted in the important study by Jones *et al.*, (1994). In this case the research focused on three areas of policy — the development of crime prevention, new policing responses to crimes against women and children and 'civilianisation' within the police service — and sought to assess the relative influence of various bodies, including the Home Office, HMIC, local authority associations, LPAs and police and community pressure groups, in each of these policy areas. Although this study was centrally concerned with policy-making at the *national* level (to be examined in chapter 6) it is of direct relevance in this chapter because of the authors' attempt to *compare* policy influence across these key agencies.

The research undertaken by Jones and his colleagues painted a mixed picture of the role of the various agencies in influencing policing and related policy-making. At centre stage was the Home Office, which was found to have exerted 'strong influence' on the initiation and develop-ment of policy in each of the policy areas (ibid:289). One key mechanism in this respect was the 'Home Office Circular', which, as was made clear in chapter 3, has become an important tool in 'enforcing' Home Office preferences and priorities. HMIC was found to have little role in the *initiation* of the policies in question, however, it was seen to have played an important part in the processes of policy implementation but only in one of the policy areas, the civilianisation of policing. They found that the local authority associations had had a 'mixed' level of influence on changes in policing policy (ibid:293). They had some success in *revising* the policy on civilianisation and had taken something of a *lead* role on raising the issue of crime prevention; however, they were not particularly successful in terms of policy *outcomes* which related to their particular agenda and preferences. The local authorities themselves they found had 'little or no influence on policy change in civilianisation, the response to crimes against women and children, or crime prevention' (ibid:296). Most significantly for our purposes, Jones *et al.* found that ACPO had an 'important' but not *dominant* influence on the policy areas in question. ACPO, they argued, had suffered some important 'defeats' (ibid:292) but had at least successfully *blocked* or had *revised* some of the policies which emerged in these areas of policing policy.

We will return to *national* policy-making, in particular ACPO's role within it, in the next chapter, but the study by Jones *et al.* does, within the present discussion, provide a useful 'comparative' reference point for our assessment of the levels of policy influence which the major national agencies associated with policing policy possess or have possessed. In order to apply this assessment to *service-level* policy-making we addressed 'policy influence' by seeking the views of *ACPO members*, as those with core responsibilities for drawing up service-level policing policies. We asked our sample of ACPO members questions about the extent of policy influence of each of the five bodies, the Home Office/Home Secretary, HMIC, the Audit Commission, LPAs and ACPO. We did this in two ways: first, members were asked to *rank* each of the bodies in terms of their relative influence over service-level policy-making; secondly, members were asked to *grade* each of the bodies in turn in terms of the extent of their influence along a three-bar scale of 'considerable', 'some' and 'negligible'.

Rank was chosen as a means of assessing how ACPO compares with other policy-shaping bodies in terms of policy influence. Each ACPO member in the sample was asked to rank-order each of the five bodies in terms of the extent to which they felt that they influence policy-making within their own police service. Rank-ordering in this context does have its limitations. 'Policy' of course can take many forms; it may be a matter of *which* policy. The rank order may vary according to the area of policy in question. Several respondents expressed some unease on these grounds; however, the vast majority found the rank-ordering of the five bodies in terms of policy influence, taking policy *in general*, fairly straightforward, in the sense that there was little hesitation amongst the sample in responding to the task. It should be noted that since the Metropolitan Police Service did not have a 'local police authority' as such at the time of the research, respondents from that Service were given the option of taking the Metropolitan Police

Committee as the nearest equivalent or other local bodies (e.g., London boroughs).

Each respondent was asked to rank order the level of influence of each body, 'one' being the highest in terms of rank order (in this sense a low numerical score indicates a more positive rating than a high score). Where scores were tied (i.e., agencies were considered to be of 'equal' influence) the scores were averaged. Figure 1 presents the aggregate scores accordingly.

Figure 1: Aggregated Rank Ordering of Influence of Each Body over Service-level Policy-making

HMIC	123.5
HOME OFFICE	88.5
LOCAL POLICE AUTHORITY	139.5
ACPO	123
AUDIT COMMISSION	140.5

Note: score of 1 = highest, score of 5 = lowest; total number of respondents = 41.

It is clear from these results that the Home Office is seen by far as the body which has most influence over service-level policy-making. ACPO and HMIC compete closely for second place, and LPAs and the Audit Commission for fourth. In the analysis of the data we also considered the rank-ordering along two variables, by *ACPO rank* and by *force/service size*. It was possible that significant patterns might be discernable in both respects. We found that the Home Office scored higher than the other bodies across the board, but that there was some slight variation in grading along rank and force-size dimensions with the other agencies. In terms of aggregate scores, assistant/deputy chief constables ranked ACPO second, behind the Home Office, whilst chief constables ranked them third, behind the Home Office and HMIC. Members from forces with less than 3,000 officers tended to rank ACPO higher on average than members from forces over 3,000: according to the points score ACPO was ranked second behind the Home Office in the smaller forces, but third, behind the Home Office and HMIC, in the larger forces. These variations are not substantial and indeed not statistically significant, so it is necessary to be cautious. Nevertheless, they might raise speculative questions: does ACPO become less important as a source of influence once one becomes a chief officer?; might this be connected with career aspirations?; is ACPO more relevant to the smaller police services?; do the bigger police services 'need' ACPO less? We shall return to some of these issues later.

Members were also asked to *grade* the five bodies in terms of whether they had *'negligible'*, *'some'* or *'considerable'* influence over local policy-making. This places the rank-ordering into context because a rank-order does not inform about the *extent* of influence as such. Figure 2 presents the results of this element of the survey.

Figure 2: Influence over Local Policy Making (%)

	HMIC	Home Office	Local Police Authorities	ACPO	Audit Commission
CONSIDERABLE	27	66	41	39	37
SOME	63	34	37	46	58
NEGLIGIBLE	10	0	22	15	5
TOTAL	100	100	100	100	100

Again these results testify to the power of the Home Office in influencing service-level policy-making. This reinforces the points made in chapters 1 and 2 about the growth in 'centralisation' although, as we have seen in other parts of this study, that growth should not be overstated or oversimplified. As regards the other bodies the picture is altogether more complicated, if not confusing. It is interesting to compare the degree of influence of the LPAs with that of HMIC, for example. Whilst LPAs 'score' more highly than HMIC in terms of them having 'considerable' influence — 41 per cent against 27 per cent respectively — LPAs do badly relative to HMIC when it comes to the percentage viewing their influence as 'negligible' — 22 per cent as against 10 per cent respectively. Clearly, there is a 'mixed message' in this regarding the LPAs. However, as we have argued earlier, this polarity in responses might reflect the extent to which the LPAs are 'on the move' in terms of policy influence as a result of the implementation of the PMCA. If, as we have seen, the role of the LPAs is an emergent one (and our research was conducted early in the life of the new LPAs), these results may reflect the fact that some police services have responded earlier than others, or been affected earlier than others, to the new 'empowerment' of the LPAs. In which case we would anticipate that the LPAs will in the future be much more centre stage in service-level policy-making.

The role of the Audit Commission is also extremely interesting. In chapter 1 we documented the strategic approach adopted by the Audit Commission to its work with and on the police service. The evidence here is that this strategy has paid off. In a very short space of time (some 140 years shorter than HMIC!) it has apparently positioned itself strongly as a source of influence over service-level policing policy, with no less than 95 per cent of respondents grading it as having 'considerable' or 'some' influence. Our research suggests that the Audit Commission 'punches above its weight', especially given that the investigative team working on the Audit Commission's work on the police is comprised only of a handful of dedicated researchers. From the point of view of the Audit Commission itself there is a degree of pride in the effectiveness of the Commission's work on the police. Two Audit Commission officials interviewed as part of our research stated:

The take-up of our recommendations is much higher in the police world than it is in the rest of the local authority sector or in the health service ... (E04).

... the work we've done on the police has been some of our smartest work. We think it's been some of our most influential work ... (E13).

However, this record is perhaps better explained in terms of the police service policing the work of the Audit Commission than in terms of the Audit Commission auditing the police service. The Audit Commission and the police service have developed particularly close relations. This closeness reflects to a significant extent the political and professional power of the police service (see chapter 6). The Audit Commission is highly dependent upon the police service (and particularly ACPO) for information, expertise, support and implementation; and consequently it tends to work with (as opposed against) the police service in its investigations. ACPO often welcomed an Audit Commission investigation to provide an external push for reform and a basis for claiming extra resources. Not only was ACPO increasingly consulted over the selection of topics for Audit Commission investigation, it was also given the opportunity to comment on draft reports to the extent that ACPO could claim a significant degree of 'ownership' of the final reports (including recommendations) published by the Audit Commission, thus demonstrating a significant degree of regulatory capture. However, there is sometimes tension between the Audit Commission and other bodies, such as those of the Treasury, Cabinet Office, Home Office and HMIC. The Audit Commission is nominally independent, though the Secretary of State for the Environment, Transport and the Regions can formally direct the Commission as he/she sees fit. No formal directive has yet been issued, although it has been threatened at least on one occasion. However, informal guidance has been evident — for example, the Home Office prevented the Audit Commission from investigating the Special Branch within the police service without recourse to formal mechanisms.

The Audit Commission has now conducted a wide-ranging series of investigations into the police. Its early papers tended to address rather 'peripheral' issues, such as vehicle fleet maintenance and the fingerprint service. However, over time it has increasingly conducted high profile investigations into often very sensitive 'core' areas of police work, such as criminal investigation and police street patrol. This shift from 'peripheral' to 'core' issues was not accidental; it was partly a learning strategy before hitting major targets, and partly a legitimation strategy to a gain a foothold into the police service. The first police-related reports written by the Audit Commission only appeared in 1988; though well over 20 reports have been published on the police service since then. Over a relatively short period of time, the Audit Commission's work has had a substantial impact upon the police. For example, two ACPO members typically observed:

The Audit Commission in my view are the people of the future. They are extremely professional people, they are well qualified and they know what they are doing. We may not like what they do, we may not like their conclusions; you ignore what they do at your peril quite frankly (M09).

... we accept them [the Audit Commission] now as I think [they are] an extremely useful, competent, objective body who do the job they do in a focused way, looking at particular issues and where we can actually get something of real benefit, we've picked up on the past and done things which have been positive and therefore if the Audit Commission produces something we take it on board quickly and fairly strongly. I think the Audit Commission has been a major success in the police service (M10).

Though senior police officers often perceive the work of the Audit Commission as 'objective', such perceptions should not be taken as meaning that the forms of 'best practice' identified by the Audit Commission are somehow brought in from 'outside' the police service. The Audit Commission makes no secret of the fact that its recommendations are often based on perceived 'best practice' found within the police service; its skill lies in identifying and disseminating such 'best practice'. However, this skill is not always valued within the police service. For example, one ACPO member said:

I have yet to read an Audit Commission report which tells me anything I didn't know already. The Audit Commission goes around and steals your best ideas and puts it in a flashy, excellently prepared and beautifully presented document ... and they always seem to be able to present it in a way that they've discovered the meaning of life and the holy grail ... (M01).

Such views notwithstanding, there is little doubt that the Audit Commission is a significant actor in shaping policing policy. Its influence stems from three key sources. First, the police service, like other criminal justice agencies, had 'remained largely immune to market-orientated reforms' when compared to other public services (Loveday, 1999:351). Significant reform of the police service was launched in the early 1990s, after the Conservative Government became frustrated with its expensive policies to reduce crime (Baker, 1993:450), and consequently the police service became targeted for new public management-inspired reforms that had already taken hold in other public services (Cope *et al.*, 1996). The Audit Commission was a key component of this reform programme, and was used by central government to introduce a performance culture into the police service. Secondly, chief constables have become more managerialist, and thus far more receptive to the work of the Audit Commission (Reiner, 1991). Thirdly, the strategy pursued by the Audit Commission of incorporating ACPO into its investigations (from design to implementation), allied with its relative dependence upon senior police officers to implement reform, greatly facilitated the acceptance of its recommendations. In general, the Audit Commission has been, and remains, a significant conduit for policy reform within the police service.

Turning now to the 'performance' of HMIC in our grading exercise, it is useful to compare our findings with those of Reiner in his earlier study of chief constables (Reiner, 1991). In some ways our 'grading' exercise replicates Reiner's in so far as Reiner asked each of his respondents (in this case they were all chief constables) to grade three agencies, the Home Office, HMIC and ACPO, in terms of whether the 'amount of influence over the chief constables' was 'a lot', 'fair', 'little' or 'none'. To begin with Reiner found clear evidence, as in our research, of the power of the Home Office — 70 per cent graded their influence as 'a lot' and 30 per cent as 'fair'. As regards HMIC he found 35 per cent grading their influence as 'a lot', 52.5 per cent as 'fair', 7.5 per cent as 'little' and 5 per cent as 'none' (Reiner, 1991:268). This is broadly consistent with our findings, indicating a sort of 'steady state' for HMIC over the period of the two pieces of research (approximately a decade). However, whilst Reiner reported a great degree of 'collegiality' between the chiefs and HMIC, with Her Majesty's Inspectors acting in effect as 'useful senior colleagues' (ibid:277), we found evidence of concern amongst ACPO members over the role of HMIC — concern just emerging at the time of Reiner's research (ibid). This may reflect the fact that HMIC, by the time of our research, was no longer a 'police only' body made up of retired chiefs; Inspectors were now drawn from senior *civilian* sources (as discussed in chapter 1). This might have disrupted the 'collegiality' of the relationship between chief officers and the Inspectorate. However, it is the arrival on the scene of the other regulatory agency, the Audit Commission, which seems to have caused most consternation. The growth in activity of the Audit Commission seems to have caused some ACPO members to think differently about HMIC. For example:

I happen to think that HMI has been overtaken, HMI as an institution has been overtaken by the Audit Commission . . . (M09).

One does have to ask what the role of the HMI is if the Audit Commission can be shown to be more influential and in time that might come about (M14).

In so far as this view is evident, this may have been due to the fact that the Audit Commission has focused on specific, cross-service issues — such as patrol, investigation and training — rather than service-by-service review. In so far as HMIC has itself begun to adopt more and more the strategy of 'thematic reviews' (see chapter 1), it is seen to be capitalising on the attractions of focused reviews. For example, when asked to comment on his grading of the policy-making bodies, one member compared the Audit Commission and HMIC as follows:

> [The Audit Commission . . .] has considerable influence . . . because of their focus on specific topics because it's in depth and we accept it as professional. HMI, some influence but I think it's [annual inspection] a procedure which is, in my view . . . becoming somewhat outdated and routine . . . the real benefit comes from a kind of thematic inspection you get with the Audit Commission and the HMIs have tended to switch to that where they produce a thematic inspection on a particular issue . . . (M10).

We must be careful not to overstate this view. During the period in which our interviews were conducted the Audit Commission was particularly active on the policing front, with a number of high profile investigations. Since that time their focus on policing has given way to concerns for other areas of the criminal justice process. In this respect any comparisons with other regulatory bodies may be 'time-bound' to an extent. Nevertheless, it cannot be denied that, as was argued in chapter 1, regulation of the police service has become 'crowded air space' and in that respect HMIC's particular influence may have been, at least partially, compromised. This leaves ACPO.

ACPO: TOEING THE PARTY LINE?

As we have seen above, it is apparent that some 85 per cent of members considered ACPO to have 'some' or 'considerable' influence over local policy-making and only 15 per cent considered ACPO's influence to be 'negligible'. It is highly interesting to compare this result with Reiner's (1991) research. Bearing in mind again that Reiner researched chief constables only, it is revealing that 30 per cent of his interviewees thought that ACPO's influence was 'little' or 'none' (ibid:269). Given that Reiner's research was conducted in the late 1980s, the comparison between his findings and ours may indicate a growth of influence of ACPO over service policy-making over the past ten years. Whichever way, our own findings point to a substantial level of influence which ACPO has over local police policy-making, again one which compares well with the formal statutory bodies. Comments such as the following illustrate the significance of ACPO for many members:

> I can't think of any occasion when we have not followed ACPO policy (M09).

> ... we would not make a policy in the force which was contradictory to anything ACPO had said and there is not one ACPO policy that we have notified that we don't sign up to and we are also signed up to policies that we initially would not have supported (M01).

> ACPO [have] considerable influence where ... a national policy is applicable ... I can't remember any Chief I've served under actually departing from ACPO policy once agreed (M10).

We have discussed in chapter 4 the organisational and cultural changes within ACPO which would appear to be behind such sentiments and which might explain how ACPO's role in influencing service-level policy-making has increased *over time*. What seems to have emerged is a much greater *consistency* in service-level policy-making over the past decade and this seems to be due, in part, to the greater influence of ACPO. Generally this greater consistency has been recognised and welcomed by the membership. When asked to comment on how ACPO's organisation and influence had changed over time, a large majority of respondents (83 per cent of the sample) were of the view that ACPO had become a more cohesive, consensual and corporate body. In this respect members expressed the following views:

> ... you're talking about a group of very independent people and each of the 43 Chief Constables in his or her own area has quite a powerful voice as an influential person there, and they don't necessarily like to lose that voice if they go to the national level ... and it would be very difficult to get unity all the time but we have made progress in that

respect, we do work more as an Association now than we did when I first came into it (M07).

... when they were operating individually and not operating as part of ACPO, people on the outside as it were, were able to pick ACPO off. Or, perhaps more relevantly got frustrated because they couldn't get the service point of view. I think things have improved enormously in the past few years and ACPO can now fulfil that function (M38).

... I think there's a recognition now of the strength of all really singing from the same hymn sheet (M06).

These sentiments are summed up by the member who saw adherence to ACPO policy as nothing less than a 'matter of professionalism' (M02). This development of a more corporate culture within ACPO is both a cause and effect of the greater influence of ACPO over service-level policy-making. The adoption of what we have called a 'presumption in favour of compliance' (see chapter 3) has been a major force in encouraging individual chiefs and their teams to toe a 'party line' and accept and follow ACPO national policy. In turn, service-level implementation of ACPO policy can also be seen as an *index/indicator* of the extent of 'corporacy' of ACPO as a body. 'Compliance' is a measure of organisational effectiveness. ACPO has become more cohesive because its members are more inclined to comply; the increasing compliance of ACPO members has made ACPO more cohesive.

What, then, is the *mechanism* by which ACPO policy is employed at the level of service policy-making? In our 'case study' research we sought to establish how ACPO policy 'informs' at the local level; we wished to determine how *particular* policies had 'fed down' at the decision-making level. This was by no means straightforward. When pressed to be specific on this issue one of the respondents stated:

The problem I have with your question is it's actually difficult to discern what ACPO policy often is ... (E20).

The same respondent said that '... there will be very rare occasions when ACPO will have something as specific as a policy'. There was little doubt that respondents found some difficulty in identifying particular ACPO policies which had informed their service-level policies recently. Nevertheless, some actual examples were cited:

> ... I can talk about where [ACPO] has influenced I suppose in the not too distant past, I mean things like pursuit policy for the force, settling informants would be good ... policy relevant to firearms and operational use and licensing issues and those sorts of things, we certainly follow those ... (E22).

In addition to these *actual* policy areas all of the respondents in the case study (and indeed many others in the general sample), cited one area of policy, 'drink drive policy' which illustrates nicely how ACPO policy functions in practice. This policy was agreed by ACPO Council in the mid-1990s, apparently after a heated debate. In essence it stipulates that the police should administer a breathalyser test to all drivers of vehicles involved in road traffic accidents. Police services have always operated differently in this area. Some left it to the discretion of the officers at the scene of the accident, some would breathalyse routinely for accidents which took place after a certain time (i.e., in the evening), others operated a 'blanket' policy of testing in each and every case. Concerned at such variations in practice, ACPO decided upon a policy which favoured the 'blanket' approach. In the case study police service, the previous chief constable had been very much opposed to this type of policy. As the serving chief stated, 'This force was totally against that [policy] under my predecessor' because the force had favoured a more 'targeted' approach to administering breathalysers. However, his successor, whilst sympathetic to the targeted approach, was confronted with the new, national, ACPO policy that tests would be administered in *all* cases of traffic accidents. His response was as follows:

> I did have to think closely about this as to whether I'd be giving the right messages to the staff and that sort of thing because there is almost an argument that you're taking away their discretion and police officers do have discretion, so I had to sell it to them as to why we were doing it and it is a national debate that I support and I agree to it as ACPO Council, that we would change our policy and I think

we were one of the last forces to do it. So we've done that and that did influence me very recently; if I put my hand up and vote for it at ACPO Council, I do almost feel obliged that I've got to accept it as policy within the force (E22).

This would appear to be an example of how service-level policy (and ultimately practice on the ground) can be shaped by ACPO policy. It is not all a matter of the chief's own particular response to national policy; some areas of ACPO policy are 'enforced' in a sense by HMIC. Indeed, the Inspectorate can act as 'enforcers' of a range of nationally-determined policies, as this particular chief explained:

When the HMIs come down and do the inspections they come with a pre-inspection list and they question our staff as to 'what are you doing about Home Office Circular so and so', 'what are you doing about the Audit Commission report' ... not that frequently though, when they're looking at the CID, they're likely to say 'well this is ACPO policy on informants, why aren't you following ACPO policy? (E22).

This point is important. We should not overstate the separatedness of the influence of each of the 'policy shapers'; as we have seen here, HMIC can be instrumental in 'facilitating' the policy influence of ACPO and the other national agencies. Yet even in this respect the chief's discretion to depart from ACPO policy is asserted. Referring to the ACPO policy on informants, the chief argued 'it's best practice, but it's a matter for me to decide whether I'm going to take it on or not'. This leads us to the wider question of the 'limits to corporacy'.

ACPO: THE 'LIMITS TO CORPORACY'

At this point we would like to open up a range of issues which qualify the case constructed that ACPO has shifted from a 'loose-limbed' to a corporate body. To begin with, many of those we interviewed expressed the view that ACPO had not gone *far enough* down the path of developing the corporate culture; there was still scope for developing corporacy further. For example, one senior figure in ACPO commented that while it was comparatively easy to gain consensus on areas of policy, such as pay and conditions of service, when it comes to others, it is a rather different picture; then ACPO becomes:

> ... a loose federation, and you will have the greatest difficulty in getting things through ... we still have the greatest difficulty in getting accord on some pretty substantial issues and it leaves us open time and time again to be picked off and picked off particularly by officials in the Home Office who have another view ... we don't have the degree of corporacy that one might expect to find from a professional body (M36).

Another respondent, while accepting that ACPO are 'definitely more corporate than they were, they're heading in the right direction', went on to say:

> I'd like to think it would have more influence, but, you know, this business of not being able to get 43 people to agree and then when they do agree and some of them resign from the position or they decide, 'well we're not ... doing that in my force' ... it requires Chief Constables to be comfortable with cabinet responsibility (M31).

The notion of *'cabinet responsibility'* was taken much further by some other members, who were of the view that while under ACPO uniformity across forces had increased significantly over the years, there is still too much permissiveness over adherence to ACPO policy. Referring to responses by chief officers to policies agreed by Chief Constables' Council, it was commented that:

> I don't mean that it [ACPO] becomes dictatorial but I do believe that people should be held to account for failing to implement the policies of ACPO freely agreed in proper forums (M26).

> That's the fault of ACPO as an organisation, because there's a big temptation to say, I heard it said, 'oh to hell with it, we're not going to do that in this force' and you can't have your cake and eat it. If you want a professional organisation like that, once the decision is taken that is the policy, then you've got to follow it. If you disagree with it, you've got to alter the argument in debate as it is being progressed, but having decided it, you can't ... say 'I am not adopting it in my

force area', which does go on. Now that is a fault of ACPO that they still have to address (M12).

The difficulty with this argument of course, and a core dilemma for a body such as ACPO, is that constitutionally chiefs have every *right* to depart from ACPO policy, given the doctrine of constabulary independence. We shall return to this issue in the final chapter of the book. At this point we need to examine further the dimensions of variance in members' interpretations, not just of what ACPO *is* but also of what ACPO *should be*. Whilst most of those whose comments have been cited above are broadly supportive of the shift to a more corporate culture, even if some consider that ACPO has not gone far enough down this path, other members are less convinced about either the extent of that shift (as we have just seen) or even the *desirability* of it. In order to draw out these strands of thought we shall turn to what might be called the 'European Parallel'.

The 'European Parallel'

One way of locating the organisational dilemmas faced by a body such as ACPO and the variant 'cultures' within it is to draw a parallel with current debates, at least within Britain, about the European Union. To an extent, ACPO is caught in a tension similar to that within Europe between those who on the one hand would wish to see a continuing shift towards a tightly knit *federation* of members under the umbrella of the organisation, and on the other, those who would prefer a much more loosely knit *confederation*, leaving greater degrees of autonomy at the level of constituent parts. Those supporting the federal route are prepared in some cases to sacrifice a degree of '*sovereignty*' at the level of individual force decision-making in the interests of the membership as a whole and of the police service in general. As such they are less likely to invoke the doctrine of constabulary independence and feel comfortable with 'toeing the party line' as laid out by ACPO. It is that sovereignty which those advocating the more confederate approach are not prepared to relinquish. While the 'professionalising' processes outlined earlier have been generally welcomed by the ACPO membership at large, there is some trepidation, even amongst those who have taken a leading role in the development of a more corporate ACPO, about that development going 'too far'. Our research indicates some interesting and possibly decisive divisions within the Association over fundamental aspects of its proper role, at least in terms of developing further in the corporate direction in which it has been going. Indeed one can push the European analogy even further (admittedly with some caution) and distinguish three schools of thought within the membership about ACPO: *ACPO-Philes, ACPO-Sceptics* and *ACPO-Phobes*.

ACPO-Philes tend to be highly supportive of the directions in which ACPO has gone in recent years, and impressed with the success of the organisation in that time:

> ... the service is actually able to present a united face now, through ACPO, to people like the Home Office, people like the Audit Commission, it has benefited the service enormously (M38).

> [ACPO] facilitated the confidence and togetherness of policing in a way that I never thought ACPO could achieve. They've done a remarkable job ... (M18)

> The policy directives and assistance coming down from ACPO in terms of crime strategies, approach strategies, personnel strategies is immense and that's a change in the last two or three years. We're actually getting first class assistance from those committee structures in telling us what we ought to be looking at in running our businesses (M18).

Not only do the ACPO-Philes enthuse about ACPO's 'new corporacy' to date, they would wish if anything for the organisation to have greater influence over its constituent forces. As we have seen above, some members refer to the importance of 'cabinet responsibility' and the need to place upon members a stronger sense of duty to adopt ACPO policies within their own forces. Furthermore, ACPO-Philes support the strengthening of the Secretariat and the Presidential Team (see chapter 3).

ACPO-Sceptics probably constitute a majority of the membership. They would also support ACPO's more cohesive approach in recent years, but would tend to begin to draw a line under that development in order to avoid damaging localised priorities. ACPO-Sceptics stress the need for balance between adopting policies drawn up by ACPO and local discretion over policies:

... the buck stops with me, if I don't like a policy which has been developed nationally then I needn't adopt it, it's a matter for me. But I do feel that there's a need for a corporate approach (M06).

This group also incudes those who feel that ACPO is in danger of becoming too 'tight' in its policy provisions:

[ACPO] spends a lot of time, wasting time, because it draws up policy guidance on things that actually forces don't want policy guidance on, I think it's much too detailed ... I need to have as little policy as possible.... So it's the level of detail about things that does concern me (M04).

I'm not knocking policy-making, what I'm saying is that sometimes we just go down to a depth that is not necessary (M43).

Furthermore, although outside of the particular concerns of this chapter, the ACPO-Sceptics would also tend to be cautious over ACPO's external campaigning activities, on the grounds of the dangers of becoming too high profile and thus exposing the Association to attack, a point to which we shall return in chapter 6. ACPO-Sceptics prefer a pragmatic approach overall to ACPO's role: organise and mobilise only as far as is necessary to secure specific objectives, but don't go too far.

ACPO-Phobes are a small, possibly dwindling, but vociferous minority who consider that the organisation has already over-stepped the mark. They are particularly concerned about the apparent 'central-isation' of the organisation in the hands of the Presidential Team and the 'assertive' approach of the central executive:

ACPO must be extremely careful not to have too strong a Presidential Team, which actually takes or gives the impression of taking away from individual chiefs their independence and their constitutional position and I think there has been a tendency for that in the last year or two ... it has caused a certain amount of resentment on occasions (M37).

I suspect that ACPO tends to be too dictatorial at times in what it says and certain chief constables would have no choice but to rebel ... (M41).

The ACPO-Phobe position is one which readily invokes the principle of constabulary independence and which tends to see the power relationship between ACPO and the service-level chief officer in 'zero-sum' terms, as one member stated:

> I'm a Chief Constable and I want to do something outside ACPO guidelines, why should I give a toss about ACPO? Once I'm a Chief Constable what do I care about ACPO? What power has it got over me? Nothing at all (M29].

> ... if they're [ACPO] saying, and this is the bit I find distasteful, is that in order to keep the ranks closed, then we really must ... compromise as ACPO, I find offensive, because that sets ACPO above the needs of the people who pay me ... I see my accountability to the people of [force named] ... I don't see my accountability to ACPO (M29).

This 'zero-sum' rationale was reflected in the response of one chief officer to the proposal for the President of ACPO to have a longer term of office:

> ... if we ever changed to that particular position I would seriously consider my position in our club because I think that would cut right across ... the independence of chief constables and what policing is about in the United Kingdom (M43).

We would not wish to overstate the extent of such sentiments; as we have seen, the majority view, which is arguably the one still in ascendancy, is one supportive of the general trend towards a more corporate ACPO, even if in many cases with some reservation. Nevertheless, the very fact that the 'zero-sum' rationale for a case against ACPO can be made along the lines apparent above is testimony to the power of the logic and utility of the doctrine of constabulary independence. This doctrine acts as a significant 'brake' on the role of ACPO as a policy-shaping body at the level of service policy-making and as such a 'limit to corporacy'. Not only can CI be employed to resist the 'intrusion' of bodies such as the Home Office or LPAs into the chief officer's sphere of policy- and decision-making; it can be extended to resist the lure of chief officer's own 'club', ACPO itself. This is an issue to which we shall return in the final chapter.

A NOTE ON THE METROPOLITAN POLICE SERVICE

On the theme of the 'limits to corporacy' we cannot leave the issue of ACPO's influence over service-level policy-making without specific comment on the position of the *Metropolitan Police Service* within ACPO. The Metropolitan Police Service (MPS) is far and away the biggest police service in the United Kingdom, with over 20,000 officers and a huge civilian staff. Its size means that the MPS is responsible for close to one fifth of the police officers of England and Wales and, in turn, close to one fifth of ACPO members. Numerically at least, it would seem that the MPS should be at the very core of ACPO's activities and that, as a consequence, there would be a great degree of symmetry between the work of ACPO and the work of the MPS. However, the policing of London and the Metropolis has always been distinct from the rest of the policing of England and Wales. There have traditionally been separate arrangements for the governance of the police in London, where, until very recently, the Home Secretary acted as the 'police authority' for the MPS — only now is the MPS to have a locally-based police authority as part of its system of accountability to the people of London. Culturally, the MPS has always had a distinct identity, with its own system for police training (which has survived intact despite the formation of National Police Training), organisational management and, regarding ACPO, its own rank structure and designations. If we are to measure the extent to which ACPO is a corporate body and influences policy-making at local police service level, then the relationship between ACPO and the MPS is a key factor. Does ACPO have a significant influence over policy-making within the MPS and, more generally, how do MPS ACPO-rank officers operate within ACPO as an organisation? Our research paid particular attention to these issues given the status of the MPS within the British policing system.

Amongst our sample of ACPO members there was a widely held view that the MPS was *not* integrated into ACPO in the sense of taking as full and active a role as one might expect given the size of the 'MPS contingent' within ACPO. Sixty-three per cent of members felt that ACPO and the MPS were effectively distinct organisationally and that there was limited influence both in terms of ACPO's influence over the MPS or of the MPS's influence over ACPO. That sentiment was even stronger amongst the MPS and former MPS members (now with other police services) of our sample. Thirteen members of our sample came under this category and of those 85 per cent felt that ACPO and the MPS operated distinctly and with little influence in either direction. In terms of the influence of the MPS *within* ACPO most members were of the view that the MPS was far less influential than the size of the MPS contingent within the organisation would seem to predict. Some comments to this effect are:

It appears to me that they [MPS] don't wield the influence that they ought (M26).

... they've disproportionately small influence, considering the vast experience of policing issues that they encounter in the Metropolis ... I'm not sure that ACPO derives all that they might derive from the Met (M13).

Normally the Met play little or no part in ACPO's professional activities, which is a pity because I mean the calibre of officers available to it, to use their skills within ACPO would have been a real benefit to ACPO (M36).

Another member expressed the same view that the MPS is less influential within ACPO than it might be, but that also, in turn, the MPS is not significantly influenced by ACPO:

The Met punches massively underweight in ACPO. The Met does not particularly shape police policy across the country. What it does is it actually quite often says 'well that's interesting but we're not going to do that' (M04).

A former MPS officer, now with another police service, repeated this sentiment and with some regret:

... the role of the Met was very uncomfortable for me, it virtually was the Met *and* ACPO instead of the Met *as part of* ACPO; I think it's slowly changing, slowly, but the Met will still do its own thing and vice versa and I have a problem with that, because if you say you have a crime strategy that's devised with something of national conse-quence that the Met *isn't* signed up to, then you're talking about nearly a third of the crime not being dealt with in that way ... (M42).

There would appear to be clear evidence of a 'limit to corporacy' in this area of a quite serious magnitude. If an organisation accounting for almost *one fifth* of the police service of England and Wales is affected only marginally by the activities of ACPO then that raises major questions about the capacity of ACPO to influence policing policy on a *national* scale. However, it is the very *size* of the MPS that is one of the reasons why ACPO seems to have only limited effect on it. Much of what ACPO can offer to the other services, particularly the smaller ones — the 'pooling' of expertise and experience, research on various policing techniques and policies and so on — the MPS is able to provide from within its own, substantial, resources. The MPS also has a number of unique problems and functions, for example in counter-terrorist work, Royal Protection and the policing of major public events (including public protest) and the sheer volume of crimes with which it deals, which add to the sense of distinctiveness of 'the Met' within the British policing context. In turn this can mean that ACPO's activities and the policies they generate have less resonance for the MPS than other police services. One member put it this way:

> The Met, like everything else, just exist in their own right and they ... do their own thing. I don't say that in a pejorative sense but they do their own thing in all sorts of ways ... they're not part of national police training ... all sorts of aspects of management ... they're self sufficient in everything basically (M20).

There is the possibility that, nevertheless, the 'uniqueness' of the MPS can be used as a means of justifying *not* to work within national ACPO policy, or for arguing that the MPS is in some way 'above' ACPO, a possibility alluded to by one member who stated that:

> ... at its most naked, it could be argued that the Met doesn't need ACPO, ACPO needs the Met (M40).

Beneath such sentiments lies something more than a calculation about organisational function, size and capacity: within the police service of England and Wales there is a form of *cultural schism* between the MPS and the other police services (often referred to, with meaning, as the 'provincial forces'). This is reinforced, but not necessitated by, the formal differentiations which support and further separate development between the MPS and the other police services — differences in forms of governance, management structures, training regimes and so on. This cultural schism results in a degree of *mutual suspicion* which pervades attitudes to, and from the MPS, in terms of the stance of the latter within the British police service. One member articulated the problem, with some degree of impartiality it must be acknowledged, in terms of (unfounded) mutual envy:

> ... [in] the relationship between the Met and the other police forces ... there's a mixture of envy from the smaller forces [towards] the Met, you know, 'London, you're always in the news' ... there's an element of that around. There's also an element of Met feeling sort of jealous of people outside, particularly if you get to ACPO level with this status issue, the Chief Constable versus an Assistant Commissioner, you know, if you're a Chief Constable of Blankshire then people acknowledge that you're incredibly important ... and there's a belief among some Met senior colleagues that life is much rosier as a result of that (M11).

Within ACPO (and indeed within the formal pay structure of chief officers), an assistant commissioner in the MPS is equivalent to the rank of chief constable in the other police services and this is reflected in the constitutional position of assistant commissioner within ACPO's Chief Constables' Council. This member alludes to the 'irony' that an assistant commissioner role within the MPS, despite the 'uniqueness' of the profile of the MPS, may be seen, by some, as somehow not as important as a chief constable's role within a 'provincial' force — however small that force might be. Yet this is only one aspect of the mutual suspicion which pervades the relationship between the MPS and the 'rest' of the police service of England and Wales. At the level of ACPO, there is a 'Met-side' view, expressed thus:

> There's an anti-Met feeling in ACPO, you know, 'the Met carry on as though no other police force existed' and the rest of ACPO are quite prepared to put down anything that comes out of the Met because it comes out of the Met ... you're left with the impression that they dig their heels in for the sake of it (M17).

... the power in ACPO is directed deliberately to keep everything away from the Met to make sure they don't get involved and get too powerful (M03).

From the 'other' police services' perspective a view was that:

... you almost get the feeling that ... if things weren't going to the Met's liking they would just decide to go it alone anyway ... (M41).

Such levels of mutual suspicion run deep within the internal culture — perhaps we should say '*cultures*' (see chapter 7) — of the British police service. Since the days when the 'provincial' police forces would be required to 'call in the Yard' when a serious crime was committed in their locality (Reiner, 1985), mutual suspicion, if not mutual stereotyping, has been the order of the day between the MPS and the other police services. At the level of ACPO this is reflected in mutual suspicion over the relevance of the MPS to ACPO policy-making and of ACPO to MPS policy-making. This is exacerbated within ACPO by two further complications. First, in terms of *career development*, work undertaken by MPS officers on ACPO committees would appear to be less relevant within the MPS as it appears to be within the other police services. For example, one of our MPS respondents stated that although ACPO committee work was a useful way of getting one 'known' around the country and therefore for career development in the 'provincial' services (as was discussed earlier in this chapter), within the *MPS* ACPO work was seen as 'not at all important' (M17). This consideration may be a contributory factor affecting the motivation for MPS officers to become as embroiled in the ACPO machinery as their counterparts in the other police services; this may have spilt over into more general attitudes to ACPO as an organisation within the MPS. Secondly, in terms of relative roles within the '*ACPO top team*', individual MPS ACPO members are placed at a structural disadvantage relative to other service ACPO members. The 'top team' of the MPS is some 30-plus strong. As such the rank of commander within the MPS, equivalent to the assistant chief constable in the 'provincial' police services, occupies a very different position within the MPS ACPO team hierarchy compared with a typical assistant chief constable. In crude terms, the MPS commander is ranked at something like (equal) fifteenth in the top team (at most), whereas his or her equivalent in the provincial forces is ranked (equal) 'third'. It was interesting to note that in our observations of ACPO conferences, from time to time the assistant chief constable was the single 'force-representative' of the ACPO team, something unlikely in relation to a commander in the MPS. This issue was nicely expressed by one MPS member:

> ... there is a real problem about being a Commander of the Metropolitan Police. If you are in the top team in any other force, you see everything that comes in at high level, you see the Home Office Circulars, you see the communication from ACPO, you see the minutes of every committee meeting. If you're a Commander in the Metropolitan Police, unless you go out of your way to get the minutes of every meeting, you won't inevitably see [them] ... you're just one of 30 ACPO officers in the Met (M31).

Again, such issues may have complicated the established cultural divide which has characterised the relationship between the MPS and ACPO. Structural imbalances between the role of ACPO for members of the 'provincial' services on the one hand and the MPS on the other, have only served to exacerbate the mutual suspicions which stem from the deeply ingrained cultural schisms between the 'Met' and the rest of the police service of England and Wales.

Within both ACPO and the MPS there has been a realisation for some time that the relationship between the organisations could be much more constructive. Within our sample, over one fifth of members expressed a wish for the MPS to play a bigger role within ACPO. From the point of view of the MPS it is significant that, during the 1990s, two ACPO Presidencies were undertaken by MPS deputy commissioners, no small measure of determination from both 'sides' to tackle the issue head-on. Indeed, under the Presidency of Sir John Smith, during the mid-1990s, whilst Sir John was deputy commissioner of the MPS, ACPO (arguably) made some of its greatest advances in becoming a more corporate body, aided and abetted it must be noted by *MPS* staff resources. Furthermore, one of our sample, speaking as a very senior member of the MPS, stated that:

> ... I'm very happy to be associated with the policy ... that the Met tries to play a full role in ACPO ... historically there have always been tensions, because of size ... I think we need to work very hard

to show that we're not abusing that privileged position *and are part of the ACPO community* (M40) (emphasis added).

However, the significance of this point is that it is expressed in terms of a *goal* rather than an achievement. It remains the case that the MPS and ACPO operate to a great extent alongside one another as policy-making entities. If ACPO's influence over local service-level policing policy is significant, but limited, in relation to the other police services of England and Wales, when it comes to the MPS it would seem to be the case that it is simply 'limited'. As such, there remains a sizeable caveat to the case that ACPO has become a fully corporate body, in so far as any such body could or should include the one fifth of the police service that is the Metropolitan Police Service.

Chapter 6
ACPO and Policing Policy: The Politics of Representation and National Policy-making

INTRODUCTION

In this chapter we will extend the analysis of the policing policy process and the role of ACPO within it to policy-making at the *national* level. As we have seen in earlier chapters, it is at this level above all that concerns have been raised about the extent of ACPO's 'undue' influence over the policy process and the implications of this for the 'accountability deficit' surrounding ACPO. We have also argued that it is possible to overstate this case: ACPO's 'past' is one more characterised by disunity and fragmentation than coherence and purpose. Furthermore, empirical research by Jones *et al.* (discussed in the previous chapter) on the role played by a range of agencies in the national policing policy process came to the conclusion that ACPO was by no means a 'big player'. In terms of the three policy areas taken as case studies in their research, ACPO only succeeded in *modifying* civilianisation, having been totally opposed at the outset, it operated only at the level of *implementation* of policies responding to crimes against women and children, and tended to play a largely *negative* role in the development of crime prevention policies (Jones *et al.*, 1994:291–13). However, such policies predated the huge debate over Sheehy, the Royal Commission on Criminal Justice and the Police and Magistrates' Courts Act 1994 which dominated the policing policy agenda from the early 1990s onwards. How did ACPO fare in this context?

In this respect we will examine the role of ACPO as a *pressure* or *interest group* (Richardson and Jordan, 1979) and the extent to which ACPO has exerted influence over the national policing policy agenda — and how that influence may have changed over time. By 'policing policy agenda' in this respect we mean not only policy and legislation relating specifically to the police and policing, but also to the wider field of criminal justice policy; as we shall see, ACPO's 'campaigns' have stretched far beyond specifically 'policing' issues. Inevitably, this will take us to the *political* role and activities of ACPO as players in the policy process. Now there are particular sensitivities regarding the interface between British policing and the political process. Unique in the public services, policing is governed, at least in principle, by a constitutional doctrine which seemingly demarcates it from 'politics'. We refer, again, of course to the doctrine of *constabulary independence* (Lustgarten, 1986; see chapter 7). Whilst the primary thrust of this doctrine is to inhibit any attempt by external political authorities to seek to control or even influence policing policies — these are to be the exclusive province of chief police officers themselves — the *discourse* surrounding constabulary independence (Savage *et al.*, 1999) draws a more general demarcation line between the world of policing and the world of politics. Not only must politics not impinge on policing, the police must not become embroiled in politics. The apparent *quid pro quo* of constabulary independence is the notion that the police should not in turn become embroiled in political affairs. However, as we have seen, not only is the concept of constabulary independence itself hugely contentious (Lustgarten, 1986), the idea that the British police have managed to stay aloof from politics is, to say the least, problematic. Against a backcloth of *'non-involvement'* in politics, the police have for many years sought to intervene in political debate, both on matters close to policing and on areas at some considerable distance from policing as such (Chibnall, 1977; Jefferson and Grimshaw, 1984; Reiner, 1992; Scraton, 1985). What is in question is how *effective* these attempts at intervention have been and by what *mechanisms* the 'police view' has been translated into policy outcomes. There is no shortage of evidence that police organisations have been 'political' in their activities; what is

less clear is how this activity is *represented* within the policy process
and how it is *reflected* in policy influence.

If we are to examine the extent to which the 'police view' has been
effective in shaping the national policing policy agenda and how the
police operate in terms of the 'politics of representation', we need to
consider the respective roles of the different *police professional
associations*. There is, of course, no 'police view' as such but rather a
variety of police *views*. It is important to understand that as well as the
question of the *absolute* extent of influence which the police exert over
the national policy process, there is the question of the *relative* influence
which each of the various police associations wield in turn. As we shall
see, there is as much competition between the police assocations for
political influence as between the police and other interest groups. We
shall therefore begin with an examination of the constitution and role of
each of the police professional associations before moving on to analyse
the internal and external policy networks which have functioned in
relation to police and criminal justice policy-making.

RANK AND REPRESENTATION: PROFESSIONAL
ASSOCIATIONS IN THE BRITISH POLICE SERVICE

An understanding of the role of representative associations within the
British police service must begin with *rank*. As with the structure of
police management, there is a rigid correspondence between the
organisational composition of police representative associations and the
rank structure of the service. The existence of a rank-based framework of
professional representation has a key role in the determination of relative
influence and the distribution of power within the 'police lobby'. This
does not necessarily always run in the expected direction. Four bodies
now reflect this framework: the Police Federation, the Superintendents'
Association, the Association of Chief Police Officers (ACPO) and the
Chief Police Officers' Staff Association (CPOSA). These organisations
have their counterparts in Scotland but, based on our research, we shall
be considering the situation in England, Wales and Northern Ireland.

The Police Federation: Strength in Numbers?

The Police Federation acts as the body representing the 'rank-and-file'
of the police service. It represents and is organised around the ranks of

constable, sergeant, inspector and chief inspector. There are Central Committees for each rank, which combine to form the Joint Central Committee, the executive body of the Federation. The Federation was established as a statutory body under the Police Act 1919 in an attempt by the Government to crush the rise of the illegal trade union which had emerged during World War I (Judge, 1994). In a real sense the Federation acts as the 'rich relative' of the police representative associations because of its sheer size and concomitant resources: it has a membership in excess of 120,000, a heavily staffed full-time Secretariat and press office, two sponsored Members of Parliament who act as spokespersons for the organisation and a monthly journal, *Police*, which presents itself as the 'Voice of the Service' (as we shall see, a claim much disputed by ACPO). Its own resources, based largely on flat-rate levies on all members, are enhanced by the arrangement whereby Federation functionaries are allowed to undertake Federation business on full- or part- secondment from their police force, effectively force sponsorship of Federation activities.

The Federation has traditionally held a position of notoriety amongst commentators on the police, particularly those on the left. This has rested largely on what has been seen as the complementary 'law and order' discourses of the Federation and the Conservative Party: if the Church of England was seen as the 'Conservative Party at Prayer', the Federation could be seen as the 'Conservative Party in uniform' (Reiner 1985). The high point in this regard, and possibly an early sign of the future blurring between policing and politics, was the infamous campaign by the Federation in the run-up to the 1979 General Election in support of 'law and order', seen by many as an open invitation to the electorate to vote Conservative (Reiner, 1985). There is no doubt that the Federation has been the most *vociferous* of the police associations and has been ever ready to state its preferences on all manner of issues and not just those relating directly to policing. Beer (1955) (quoted in Jordan and Richardson, 1987) felt that it was more important to study the groups that had quiet but regular access to government rather than a focus on the 'noisy threats and loud demanding claims' of other groups. Yates refers to this as 'silent politics' (1982:87; quoted in Jordan and Richardson, 1987). Therefore what is less clear is how *effective* it has been in influencing the policy agenda. Whilst some have viewed the Federation as a darkly subversive force of reaction (Scraton, 1985), others have been more sceptical. Kettle, for example, argued that the

Federation tends towards '... tilting at windmills, forever launching grand schemes which have no real chance of fulfilment ...' (Kettle, 1980:32). Brogden in a similar vein stated that 'The Federation raises issues in the public domain as a substitute for direct access to the corridors of power' (Brogden, 1982:95).

In the wake of Federation campaigns subsequent to these judgments such assessments of the effectiveness of the Federation as a lobbying body may need to be revised. In a recent study by McLaughlin and Murji (1998) it has been argued that the Federation has over time enhanced its capacity to put its own particular version of the 'police view' across and in doing that has managed to transform its representative status. It has shifted, they claim, from being a 'toothless tiger' to becoming an influential and powerful pressure group (ibid:371). They present this transformation as being two-pronged. On the one hand the Federation has enhanced its *private lobbying* skills and activities. This includes direct briefing to politicians; issue-based lobbying of Members of Parliament; the creation of Federation-funded special 'advisors' in Parliament (now involving one Member of Parliament from each of the Labour and Conservative Parties — before it was just one); targeted lobbying at 'neutral' or sympathetic opinion formers; 'off-the-record' briefings to selected journalists; and the formation of *strategic alliances* with other groups on specific issues — as we shall see later, this has included the other police associations.

On the other hand, McLaughlin and Murji argue, the Federation has pursued a programme of *public campaigning*. This has included strategies such as:

(i) Protest meetings; (ii) issuing press releases; (iii) establishing a higher media profile for their annual conferences and making them more 'media friendly' (iv) vociferous campaigning against various 'anti-police' critics; (v) submitting evidence to public inquiries, commissions and committees; and (vi) placing advertisements in newspapers to appeal to the general public on particular issues (ibid).

In this respect McLaughlin and Murji trace the role of the Federation through a range of campaigns, including those linked to police pay, 'law and order' and penal policy, police complaints procedures and police powers and capital punishment (ibid:375–386). However, even these highly public campaigns look tempered in the light of the Federation's activities during the debate on 'Sheehy'. In 1992, the then Home Secretary, Kenneth Clarke, launched an inquiry into 'police roles and responsibilities', a root-and-branch review of police functions, pay and conditions of service. The inquiry reported in 1993 with a highly controversial set of recommendations for reform of the service (Home Office, 1993a). We shall return to the case of Sheehy later, when we consider police association activities around the wide-reaching police reform agenda which was formed under the Conservatives in the mid-1990s. At this point what is of note is that prior to and after the Sheehy Report was published the Federation was seen to employ the full panoply of lobbying machineries as a means of resistance and opposition to the emerging framework for reforms of police pay and conditions. This included the use of a public relations company to lobby the media, a huge protest gathering at Wembley (with over 20,000 officers in attendance), strategic alliances with other police associations, commissioned research involving academic consultants and an elaborate programme of media advertising warning of the threat posed by Sheehy to the 'fundamental traditions of British policing', including statements of support from high profile political figures (McLaughlin and Murji, 1998:392 *et seq*). The fact that Clarke's successor Michael Howard was at pains to distance himself from the main thrust of Sheehy, such as the support for fixed-term contracts for police officers and performance related pay (Leishman *et al.*, 1996), was due in part at least to the Federation's energies in lobbying against Sheehy at every point. If ever there was a campaign which the Federation felt to be successful, it was that surrounding the Sheehy agenda. From our own research one senior member of the Federation saw the Sheehy campaign as a watershed in the organisation's lobbying capacity:

... we came of age in ... [our] ... political lobbying style ... we took on lobbyists as well as communication groups in London, so we knew who to target (E51).

If the Federation has traditionally been the most *vociferous* of the police staff associations — and it can certainly enforce that with the huge resources at its disposal — what is less clear is whether it stands as the most politically *effective* of the police staff associations. As we shall see later, in recent years ACPO has laid claim to that mantle. In terms of policy networks (see chapter 1), what is at issue here is the *relative* power and influence of the police associations, what might be called the 'horizontal' distribution of power *between* those associations. Increasingly integral to this distribution are the articulations of rank and the growing significance of a divide, both cultural and functional, between 'management' on the one hand and the 'workforce' on the other, a divide exacerbated by the rise and rise of 'new public management' (Leishman *et al.*, 1996). With reference to the relationship between the Federation and ACPO, a senior Federation member interviewed as part of our research referred to ACPO's attitude as 'the philosophy that "I'm the boss and you're the workers"' (E51). In this respect we can now move on up the 'rank hierarchy' and consider the role of the Police Superintendents' Association.

The Police Superintendents' Association — 'Piggy-in-the-Middle'?

The Police Superintendents' Association (PSA) was formed in 1920 and currently has a membership of approximately 1,500 officers of the ranks of superintendent and chief superintendent (a membership much reduced over recent years with the shedding of superintendent's posts as part of the drive to 'de-tier' police management). The work and activities of the PSA have not attracted a great deal of attention from observers of British policing, perhaps some recognition that the organisation in a sense sits 'in between' its sister associations. It cannot compete easily with the size and resource-base of the Federation nor can it boast the level of seniority of ACPO. Brogden (1982) has expressed it thus:

> Neither the master or servant, the Police Superintendents' Association can at most only make a marginal contribution to the development of the power of the police institution within the State.

The PSA in this sense suffers a structural weakness as the 'piggy-in-the-middle' of the police staff associations. However, we should be careful not to underestimate the influence which the PSA has had on policy-making, particularly in recent years. The police reform agenda of the mid-1990s, embracing everything from police pay and conditions of service through roles and responsibilities to police accountability, created fertile ground on which all of the police associations could set out their wares and the PSA was no exception. This was soon coupled with a growing tendency of politicians to take heed of the 'police view' on all matters relating to criminal justice policy, a tendency symbolised above all by the then Home Secretary Michael Howard but matched speech-by-speech by his opposite number in the Labour Party, Jack Straw. What emerged was an environment in which the associations found themselves being courted by senior politicians bent on appearing to support the forces of law and order (Charman and Savage, 1999). As doors were being opened the PSA was quick to step inside.

It is never clear whether an organisation's 'success' in the lobbying business is due to environmental factors — in this case an environment more receptive to the 'police view' — or factors relating to the organisation itself, such as the growing 'professionalism' of its representative capacities. Government, through its policy changes, may adopt ideas and suggestions from a pressure group but this does not translate into success for the group. Pluralists, in particular, tend to ignore the notion of ideology within politics (Smith, 1990, 1993); a group's policy ideals may 'fit in' with the ideology of the government — who then is successful? For example consider the supposed 'success' of the Institute of Directors during Thatcher's period as Prime Minister (Holliday, 1993). If success within pressure group activity is, in part, having coincidental interests then the resources of that group (financial or otherwise) become less relevant. In that case, Ryan argues that it is not the resources of the group that are important but its 'clout' (1978:13). This has as many implications for the large and heavily financially resourced Federation as it does for the smaller and less well financially resourced PSA and ACPO.

It has been argued (as with the other police associations) that the PSA has 'geared up' its lobbying activities and political skills in recent years. A senior PSA role holder interviewed as part of our research argued it thus:

In recent years, not to put too fine a point on it, we've [the Superintendents' Association] moved from a fairly benign officers' dining club, more than anything else, to becoming a ... proactive organisation which is able to exert considerable influence not only on policing but on conditions of service ... and the criminal justice system generally.... We have had to turn around from basically being innocuous ... to being what we consider we are now, a major influence on policing in general (E31).

The implication here is that in so far as there has been an increase in the PSA's influence over policing and criminal justice policy, this has not simply been the result of a more receptive environment but is also an expression of a more proactive and concerted organisational approach to the art of lobbying. Of course, we need to be cautious about such claims; there is perhaps an inbuilt tendency of senior role holders of an organisation to portray that organisation as being more effective than it had been in the past — it is in a sense self-supporting to do so! However, there does seem to be a plausible case here. Certainly in terms of media exposure, the PSA did score quite heavily in the law and order debates of the mid- to late-1990s.

It was certainly noticeable that the President of the PSA throughout this period, Brian McKenzie, made more radio and television appearances than either of his equivalents in the Federation and ACPO. This was clearly something of which the PSA was proud, as our interviewee in this area made clear:

A recent example is where Dimbleby wanted someone on his programme and it was Brian McKenzie, our President, who went on as opposed to somebody from the Federation or somebody from ACPO (E31).

During the period of our research, it was clear that the PSA was notably successful in gaining air space and column inches to represent its views on a wide range of issues, some of them only indirectly concerned with policing. It was also apparent as well that the 'PSA line' on such matters had a tendency to find its way to the ears of senior politicians. Undoubtedly part of the reason for this rested with the personal media skills of McKenzie himself. The fact that on retirement he was made a life peer by the new Labour Prime Minister could be seen as some measure of that! It will be interesting to see whether this high profile scheme of the PSA will be able to continue with a different character at the helm. Nevertheless, there is an important *organisational* phenomenon here which could be significant to pressure group analysis, at least as it applies to the police.

We have made the point that the PSA lacks both the size of the Federation and the seniority of ACPO, factors which together could act to diminish its 'clout' in pressure group terms. However, these very 'disadvantages' could in other senses act as sources of organisational strength. There are group theorists who believe that organisation is far more important than size (Richardson and Jordan, 1979) and those who argue for the importance of small groups (Grant, 1984). Smaller groups can be more effective than larger groups because of the pressure to contribute in a small group whereas in a large group anonymity can result in inaction (Olson, 1971). So on the one hand the *smallness* of the PSA can enable it to move quickly, particularly in rapid response to a crisis or the sudden emergence of a new policy agenda — something that was happening frequently during the police reform era of the mid-1990s. What this means is that, unlike a large and complex organisation like the Federation, which represents tiers of police ranks with potentially conflicting interests, the PSA does not have to 'refer back' to the central Executive before any commitment is made or any view expressed. A high degree of autonomy is granted to key role holders in taking the lead on key issues, as the senior PSA respondent stated:

What actually happens is that we are given the discretion by the National Executive Committee to make decisions on the hoof (E31).

On the other hand this very discretion benefits the PSA relative to *ACPO* precisely because of its *lack of seniority*. As we have seen in chapter 3, a crucial feature of ACPO as an organisation is the constraining effect of the discretionary powers of individual chiefs over the formation and adoption of 'collective' policing policy. Because of the doctrine of 'constabulary independence', chiefs frequently assert their right to individually judge each and every matter of policing policy and decide upon its merit. The whole machinery of ACPO policy-making is skewed to take heed of this 'right of *chiefs*'. One consequence of this is that the President of ACPO and even the ACPO Executive would never take it upon themselves to formulate ACPO policy without full reference back to the full committee of chiefs — Chief Constables' Council — and, as we have seen, even policy thus approved can be subject to non-compliance by individual chiefs. What this means is that the sort of 'policy-making on the hoof' open to the PSA and, to a lesser extent, the Federation, would be unthinkable in the context of ACPO. Olson (1971) argued that groups which existed for reasons in addition to their pressure group role (for insurance, access to facilities, employee protection etc.) as the Federation and the PSA do, required less consultation than other groups.

His 'by-product' theory stated that leaders of these groups can act without the consent of its members in the knowledge that members will tend not to leave the organisation in protest. Salisbury (1984) supplements this by adding that leadership of these groups is more autonomous and that the actions of these leaders are less likely to be justified for membership approval. The result is a 'captive membership' (Olson, 1971:133). We shall return to this issue concerning ACPO later. At this point what is of relevance is that this 'discretionary freedom' gives the PSA a distinct advantage in responding immediately to new agendas, particularly in terms of responding at short notice to media requests for comment and a 'party line' on this or that matter of policing and criminal justice policy. It enables the Association to keep itself in the media spotlight at times when ACPO would be forced to adopt a low-profile or non-committal stance. It would be interesting to determine the extent to which this pressure-group variant of the thesis that 'small is beautiful' has resonance for other policy sectors.

It is however only in recent years that this organisational advantage in so far as it exists has been brought to bear. As with the Federation's 'coming of age' in terms of lobbying skills and activities, the Sheehy agenda appears to have been the major spur for this. The PSA had much at stake with Sheehy: one of the central proposals of the Sheehy Report was to abolish the rank of chief superintendent, one of the two ranks represented by the PSA. The reform agenda more widely pointed to the 'thinning out' of middle management within the police service — a process which was directed more than anything at the superintendent level of the police organisation. The PSA were spurred into action as a result and were forced at short notice to sharpen their lobbying skills. This entailed the adoption of a higher media profile, mainly through the public presence of the PSA's President, as we have seen, together with direct lobbying of politicians and members of the House of Lords — who happened to have in their ranks a small number of retired senior police officers (who were also to prove useful to ACPO). The main focus of this campaign was on retaining the middle management ranks threatened by Sheehy. Ironically, it could be argued that it was the *Federation* rank of chief inspector, rather than the rank of chief superintendent — for both were seen as disposable in the Sheehy Report — which was to become the PSA's success story. It has been claimed that, in effect, the PSA were given a choice between the two by supporters in the Lords ('one or the other could be saved') and in the end the association opted for the chief inspector rank:

We saved the rank of chief inspector. Absolutely down to the Superintendents' Association that was … when the Police and Magistrates' Court Act wanted to abolish the ranks, we argued long and hard that was a step that shouldn't be taken. We wish we could have saved the chief superintendent rank as well but we weren't successful. We certainly saved the chief inspector rank (E31).

Whilst the other associations may also claim some responsibility for this 'success', there seems little doubt that the noise created by the PSA had at least some impact on the eventual policy outcome. This taste of the lobbying action became an acquired one. As was to be the case with ACPO, as we shall see, the police-focused successes over Sheehy were to act as a spur to more wide-ranging and diffuse campaigns by the PSA. The Association successfully campaigned for the establishment of a 'paedophile register', a local listing of sex offenders convicted of offences against children which could be used to monitor the movements and actions of those listed. The PSA also took a lead role in the shaping of gun controls and in particular controls on the possession of handguns (in the wake of the massacre of 16 children in Dunblane, Scotland). In both cases the PSA was quick to pounce on the opportunities presented by huge public concern and high intensity media coverage of the issues and stamp its mark on the emerging policy agendas. Relative success had bred relative success.

These cases notwithstanding, it is important not to overstate the PSA's role in the policing policy network. It is perhaps best to depict the PSA as more of a 'policy-sniper' than a 'policy-shaper', able to score on specific but relatively marginal targets but not well placed to take a leading role in police policy-making more generally. It is ACPO which has positioned itself most effectively in this role.

THE ASSOCIATION OF CHIEF POLICE OFFICERS: THE VIEW FROM THE TOP

If the Federation has acquired notoriety in the eyes of some for its vociferous and *high profile* campaigning (typically in pursuit of anti-liberal causes — opposition to new police complaints procedures, support for capital punishment, etc.), ACPO, as we have seen in chapter 4, has attracted critical attention over its *covert* activities. The concern over ACPO has been less about 'tub thumping' than about 'behind the scenes' agenda-setting and lobbying. For example, Geoffrey Robertson, writing in the late 1980s, claimed that:

'ACPO ... has become the most powerful club in the country, promoting policies agreed amongst its members, resisting attempts to introduce measures for accountability and *actively entering the political arena*.... It reports directly to the Home Secretary, and has the capacity to become a centralised intelligence agency, without any charter to limit its operations (Robertson, 1989:24–25 (emphasis added)).

The image painted here is of an organisation working concertedly but discreetly in the corridors of power to shape the policy agenda in what it considers to be its best interests. This was a common reading of the role and activities of ACPO throughout the 1980s, particularly in relation to controversies over local accountability of the police (Scraton, 1985; Jefferson and Grimshaw, 1984). We have challenged this view as an overstatement of the capacity of ACPO, at least in the past, to act cohesively and effectively in pursuit of any apparent goals (see chapters 3 and 4). We have argued that, on the contrary, ACPO's history has been one of *disunity* rather than cohesion (Savage and Charman, 1996a). This applied both to ACPO's ability to hold its own members together in adopting common policing policies across individual police forces (as argued in chapter 5) and its capacity to conduct united and strategic campaigning in terms of its external representational activities. ACPO members revealed to us their concerns that all too often ACPO had been side-stepped and outmanoeuvred when it came to public campaigning, particularly in comparison to their main rival for media attention, the Federation. For example, one commented that:

... when something happened they [the media] would go to the Federation and whoever was the Secretary of the Federation would speak for the country's police service (M38).

That the body representing the 'rank-and-file' could enjoy more media attention than ACPO, representing the 'police elite', was clearly a cause of much frustration:

... we get infuriated by the Federation being known as the 'voice of the service' ... (M15).

If this was the case, it has become less a source of concern over time. Most ACPO members were of the view that in recent years ACPO had managed to position itself much more effectively in terms of media exposure and political impact. Again, this is presented in terms of the relative influence of ACPO in relation to the Federation. As one member stated:

I think ACPO is now far more powerful and influential in terms of the media than it ever was. I think the Home Secretary and the media are far more likely to go to talk to the President [of ACPO] about the issues of the day than they would to talk to the Chairman of the Federation ... (M18).

We would argue that both in terms of the *relative* influence of ACPO as a campaigning group *vis-à-vis* the Federation and the *absolute* effectiveness of the organisation in shaping the policy agenda ACPO has become a much bigger player in recent years. More specifically, as we shall make clear later, ACPO has managed to shift from the position of relative *outsider* in the policy process to one very much of an *insider* (Grant, 1989). This transformation became most apparent during the police reform agenda of the mid-1990s, but has its roots in the key organisational changes which took place some years before. We have considered these in detail earlier (see chapter 3), but in this context we shall return to two of these devolopments, the formation of *media management* and the *split in ACPO*, in the light of their specific impact on ACPO's capacity to engage in the *politics of representation*.

One of the key steps taken by the ACPO as part of its media management strategy was the establishment of the ACPO Information Office. This Office manages responses to requests from the media for information and comment and also maintains close links with information offices around the forces with the aim of presenting a 'common face' to the media and with developing a more *proactive* approach to media management. The origins of this could be found in a paper written by ACPO in the mid-1980s entitled *A Clearer Voice for ACPO*, which had stressed the 'mistakes of the past' and which argued for a much more proactive approach to media relations. It acknowledged ACPO's past 'delayed, diversified or sometimes non-existent response to media demands' and warned of the dangers of a slow response to the media:

> Delay allows inaccuracies in stories to become established in the public mind and other voices are heard instead. These may be the voices of staff associations, with a particular angle to push or lacking in some aspects of finesse ... (ACPO, unpublished).

This was a clear enough reference to ACPO's media key rivals, the Police Federation. It took some years before the paper's message was put into effect. This stressed the need for an information base of statistics, common lines of criticism and agreed lines of response. Each ACPO committee, it was argued, should have a media strategy item placed on every agenda. A list of agreed media 'voices' was also seen as essential and the report continued in this vein right through to the recommendation of news release headed stationery. In 1994, the establishment of the Media Advisory Group, a free standing body with a link to the Presidential Team, made clear ACPO's commitment to an informed media strategy. Tactically, this has included the national distribution of 'fact sheets', for example, a series entitled *Your Police: A Service to Value*, the first one of which presented the case that the police service is good 'value for money' and which was aimed at increasing public support for the police at a time when economies and efficiency-savings within the police were creeping up higher on the Government's agenda (ACPO, 1994). Following on such diffuse campaigns was the publication of the more strategic document *In Search of Criminal Justice*. This set out, in effect, a 'shopping list' of the criminal justice changes ACPO wished to see introduced, including advance disclosure of the main platform of the defence case and changes to the rules of evidence to admit previous convictions and hearsay, measures heavily opposed by civil liberties bodies and criminal lawyers (ACPO, 1995). The publication of this document signalled more than any other the arrival of a *proactive* campaigning strategy for ACPO in place of the primarily reactive approach of earlier ACPO activities. Following on from this, ACPO produced *In Search of Justice: Three Years On*, which provided a progress report of the 'shopping list' plus some new proposals which included 31 recommendations for the future of the criminal justice system (ACPO, 1998). We shall return to this issue later.

In addition to the newly empowered Information Office, the media management strategy within ACPO embraced programmes of media training for its members, such as 'Media Skills', 'Broadcasting Skills' and 'Facing the Press'. This new approach to the media enabled ACPO to 'compete' more effectively with the Police Federation whose media and public relations machinery was already firmly in place. This process also involved persuading reluctant ACPO members that they could comment on an issue that was not only related to their force area. This has meant that increasingly ACPO members have been made available to respond to media requests, so that the media do not simply have to turn to the Federation, who were always there to offer what one member called 'red meat'!

However, the second organisational development within ACPO referred to above may prove to be the most significant in the long term, at least in terms of ACPO's position as a police pressure group — the split of ACPO into two distinct bodies, a 'staff association' and a 'professional body' (see chapter 3). The decision made in 1994 by ACPO to divide the organisation into two bodies, one concerned with its members' pay and conditions of service — CPOSA — the other concerned with developing policing policy and with representing the 'professional' view of the police — ACPO itself — was strategic in a number of ways. However, in one specific way it acted at a stroke to strengthen ACPO's hand as a campaigning group, certainly relative to the Federation and the PSA. The case could now be constructed that ACPO was there to represent the 'professional' view of the police service, not only to advocate sectoral 'vested interests' — the accusation that could now be levelled at the other police associations. With this framework established, ACPO could claim that whilst the Federation and the PSA acted primarily with their own 'interests' at heart when they adopted their position on this or that policy, ACPO, now free from such 'vested interests', was the only body genuinely concerned with the service *as a whole*. In the discourse of public campaigning ACPO could claim that it alone had its hands 'clean' of narrow, sectoral interests. We shall return to this later.

The development of media management and the organisational split have done much to assist ACPO as a pressure group. However, it was a *tactical* rather than organisational measure which appears to have been particularly effective during ACPO's campaigns on the police reform. We refer here to the role played by '*strategic alliances*' formed by

ACPO in furtherance of its goals relating to Sheehy and the Police and Magistrates' Courts Act 1994. With policy arenas becoming increasingly overcrowded, governments are more than happy to reduce the numbers of groups that they need to consult. Close knit policy communities have extremely restricted access so the fewer the groups within them the more successful the policy community is likely to be (Smith, 1993). McRobbie (1994) lists 'alliances' as one of the four requirements for pressure politics. These 'strategic alliances' have been established with other national bodies, in furtherance of campaigns around policing and criminal justice issues. On the one hand alliances were formed with the *other* police associations to further specific aims, mainly relating, not surprisingly, to Sheehy. As a member of HMIC stated:

I think ACPO really started to pull its weight when it worked with the Police Federation and the Superintendents' Association to a certain extent, to influence discussions on Sheehy, the police reform programme, all the changes that were taking place at that stage and started to have an impact over the House of Lords and House of Commons (E07).

On the other hand, perhaps more crucially, ACPO chose to work closely with the local authority associations (LAAs), such as the Association of County Councils (ACC) and the Association of Metropolitan Authorities (AMA) — now reformed under a joint body (see chapter 2) — during the debate over aspects of the Police and Magistrates' Courts Act 1994. This Act offered plenty of scope for ACPO and the LAAs to find common ground — most obviously, over the threat to the 'local' element in the accountability structure (Loveday, 1995). In this respect the leadership of ACPO effectively 'bought into' the established political skills and political networks of the LAAs as it sought to amend certain dimensions of the planned reform of the police authorities. One past President interviewed in our research said:

We didn't have any experience in lobbying at all in the Houses of Parliament; the ACC and the AMA had considerable experience in that and so we worked well with them ... which created this enormously powerful alliance of interests, and that still exists (PO4).

Another respondent, a civilian with close links with ACPO, put it this way:

> They [ACPO] did not know how to lobby, but the people who knew how to lobby were the local government people ... and they said 'we'll help you' because they had concerns too. Their concerns were about the size of the police authorities and the fact that they wouldn't have proper representation on them ... (E48).

On this basis an alliance was formed in which ACPO were very much a beneficiary, as the same respondent explained:

> ... we [ACPO] did make use of their expertise and their offices and their arrangements ... we were riding in on their expertise because we were babes at it.

We should note at this point that there is an indication again here of how *weak* ACPO had been in the past at the art of politics, despite the views of commentators at the time. Another point to make is that there are certain ironies associated with such alliances, not least because they entailed ACPO 'getting into bed' with former adversaries. During the 1980s ACPO had fought pitched battles with the LAAs, particularly the AMA, over their attempt to gain more control over chief constables by granting more powers to the LPAs in relation to police policy-making (see McLaughlin, 1994). Whereas on those occasions the main line of opposition to the proposals came in the form of chiefs defending the 'independence' of the police, this new alliance chose to rally around the *defence* of the local nature of policing and the need to keep the LPAs 'close' to their local communities. Whatever the ironies involved, the strategic alliances formed around the police reform agenda served both to achieve specific short-term goals, particularly the victory over who should select the chairs of the new LPAs — now to be chosen by the LPA itself and not the Home Secretary — and to equip ACPO with longer term skills in the art of lobbying. Political skills were acquired during the police reform debate of the mid-1990s which ACPO was to employ again.

Looking across the three police associations as they have operated during the 1990s, there appears to be a common theme. Each body claims to have enhanced its own capacity to lobby and campaign on the policing and criminal justice front and to have competed more effectively with the other police associations within the policing policy network in the battle to represent the 'police view'. In this respect two notes of caution should be stated. First, there is something of an 'organisational imperative' for senior figures within representative bodies to claim to have overseen a process of 'professionalisation' of that body. This can take the shape of comparing a relatively unsuccessful past with a much more effective present, which in turn reflects positively on the figures who were at the helm during that process. We should for this reason be circumspect about such claims; analysis must assess the evidence that such enhancement has taken place. Secondly, we should not underestimate the extent to which the environment of the early to mid-1990s was one in which the 'police view', however and by whoever it was articulated, was virtually guaranteed to have been well received (Charman and Savage, 1999). The political contest between the Conservative and Labour parties in the long run-up to the 1997 General Election was one which frequently embraced 'law and order politics' (ibid; Reiner, 1997); the parties competed for the title of 'toughest on crime' and in that environment the 'police view' was one sought out at every point. As a consequence the police associations were courted by senior figures in both of the main parties, who were more than ready to appear at the annual police association conferences and pledge their support for the police. In this respect whether any increased 'influence' of the police associations is due primarily to their own endeavours or to a more receptive environment is a question we should constantly bear in mind.

These issues notwithstanding, we shall now proceed to draw more general conclusions about the role of the ACPO and the other police associations within the police and criminal justice policy network.

CAUGHT IN THE ACT: POLICE CAPTURE OF THE POLICY AGENDA

We would argue that the police staff associations in general and ACPO in particular, have, over the past decade or so, managed to relocate their position within the criminal justice policy network. The 'Bobby Lobby' has enhanced its status as a player with influence over the policy agenda and, significantly, that influence has extended beyond the *policing* policy agenda and has penetrated more effectively than before the wider *criminal justice* policy agenda. The pattern which the relocation of the police lobby has taken is directional: it takes the form of a three-stage movement, from *agenda resistance*, through *agenda re-shaping* to *agenda setting*. This movement has been uneven and does not lend itself easily to periodisation, but it is, we would argue, a movement evident in policy outcomes.

From Agenda Resistance to Agenda Setting: Forming the Policing Policy Network

If there has been a discernable movement in the effectiveness of the police lobby, that has been due largely to the role adopted by ACPO within the police staff associations as increasingly the lead body in the representation of the 'police view'. By means of the organisational mechanisms outlined earlier, ACPO has strategically and successfully relocated itself within the policing and criminal justice policy-networks to occupy a position more centre stage than had ever been the case. In that sense the path of ACPO's ascendancy involved two major steps. First, ACPO set out its stall *internally* by deliberately attempting to present itself as *the* police professional association. The split within ACPO between the 'staff association' and 'professional' wings of the organisation's roles referred to above was a crucial element in that strategy. By seeming to separate out the 'professional police view' from 'vested interests', ACPO could more easily distinguish itself from the other police associations whose interventions and posturings could, when convenient, be labelled as sectoral and interest-driven. According to this logic, only ACPO — now stripped of its organic connection with its own members' interests in terms of pay and conditions — could advance itself as the only essentially *'professional'* police association, one which could thus speak on behalf of the whole service. It was also, of course, the senior association in terms of police rank. In terms of gaining legitimacy, these rationalisations could be powerful instruments. The second step was *externally* oriented. It was to move the organisation from a *reactive* approach to policy-shaping to one that was increasingly *proactive*. As pressure group theorists have long argued, in order to be 'successful' groups need to be organised in two ways — internal organisation and organisation in terms of contact with government (Richardson and Jordan, 1979). Not content with being more or less effective in combating policy agendas set in motion by other parties outside of the police service — as was evident in the research discussed earlier by Jones *et al.* (1994) — ACPO began to adopt an approach which more and more took the initiative in policy formation. We shall develop this argument by means of specific areas of police-related public policy and present the activities and ACPO, and to a lesser extent the other police associations, in terms of three configurations of policy-shaping as they have emerged during the 1990s. These cannot be easily or accurately articulated in a temporal framework as they were to an extent coterminous; however, the incremental and directional nature of the shifts in question allow some form of periodisation.

Phase One: Agenda Resistance

There is little doubt that the policing policy agenda which emerged during the early 1990s constituted a serious threat to the status quo of the British police service. Having enjoyed very much a privileged position within the public sector throughout the 1980s in terms of levels of funding and non-interference in the management of its affairs, there were clear signs that government had now reached the point of 'the party's over' (Savage and Nash, forthcoming, 2001). Conservative ministers were beginning to become restless that there appeared to be no clear 'pay off' for the years of generous funding directed at the police service and pointed to continuing rises in recorded crime as evidence that the police were failing to deliver. It was in this context that Kenneth Clarke took over as Home Secretary. Clarke was noted for his refusal to treat public sector professional bodies with kid gloves and was quite prepared to 'tough it out' with what he clearly saw as bastions of self interest. This was apparent in his approach to his first Police Federation conference as Home Secretary in 1992, when he threatened to undermine tradition by not attending. He said to the Federation Chairman:

> I didn't go to the teachers conference, not the BMA's. I don't have to go to yours. I've looked up my legal obligations towards the Federation. I am only obliged to consult you. No more no less (Quoted in Judge, 1994:468).

This 'cooling down' of relationships between the Conservatives and the police was to become more apparent with the police reform agenda which emerged, initially at least, under Clarke. As has been mentioned, amongst other things this entailed the Sheehy Inquiry on police pay and conditions which set out to challenge in fundamental ways some of the basic arrangements for the employment of police officers. The absence of any police representative on the Sheehy team signalled the tone of the Inquiry; quite clearly the police service was in for a shock. In policy terms this was to take the form of recommendations for *fixed-term contracts* for officers and support for schemes to introduce *performance related pay*, both designed to strengthen the 'right to manage' within the police and overhaul the rewards and sanctions framework of the service.

There is little doubt that the police representative bodies had been 'side-stepped' by Sheehy and forced onto the defensive; the new agenda was dominated by employment philosophies which took little notice of tradition and showed no sympathy with precedent. However, the speed and effectiveness with which they responded to the agenda thus *imposed* was to prove crucial. In this respect what was at issue was the capacity to launch a campaign of *agenda resistance* and in that sense the police associations did so by means of an *intra-organisational policy network*. ACPO, the Police Federation and the Superintendents' Association, operating as an *internal policy network*, began to work together to challenge, oppose and undermine the Sheehy agenda. Fixed-term contracts and performance related pay were to be the main targets of this campaign. Joint platforms and shared information and research fur-thered the capacity of the associations to lobby against the introduction of such measures within the police, on the grounds that they would fundamentally alter the type of service which has been the tradition of British policing (McClaughlin and Murji, 1998). That the Conservatives eventually dropped both schemes (at least for all non-ACPO ranks) bore witness to the effectiveness of that campaign — although the subsequent arrival of Michael Howard as Home Secretary, noticeably more 'pro-police', played its part (Savage and Nash, 2001). ACPO itself played a key role, as one ACPO member interviewed expressed it:

When we were most under attack from Sheehy ... you saw ACPO as a fairly strong lobby breaching the political line ... we did I think become a very strong political lobby at all levels ... with local MPs and local politicians and very successfully so ... (M06).

Whichever way, there is little doubt that Sheehy forced the police associations into what another member described as 'on the back foot defending our position' (P06). What was at issue here was their ability to *resist* agendas set by others. The early- to mid-1990s were also to witness the capacity of the associations, and ACPO in particular, to *shape* or at least *re-shape* agendas.

Phase Two: Agenda Re-shaping

Alongside the reform agenda directed at police officers' pay and conditions was another, overlapping agenda concerned with the structures of police governance, police management and police roles and responsibilities. As was made clear in chapter 2, during the early- to mid-1990s, two major reviews were undertaken which set out to challenge in radical ways the reorganisation of British policing; the White Paper, *Police Reform: A Police Service for the Twenty-First Century* (Home Office, 1993b) and *Review of Police Core and Ancillary Tasks* (Home Office, 1995a), known generally as the Posen Inquiry. The White Paper and Posen were intended to undermine the status quo of British policing in different but fundamental ways; both were to be blunted by the concerted efforts of the police associations in general and ACPO in particular.

The White Paper was concerned primarily with the question of police governance and set in motion what was to become the Police and Magistrates' Courts Bill (1993) and eventually the Police and Magistrates' Courts Act 1994 (the PMCA). It is difficult to overstate the strength of opposition to the White Paper's key proposals and to doubt that they sent shock waves throughout the police establishment and beyond. The two central issues were on the one hand the plans to reform the local police authorities by reducing them in size and by replacing part of the directly elected element by 'independent members', and on the other the plan to create new powers for the Home Secretary to set out 'national objectives' for the police service. These proposals opened up the Government to attack (Loveday, 1995) that it was guilty of both diminishing the *local* nature of policing, by reducing the involvement of local councillors on the police authorities, and at the same time by *centralising* controls over the police through the new powers of the Home Secretary not only to set national objectives but also to select the chairs of the new police authorities. Senior police officers saw in these proposals therefore a dual threat to their position: the Home Secretary would be able to *impose* policing objectives and thus reduce their own discretion to determine policy; the externally appointed chairs to the police authorities could overturn established working relationships between chief officers and their local chairpersons, relationships which had allowed considerable autonomy to those chief officers.

The response of chief officers to the emerging agenda was concerted and effective. As has already been stated, ACPO sought out and formed *strategic alliances* with LAAs and key figures in both Houses of Parliament to put pressure on the Government to pull back from some elements of the Police and Magistrates' Courts Bill. With their partners in the campaign they forced concessions from the Home Secretary over the selection of chairs to the police authorities — these would now be selected locally — and the setting of national objectives, which would now only be formed after formal consultation with chief officers themselves. These were seen as at least partial victories over the policy agenda as originally set out. The 'lobbying' had paid off, as one member put it:

> ... the new Police Act had a lot more teeth and a lot more danger in its draft form ... there was an awful lot of lobbying which went on with local MPs and local politicians and ... very successfully so. Probably quite worryingly so from the Home Office perspective (M06).

There appeared to have been a subtle shift in comparison to the response to Sheehy: ACPO were now *re-shaping* the policy agenda and moving on the *offensive* as a campaigning body. A central mechanism of this was the *policy network* involving ACPO, the local authority associations and key allies in the Houses of Parliament. Without this network it is difficult to imagine that the Home Office would have been forced to concede in the way it did on central platforms of its legislative plans.

The *re-shaping* process was to become even more apparent in relation to Posen. The Inquiry set out to identify policing functions which were 'core' in the sense that they could only be undertaken by sworn police officers and those which could be classified as 'ancillary' and which potentially could be undertaken by other bodies and agencies, perhaps through 'out sourcing'. Chief officers initially saw in this agenda the spectre of 'stripping' down the police service and of the privatisation of policing functions; again a campaign was launched by ACPO, using the same allies assembled against the PMCA, to counter this threat. What transpired was that, almost by a process of stealth, ACPO managed to position itself in the Inquiry in such a way as to gain a significant degree of *ownership* of the eventual recommendations contained in Posen. Key ACPO members were granted full participation in the proceedings and allowed not only to comment on, but to take an active role in, the drafting of particular sections of the Inquiry Report. Indeed, ACPO effectively provided much of the 'research' on which the final recommendations of Posen were based. ACPO's own preferences on core and ancillary functions were clearly evident in the final report (see Leishman *et al.*, 1996). As with the PMCA, the final outcome of the *Posen* agenda was considerably less threatening to the *status quo* of policing than might have been the case. It is appropriate to view this as a process of *agenda re-shaping* rather than straightforward *agenda-resistance*; ACPO was in this case fully and actively on the *inside* of policy formation and not, as with Sheehy, forced to defend *ex post facto*.

The successes over the PMCA and Posen were, however, over concessions forced from agendas *imposed* on the police service. Throughout and subsequent to these campaigns ACPO was also moving strategically into the business of *agenda setting*.

Phase Three: Agenda Setting

There is something of a paradox in the lobbying track record of ACPO and the other police associations as it unfolded through the 1990s. In relation to issues pertaining directly to the police service, such as pay and conditions, roles and responsibilities and police governance, they were forced on the defensive and managed at best to re-shape agendas set by others. Yet in relation to areas less within their remit of responsibility and control the police associations have to some extent been more successful in actually *setting agendas* for others to respond to. Nowhere is this more apparent than in relation to the highly controversial debate over the *right to silence*. The background to this lies with ACPO's handling of the *Royal Commission on Criminal Justice*, known generally as the Runciman Commission (RCCJ, 1993).

ACPO's tactical response to the launch of Runciman, set up in the wake of a series of miscarriages of justice in the 1970s and 1980s, contrasts sharply with the organisation's earlier approach to the Royal Commission on Criminal Procedure (RCCP) set up almost a decade before, again a response in part to concerns over abuses of police powers and the miscarriages of justice which followed. ACPO did submit evidence to the RCCP on issues like police powers and the rights of suspects but it did so more on the basis of stated *preferences* than on the basis of a constructed *case*. There was no apparent strategic or tactical approach to the emerging agenda, more a defensive and negative *resistance* to the proposed changes to police powers which were winning support within the Commission. It was not until the Commission's recommendations were drafted into legislative form that ACPO and the other police associations really began to mobilise. With Runciman, however, ACPO adopted a very different strategy: it decided to *steer* the agenda, to some extent, in the direction which it preferred and to operate *proactively* by deciding both what it wanted out of the Commission and how it was to achieve it. This was reflected in the use of 'evidence' and 'research' in support of its preferences, something which had clearly not been employed in response to the RCCP. One past President of ACPO compared the two different approaches in this way:

> ... whereas a couple of years ago we would have probably grumbled about what we saw as major deficiencies in the criminal justice system, now we proactively try to get something done about it ... (P01).

Research thus becomes a tool in this 'proactive' approach to setting agendas. This signalled a departure from past practice, as another past President explained:

> ... if you look at the Royal Commission on Criminal Procedure ... there is a criticism in that report saying that they were concerned that the evidence given by the police was largely anecdotal ... was not based on sound research. I think the Runciman Commission ... would say they were impressed by the evidence that was prepared by the police because it was extremely well prepared, was based on good research and indeed there was marked absence of anecdotal evidence ... (P05).

The effect, according to this respondent, was evident:

> ... we have evolved a much more professional approach to this in that we research it ourselves very thoroughly, we debate an area of change

that we think we would like to see and then we market it to
government, to members of Parliament whatever, to try to achieve
that change (P01).

What was even more remarkable was that despite the fact that Runciman
was established primarily because of concerns about abuses of police
powers, the final Report put 'blame' elsewhere, as one ACPO member
(from our 'case study') put it:

the Royal Commission had been set up on the basis that the police
were the bad boys and the Royal Commission was going to put that
right . . . I think the police walked away from that Royal Commission
with a fairly reasonable clean bill of health whereas the finger was
then pointing to the other bits of the criminal justice system which
weren't working very effectively . . . (E20).

In their evidence to the Royal Commission ACPO argued for a range
of changes to the criminal justice system (ACPO, 1995) including:

(a)   Greater openness in investigation and trial.
(b)   Better police investigations.
(c)   Videoing of police interviews.
(d)   Defence disclosure.
(e)   Courts to be able to draw inferences from silence.
(f)   Previous convictions to be admitted in evidence where the
defendent denies intent.
(g)   Greater use of DNA evidence.

It must be noted at the outset that some of these changes at least come
under the umbrella of improving the quality of policing through more
vigorous procedural requirements for police officers. Others, however,
are very much classic 'police preferences', such as the admissability of
evidence of previous convictions. In advancing its case ACPO submitted dossiers of research-based literature in support. For example, in
support of the amendment to the right of silence, ACPO undertook a
survey which 'suggested that silence was the refuge of the experienced
criminal facing serious charges' (ibid:6). When the Royal Commission
reported in 1993, it accepted a number of key ACPO recommendations,
including the extension of the use of DNA and the setting up of a DNA

database and introduction of a requirement on the defence to disclose their case. It also recommended a review on the rules revealing previous convictions (RCCJ, 1993). By any standards this was a high success rate. However, even this was seen as only a partial victory. The central target in this strategic campaign was the *right to silence*. The police service had long held that the unfettered use of the right to silence had given excessive protections to suspects of crime and that this had led in turn to the manipulation of the criminal justice process by 'guilty' defendants. The launch of Runciman, amongst other things, was taken as an opportunity to fight for the abolition of the unfettered right to silence. ACPO set out in this direction by assembling research evidence in support of its case and by constructing powerful counter-arguments to the traditional objections to interference with this right. It had even prepared a drafting of the statute which could be part of the legislation replacing the existing case law on the right to silence. A member of ACPO even learned the formal skills of statute writing in order to assist ACPO in this aim. ACPO knew what it wanted to achieve and marshalled the case to win over enough of those who needed to be convinced, a case supported with a targeted media campaign, again attached to documented research and evidence in favour of the proposals. It was a case they lost, but only temporarily. Although the Royal Commission rejected the case, a minority statement gave its support. The proposal, with its supportive evidence, had gained some support in the 'right places': the campaign continued and accordingly the amendment to the right of silence was enacted through the Criminal Justice and Public Order Act 1994, together with many of the other measures advanced by ACPO. In the words of ACPO itself, the Act 'accepted the police service's arguments on DNA and the right to silence' (ACPO, 1995:6). Again, we have to be clear what was achieved in this respect. A Royal Commission set up initially in response to abuses of police powers and miscarriages of justice was persuaded *by* the police to transform the criminal justice system in directions *the police service* preferred. In *In Search of Criminal Justice: Three Years On*, ACPO voiced its approval of this change in law:

The changes in the law around the right to silence were in particular welcomed by ACPO, who had pressed for some considerable time for such a change as a counter to 'ambush defences' which were becoming increasingly prevalent' (ACPO, 1998:3.5).

We would argue that what was involved in this context was a process of *agenda setting* and a strategic approach to that process. In some respects it left other more 'established' criminal justice pressure groups, such as the legal professions, floundering. ACPO, rather than the legal professions, had the 'ear' of government and had as such manoeuvred itself *within* the governmental policy network. It had become an *insider* pressure group (Grant, 1989), arguably for the first time.

What we have mapped out here are *three configurations of policy formation* within the policing policy network, with ACPO playing the 'lead' role in each case. These configurations do not fall neatly into a temporal framework but rather involve overlapping and at times consequential processes. We can portray them in tabular form as follows:

Three Configurations of Policy Formation

POLICY INFLUENCE	POLICY AREA	POLICY NETWORKS
Agenda resistance	Fixed-term contracts	ACPO and Police Federation/PSA
	Performance related pay	(Intra organisational network)
Agenda Re-shaping	PMCA (appointment of Chair of Police Authority) Performance Measurement	ACPO and local authority associations (AMA, CoLPA) HMIC Audit Commission
Agenda setting	Right of Silence	Direct influence over Home Office and 'hostile' networks (legal professions)

We would want this framework to be seen as *context-* and *time-bound*. Whilst there may be a general process of 'movement' here, *from* agenda resistance *to* agenda shaping, this should not be seen as an immutable process. It was revealing that ACPO's subsequent campaign over the police use of 'intrusive surveillance' (Savage *et al.*, 1997) largely failed to achieve its objectives. In 1996 ACPO had set out to gain statutory powers for chief police officers to decide on the propriety of intrusive surveillance by the police of private premises, very much in the 'agenda setting' mould. It fought a campaign which employed many of its recently acquired political skills and which at one point appeared to have gained cross-party support. However, at the eleventh hour Labour support was withdrawn — after heavy lobbying by those old hands, the legal professions — and, given the frailty of the Conservatives' majority in Parliament, the case was lost. Some members of ACPO saw in this a sense of 'one battle too many' and the need to 'turn down the steam' after a run of successes (ibid). However, it may also have signalled something of a reversal of fortune. The heavily 'pro-police' atmosphere which cut across party lines in the run up to the 1997 General Election may well have given way to a more even handed, perhaps even guarded, approach to ACPO by the Labour Home Secretary. This reversal was fairly rapid. In 1997 commentators were bemoaning the attention that ACPO was receiving:

> Labour . . . increasingly appears to be listening to a few select voices. In the criminal justice area the tough-on-crime policy translates as hearing the demands only of the Association of Chief Police Officers (Donovan, 1997).

By 1998 Jack Straw was arguing that single issue pressure groups had taken over control of the Labour Party in the 1980s and he was not going to let that happen again. He would instead be concentrating his attentions on 'local communities and their elected representatives' who were worth 'a thousand pressure groups' (Straw, 1998). However, it is extremely doubtful that the 'insider' status of ACPO as a pressure and interest group is, or will in the future be, seriously under threat. Nevertheless, there is a game of high risk involved here which we can express in terms of the 'ACPO Dilemma'; it is on this issue that we shall conclude this chapter.

CONCLUSION: THE ACPO DILEMMA

In the previous chapter we traced the processes by which ACPO has become a more central player in influencing service-level policy-making and through which ACPO has formed into a more corporate agency. We also closed that discussion by examining what we called the 'limits to corporacy', the factors which present structural and/or cultural obstacles to ACPO going much further down the path it has gone in recent years: ACPO can only go 'so far' in influencing service-level policy-making before a range of fundamental issues begin to emerge which call into question the *status quo* of British policing. Central in this respect was the doctrine of constabulary independence. We would argue that equivalent, if not overlapping, obstacles to ACPO's influence are evident at the level of *national* policy-making. Equivalent, because it is clear that ACPO can only go 'so far' in its lobbying activities before opening up a Pandora's Box of problems and challenges to its role and authority. 'Overlapping' because the doctrine of constabulary independence also lies at the heart of ACPO's 'dilemma' surrounding its influence over national policing policy.

The interrelationship between the doctrine of constabulary indepence and the ACPO dilemma is evident in this statement by one ACPO member:

> I have concerns about our lobbying role. The one thing about us compared to a lot of other organisations is our political independence. I worry that if we are seen as an overtly lobbying body, as we were with Sheehy to an extent, we will very quickly lose that independence ... I think in the long term we will lose more than we gain (M23).

This statement is rich in significance. It reflects a sentiment which was reflected in many of the interviews we conducted, particularly those involving the most senior members of ACPO. There is no doubt that, however much members have welcomed ACPO's greater assertiveness and effectiveness as a lobbying organisation, that welcome is surrounded by attitudes of caution and reservation; even those central to ACPO's success in this area expressed a certain unease. What seems at stake in this respect is the *quid pro quo* which is associated with constabulary independence. If policing is to be kept free from 'political interference', as constabulary independence appears to assert, then in turn the *police* must not interfere in 'politics', or at least not be *seen* to interfere in politics. 'Independence' bites both ways; the sustainability of the notion of 'keeping politics out of policing' is dependent, for legitimation purposes, on some *quid pro quo* of 'keeping the police out of politics'. This is the crux of the dilemma: the more assertive and effective ACPO becomes in lobbying to resist, shape or set policy agendas, the more difficult it is articulate the case for the 'special' or 'unique' nature of policing in terms of operational independence and its inherently 'non-political' character. Returning to the statement cited above, what might be 'lost' as ACPO becomes more assertive is not so much 'independence' as such but the capacity to *claim to be independent*.

There is evidently a degree of *political calculation* at work in this respect in the 'caution' surrounding ACPO's greater effectiveness as a lobbying organisation. This relates to a concern within ACPO that it is possible for the police to be too successful, too effective and too explicit, because evident success and effectiveness might lead to adverse reactions from other parties in the policing policy process. As one member put it:

> We got reverses on almost everything [on Sheehy] . . . I think that was a very dangerous route. I hope it's finished . . . I think we really ought to keep apart from lobbying and the due process of Parliament (M03).

Implicit in such statements is some notion of 'excessive' levels of activity and effectiveness. What appears to be at stake in this respect is a type of (unspoken) 'concordat' about 'appropriate' forms and levels of activity within which the policing organisations in general and ACPO in particular should be concerned to operate — to step beyond those forms and above those levels is a dangerous game. This is not simply a one-sided, ACPO, view. One of the former Home Secretaries we interviewed reinforced this notion of 'appropriate' forms of activity and the dangers of stepping outside of them:

> My own feeling is that ACPO's lobbying should be done very quietly and very discreetly because they will take views which at times will not be possible for any Home Secretary to meet (E01).

Referring to a recent ACPO 'campaign' on sentencing he went on to say:

> [ACPO] . . . have an agenda on sentencing, which is getting into a very tricky area if they become too public on all that because then you'll get judges having a view on sentencing. . . . The judges are now going public and I think it's very bad to have the different elements of the criminal justice system arguing against each other in public. Very bad indeed. . . . These things are much better conducted discreetly.

It is interesting that comparisons with the judiciary were made: they too occasionally rely on the notion of 'independence'. The point however is that ACPO, at least according to some, often very senior, members had come very close to overstepping the boundaries of 'appropriate' forms of activity. The rationale behind this was spelt out by a former chief constable who, when asked whether he thought there would be any dangers in ACPO being successful as a lobby group, stated:

> Yes, there would be; they don't have a constitutional position and if they became too successful too often I think they would attract a lot of undue interest in them and you could find their wings clipped in some way (E39).

This respondent went on to refer to the views of a very senior member of ACPO which were expressed to him:

> [person named] . . . said to me, and I agree with him . . . that he thinks it's high time ACPO became a little less successful in that area [lobbying] for a while, lower the profile, don't let's have too much success . . . because there would actually be a reaction against it. I think it's wise advice.

'Lowering the profile' (expressed by one former President of ACPO as 'turning down the steam'), was seen as a necessary antidote to the run of success which ACPO had enjoyed over the range of areas considered earlier. Why? Apparently because 'too much success' would call both ACPO and the principle of 'independence' into question. The more active ACPO becomes, the more its non-constitutional status could be the subject of concern. The more active ACPO and the police organisations become in lobbying on the political front, the more difficult it is to sustain the notion of the independence of the police from politics. Herein lies the 'ACPO dilemma'.

We shall deal further with both ACPO's non-constitutional status and the notion of 'independence' in the following chapter. In this chapter we need, finally, to draw out another element of the 'ACPO dilemma' which explains further the attitude of caution and concern surrounding ACPO's record of success. This relates less to political calculation and more to a distinctively British form of police discourse. We refer here to the notion of 'winning by appearing to lose'.

What appears to lie behind the idea of 'lowering the profile' of ACPO and operating 'discreetly', is in many ways a senior management equivalent to the operational policing tactic of the 'minimum use of force'. Reiner (1992:64–67) has documented how the notion of 'policing by consent' as attached to the 'British policing model' rested on the employment of a range of ideological and tactical instruments, one of which was the miminum use of force. In the operational sense the rationale was that the key to successful policing — the 'traditional British style of policing' — lay in a cautious and low key response to incidents, avoiding the possible reaction an aggressive approach might invoke. The logic is that this style and approach to policing was all the more effective for it being 'low key'; in Mark's words, 'The real art of policing a free society or a democracy is to win by appearing to lose' (quoted in Reiner, ibid:64). The doctrine of the minimum use of force has seemingly permeated the discourse surrounding the British police well beyond the operational sphere. In an interesting way this philosophy is transposed onto *ACPO* as an organisation and used by some, including key role-holders within the Association, as a form of framework for organisational style and strategy. This is expressed in terms of the need to ensure that ACPO does not go 'too far' down the road of professionalisation and assertiveness, whether that be in the context of external or internal activities. One senior member of ACPO stated the case clearly:

The danger is that we're too fast and too slick, because I think that you can win, as ever, by being too professional, and in a sense you can lose by being too professional, that's another factor in British policing. I mean, it's the dustbin lid syndrome, when the riots are going on and all you've got is a dustbin lid . . . the best example I can think of and this is in the early, middle sixties, up in the [area identified] we had a police inspector shot and that was a fairly unusual event then and still is thank God but was even more unusual then. We had the situation, almost, where Police Officers were saying 'who's been in the army and who can carry, who knows about guns, come and get a gun and we'll go and find this fellow' . . . and a big exercise went on and it was hardly more professional than that, I exaggerate, but you get the feeling. . . . That wouldn't happen now, what happens now is we make one telephone call and I've got the equivalent of the SAS who will turn out, in two or three vans, all in black suits, all with sub machine guns, all looking extremely professional, they will do an extremely professional job and they'll get the job done, and that doesn't mean shooting the guy, it probably means less, much less likely to shoot the guy, but to get him arrested and into custody. Much, much more professional but which has the most public sympathy? Which catches the public imagination most? And we've often through the years won by losing, the dustbin lid in the riot ... it's the traditional police officer that's caught up in this. He's not now, he's in all his gear and he's got his sticks and his batons and his gas and God knows what. ACPO's a bit like that, we sort of bumble along and get ridden over as we were in the past but we can become too professional, too slick, we're on *Today* programme every other morning, we're talking to all sorts of people and making policy and making things happen because of the influence that we have, a very strong influence that we have, and in so doing we can get too strong and lose and that's what a lot of this project's about. And I constantly will say we're very much aware of that ... (E02).

This statement expresses better than most the crux of the 'ACPO dilemma'. On the one hand there is an element of *political calculation*, in the sense that ACPO is seen to be treading on dangerous ground if it becomes too professional, too strong and too effective, ACPO might 'lose' in the end — support would be lost and other bodies would react competitively to ACPO's increasing power. On the other hand there is the belief that a 'fast and slick' ACPO is *undesirable*. ACPO should go no further than absolutely necessary down the path of 'professionalisation'. It must ensure that the 'traditions of British policing' are secured and not compromised by its activities — a parallel here with the insistence on the 'local' nature of policing as discussed in the previous chapter. The balance that needs to be struck is between the need to have the 'police view' adequately represented in the process of policing policy-making and the need to preserve traditional arrangements, characterised by independence, a low, minimalist profile and localism. As ACPO has become more professional, high profile and effective in the art of representation, it is that balance which, some would argue, is under threat.

From a perspective outside of ACPO, however, the growth of ACPO's influence over the policing and criminal justice policy process is of much wider resonance. The serious danger with the enhanced lobbying activities and effectiveness of the police staff associations witnessed in recent years lies with distortions it can create within the criminal justice system. Researchers have long argued that the police and police actions dominate the criminal justice process in terms of governing outcomes in the pre-trial and trial stages of the justice system (Sanders, 1997). This will be made only more problematic if the police (through their associations) also dominate the *policy-process* which defines that justice system. That in turn raises again the whole question of *accountability*, a central concern of our final chapter.

Chapter 7
Conclusion: ACPO — Getting Their Act Together?

INTRODUCTION

This study set out to examine the role of ACPO as an organisation, the extent to which ACPO had changed over time and the impact of ACPO on the policing policy process. The spur for the research was the apparent 'gearing up' of ACPO as an organisation as it sought to influence and shape the policing policy agenda during the highly charged debates surrounding the criminal justice and police reform programme, which emerged in Britain in the early- to mid-1990s. Crudely, we set out to assess whether ACPO was 'getting its act together', as many of those we interviewed have put it.

We have taken three, closely interrelated, 'measures' or 'indices' of this process. First, we examined the extent to which ACPO has developed into a more *corporate* body, in the sense of mobilising its constituent parts to operate strategically and cohesively. Secondly, we sought to assess the extent to which ACPO has been able to *influence service-level policy-making*, in terms of the relationship between ACPO policies for policing and policy-making within the individual police services of England, Wales and Northern Ireland. Thirdly, we researched the extent to which ACPO has been able to *influence national policing and criminal justice policy* — the 'external' manifestation of ACPO's activities. The empirical basis to these assessments stemmed from interviews with former and current members of ACPO and with a wide range of 'outsiders' associated in various ways with British policing. In all three respects we would conclude that there seems to have been clear evidence that ACPO had indeed 'got its act together', that, compared with its role in the past, ACPO had moved on to a different level of organisational effectiveness and that this was expressed in a variety of ways in terms of the policing policy process. However, we would argue that this development has, in a number of respects, been one subject to significant, if not fundamental, constraints, which are analysed further below.

Our examination began with an historical review of the ACPO in terms of its organisational and cultural characteristics and development. Despite the views of its critics, who in many cases saw in ACPO an organisation with immense power and purpose, we have argued that ACPO was, until relatively recently, characterised by *disunity* and organisational fragmentation. Above all, ACPO was to be seen as an organisation seemingly incapable of 'getting its act together'. It was often incapable of presenting itself as a coordinated and cohesive body which could speak on behalf of its constituent members. We have gone on to argue that, since then, a series of organisational and cultural developments within ACPO, driven in part by environmental factors, began to transform ACPO into a much more corporate body, one increasingly characterised by internal cohesion and organisational 'mission'. Key in this respect (see chapter 3) were developments such as the establishment of the permanent Secretariat, the introduction of the principle of what we have called the 'presumption in favour of compliance' and the emergence of a 'new breed of chief'. In relative terms at least, organisationally ACPO had indeed begun to 'get its act together'.

One measure of extent to which ACPO is to be seen as a 'corporate' body lies with the degree to which ACPO members, within their own police services, follow ACPO policy as they form policies at the local level. In chapter 5 we set out to assess the role of ACPO in terms of its influence over service-level policy-making. There was every indication that ACPO's influence in this respect had grown over time; members were now more prepared than their predecessors to fall in line with ACPO policy framed nationally and allow that policy to inform and guide policing policies within their own local police services. This has been both an absolute and a relative development: absolute in terms of the net increase in influence of ACPO at service-level over time; relative in terms of ACPO's growing influence relative to some other national agencies, for example Her Majesty's Inspectorate of Constabulary (HMIC). It would seem as if the wholly permissive approach by chief officers to ACPO policy in the past — they would tend to 'do their own thing' irrespective of ACPO policy — has given way, with certain exceptions, to an approach which is inclined towards ACPO policy as a matter of course, again, what can be called the 'presumption in favour of compliance'.

Our third measure of the extent to which ACPO has 'got its act together' was based on assessment of the nature of the influence ACPO has been able to exert over *national* policing and criminal justice policy. In chapter 6 we concluded in this context that it was possible to trace ACPO's activities along a developmental path characterised by a growing capacity, aided and abetted by a sympathetic political climate, to influence the policy agenda. This path is one that had moved from the tendency for ACPO to (more or less successfully) resist agendas advanced by other parties, through to an ability to *shape* agendas initiated by other parties, to the capacity for ACPO to actively (and proactively) *set* agendas for policy and thus institutionalise the 'police view' within the policing and criminal justice policy process. Again, this has involved both an absolute and relative shift: ACPO has been able to exert a much more direct and instrumental influence over policing policy than was the case in the past, with a number of identifiable 'successes'; ACPO has also been able to hold its own relative to other police associations and in particular relative to the Police Federation, which has had to concede some ground on the right to be able to represent and lobby on behalf of the 'police view'.

As we have examined each dimension and expression of ACPO's shift to a more corporate culture and organisation, we have also discussed a number of caveats. Whether it be in terms of ACPO's capacity to develop 'corporacy', ACPO's influence over service-level policy-making, or ACPO's representational and lobbying abilities, we are confronted with *limits* and *boundaries*, including what we referred to in the last chapter as the 'ACPO dilemma'. Of course, this may come as a relief to those outside of ACPO who have watched ACPO's development with trepidation if not serious concern. It is not just a question of how far ACPO *has gone* as an effective corporate body, but of how far *should ACPO be allowed to go*. This relates to the whole question of the *accountability* regarding ACPO, to which we shall return to later. At this point we shall attempt to examine further these 'limits' and how and why they are articulated. Central in this respect, once again, is the doctrine of constabulary independence.

ACPO AND THE DOCTRINE OF CONSTABULARY INDEPENDENCE

As we have seen, 'constabulary independence' is a principle which lies at the heart of much debate on British policing (Marshall, 1965 and 1978). It runs through the machinery of police governance and structures the processes of police accountability in Britain. It also permeates the workings of ACPO as an organisation and the relationship between ACPO and its constituent parts. The doctrine has enjoyed the status of a 'given', an unquestioned if not unquestionable 'absolute' which can draw a line beyond which it is not possible to step. Chief police officers need only invoke the principle for others to retreat, or be encouraged to retreat, whether they be local police authorities, the Home Office, or ACPO itself.

Constabulary independence (CI), we would argue, should be deconstructed and opened up for close scrutiny. We have already referred to the *legal* critique of the doctrine (see chapter 5; Lustgarten, 1986). In this context we shall not pursue the 'legal case' for the deconstruction of CI, but rather approach CI as a form of *policing discourse*. We would argue that CI should be seen as more than a legal doctrine; CI is a discursive form articulated by senior police officers and presented in certain scenarios and debates as way of framing 'what is' and 'what is not' possible.

Constabulary Independence as Discourse

Most certainly the discourse of senior police officers is riddled with 'Denning-type' interpretations of the role of the chief officer and his/her relationship with other authorities. Put simply the doctrine of CI presumes that chief police officers are fully independent from other bodies when it comes to a matter of police decisions or policing policies.

Our research follows that of Reiner (1991) and exposes a deep seam within the discourse of chief officers which constellates around the construction of CI. For example one chief officer stated:

> the Chief Constable is autonomous in his [sic] command and that is a very important aspect of the constitution of this country ... the Chief Constable's operational command ... cannot be usurped by anybody apart from a court of law ... this independence of the police service is unique to this country ... and I think that is the strength of the British police service, that it is not politically directed or manipulated ... it is a very sacred thing (P12).

Notwithstanding the debate over the constitutional legitimacy of the principle of CI, it is the discursive functions of CI to which we shall pay attention. In doing this we seek to contribute to the growing literature on police culture as a discursive form (Chan, 1997; Shearing and Ericson, 1991; Waddington, 1999). In this particular context we draw upon the notion of *variations* in police culture (Chan, 1996) and the patterning of police culture which addresses not just 'street' culture (Reiner, 1992) but also *senior management culture* (Chan, 1997; Manning, 1993; Reuss-Ianni and Ianni, 1983).

In this respect we find that Chan's development of the notion of 'axiomatic knowledge' as the most fundamental dimension underpinning police culture to be of particular significance. Axiomatic knowledge:

> ... represents the fundamental assumptions about 'why things are done in the way they are' in an organisation. Axiomatic knowledge, often held by top management constitutes the foundation for the shape and future of the organisation (Chan, 1997:68).

In this particular case the notion of axiomatic knowledge is applied to the elements which make up 'the police mandate' (Manning, 1978), that is police discourse on 'the war against crime', maintaining order and 'the thin blue line'. We would argue that a feature of the axiomatic knowledge of at least *British* senior police management extends to the notion of CI — together with notions such as 'policing by consent' and, as discussed in the previous chapter, the rationale of 'winning by appearing to lose'. This reads that chief officers are to be left alone to determine policing matters and to formulate policing policy with no *direction* from other authorities, local or national, other than 'the law'. In other words CI forms a central component of the constructed discourse of chief officers in Britain; CI has become 'a core assumption' of chief police officers and is articulated in a variety of contexts and scenarios (Chan, 1997). This discourse is reinforced at least to an extent by the various 'audiences' to whom it is presented, such as the Home Office, which has (in the past at least) allowed 'space' for CI to operate and the local police authorities, which in the main have left the principle unchallenged. In this respect it is a discourse whose very expression generates silence from its recipient audiences. Indeed the principle of CI almost denies its audiences the right of reply — to do so might impinge on the territory marked out by the principle itself.

We would go further and argue that, in the same way that 'street police cultures' are seen to be reinforced by the group (Punch 1983; Skolnick, 1966), the axiomatic knowledge expressed within senior management culture within the police is reinforced by the group elite which is made up of chief police officers. In the British context this takes the form of ACPO. ACPO, by its mode of operation and internal functioning, persistently reinforces the core assumption of CI — even when, as we have seen at various points in this study, CI serves to inhibit ACPO itself from enjoying service-by-service compliance. Amongst the core assumptions reinforced by the work of ACPO is the sanctity of CI as a basis on which chief police officers are prepared to 'do business'. Indeed there is a sense in which, with some irony as we shall see later, ACPO has helped to create a protective ring around CI. Because of ACPO's growing mandate to deliver consistency and consensus around policing policy across its 43 member services, it has been possible for ACPO to argue that further interference by outside bodies in policing policy is not necessary. As we have argued elsewhere, ACPO can be seen as a centralised body which protects a *decentralised* policing system (Savage *et al.*, 1996 — this issue will be examined later). Within this mandate the operation of CI is heralded, yet accommodated within a collectivist ethos. Consistency of policy across police services has been accepted as a matter of principle within ACPO but always with the proviso that in the final analysis CI will overrule any 'party line' if individual chief officers wish it to. 'Consistency' of policy can thus survive hand-in-hand with CI, as two members expressed it:

I don't think that any local influence is diluted by national response
... they [chief constables] will fight tooth and nail ... that they will
not lose independence at all ... it's not a question of acquiescing to
ACPO centrally, it's merely complementary to what they do ...
(M09).

... local independence will never be compromised by the ACPO ...
(M18).

If ACPO serves to reinforce and restate the principle of CI it is, we
would argue, as a *group* response to perceived threats or challenges
from the working environment of senior police officers. Just as the
formation and configuration of 'street' culture relates to a group or
collective accommodation of perceived threats or challenges stemming
from the policing environment of street officers (Skolnick, 1966;
Waddington, 1999), so the working environment of senior police
officers creates the context (or 'field' (Chan, 1997)) for the formation of
senior management culture. That environment includes challenges to
chief officers' authority and discretion. It includes the rise of 'new
public management' (Leishman *et al.*, 1996), the development of
regulatory governance (see chapter 1; Rhodes, 1997) and incursions
from central and local government. In all of these respects CI forms part
of the cultural 'tool-kit' (Shearing and Ericson, 1991) at the disposal of
both individual officers and their collective body.

We can now move on to examine in more detail how, within the
'tool-kit' of senior management discourse, CI functions. We would see
CI as fulfilling two linked discursive functions: first as a means of
furthering professional closure and secondly as a means of *marking out
disputed territory*.

Constabulary Independence as 'Professional Closure'

In this respect the literature on professions and professional power is of
significance (Johnson, 1972). It has been argued that strategies
employed by the 'professions', in particular the 'established' professions (law and medicine), to maintain professional power and autonomy
are oriented to forms of 'professional closure' (ibid). Professional
closure is concerned with one profession/occupation seeking to close off
other groups of operatives from becoming recognised, or 'licensed'

practitioners in their area of work. Closure is a means of denying access or legitimacy to competing practitioners. Central to this strategy is the reference to *unique knowledge and expertise* which only the established profession possesses. Only those who have progressed through the machinery of education and training legitimated and accredited by the professional body itself are presented as capable of being licensed and to practice in that area of work. Thus practitioners of 'alternative medicine' are denied legitimacy on the grounds of the weakness of their knowledge base and absence of appropriate expertise (Saks, 1992; Turner, 1987).

CI can be employed in an equivalent fashion to that of 'unique expertise' as a means of securing and defending the professional closure of policing. The policing profession does not have at its disposal a machinery of licensed practice and accredited knowledge as is the case for professions such as the legal and medical professions. Due in part to its 'artisan' origins (Reiner, 1992) there is no equivalent cultural store of legitimated knowledge and 'identifiable' expertise. However, CI can act as a surrogate rationale in the defence of professional autonomy of senior police officers. Whereas other professions can legitimate professional autonomy and exclusivity through reference to the unique possession of a specialist knowledge and technique, chief police officers in Britain at least, can turn to a *constitutional* rationale for their own autonomy. It is what one ACPO member described as a 'flag of convenience' which senior officers can display at appropriate moments:

> ... you will still have this potential for chief constables to declare UDI [unilateral declaration of independence] ... that always exists and they always fall back on their independence as chief officers, it's wonderfully convenient at times, it really is (M09).

In this sense CI can be employed in the tool-kit of senior police managers as the equivalent of the medical doctrine of 'clinical freedom'. In the case of the latter, non-interference in professional judgments is justified on the basis that medical training and accreditation guarantee sound judgment (Turner, 1987). In the case of policing, non-interference is justified on the basis of the unique *status* of the chief police officer as possessor of the role of sole authority in his/her area of work. As one chief officer expressed it:

... this cherished operational independence is something that is in my view quite the strongest point of a very good police service (M34).

This logic is particularly in evidence when it is a matter of perceived threats and *challenges*; in this context CI can be articulated in terms of *territory*.

Constabulary Independence as 'Marking out Disputed Territory'

There are numerous stakeholders in the policing world. At the most senior levels these include agencies attached to local or central government, regulatory bodies and other public services. In the working environment of the senior police officer these agencies can be perceived as constituting a threat or challenge to his/her authority over policy and decisions. That environment appears to be changing to one of increasing competition of stakeholders for power and influence, as we shall see later. At this stage we are interested in how CI is employed as a means of marking out and protecting territory as that competition increases.

One agency whose assertiveness has clearly increased in recent years is the regulatory body HMIC (see chapter 1; Reiner, 1991). Given the division of policing in England, Wales and Northern Ireland into 43 relatively self contained police services, consistency of policing practices and organisational structures rests in part on the role of HMIC. With the increasing influence of 'new public management' and regulatory governance during the 1980s and 1990s, as we have seen, HMIC has 'flexed its muscles' as it has engaged in its inspection processes. As a result inspections have become more 'directive' and less 'suggestive' in terms of recommended reforms and policies. This has not been lost on individual chief officers, who in some cases claim this to be encroachment on their territory and an undue incursion on their own territory of command. Thus one chief constable could argue:

You can't have former colleagues of mine coming in here and doing an inspection ... I am still the demagogue that I ever was, in that I know what I believe is right for the force (M34).

Even the Home Office, accepted as the major source of influence on chief officers' policy-making (Savage *et al.*, 1998) is viewed with some trepidation, as one former President of ACPO put it:

... if we became too friendly, if we became too close [to the Home Office], then the independence on which we rested so much for policing successfully would become suspect (P14).

Strategies of resistance are, however, most in evidence when it comes to the role of the local police authorities. The role of police authorities has of course been the subject of voluminous debate (see chapters 1 and 5) but if there is something approaching a consensus on this role it is that the police authorities are the 'poor relation' in the 'triangle' of accountability between ACPO, the Home Office and the local authorities themselves. Longer-term analyses of the role of police authorities refer to a diminution in influence over time (Loveday, 1995; Lustgarten, 1986; Wall, 1998). Despite this, chief officers feel it necessary to draw lines between the 'legitimate' role of police authorities and their own responsibilities. In our research we found expressions of this raised in the context of the emergence of the new police authorities as constituted by the Police and Magistrates' Courts Act 1994 (Jones and Newburn, 1997). Again, a central tool in this process of denial of legitimacy is the principle of CI. Referring to the role of 'policing plans' as set out under the Act, the same chief officer, as we have seen in an earlier chapter, argued:

> ... it was the chief constable's plan by law ... but then they [the police authority] publish it and say this is what the police service is going to do this year. Now there is an intrusion and there is impinging on operational independence to a degree in that ... local authorities don't inform my policy ... I try not to let them ... (M34).

Now this strategy of 'marking territory' also applies to ACPO itself. ACPO serves to be both a 'reinforcer' of CI and, to an extent, a *victim* of it. CI has been employed to strengthen individual officers' capacity to deny *ACPO's* own activities, where convenient. In other words ACPO members can employ the discourse of CI as a tool of resistance towards ACPO's own attempts to develop a more corporate policing framework. An expression of this logic is:

> [ACPO] has got to be very careful that it doesn't try and take away from individual chiefs ... their independence and their constitutional position (M37).

Referring to the proposal to strengthen the office of President of ACPO with a longer term of office than one year, another chief commented:

> ... if we ever changed to that particular position I would seriously consider my position in our club [ACPO] because I think it would cut right across what the independence of chief constables and what policing is about in this country (M43).

Applying this form of rationale, a former President insisted that ACPO should aspire to be not much more than an 'advisory body':

> I don't think it could ever be more than that because of the legal independence of chief constables, which you know I would sort of die in the trenches to support (P01).

'Independence' in these contexts is presented as essentially a matter of *professional autonomy* and any body which threatens to circumvent that autonomy, even the body representing chief officers, is presented as confounding a very sacred principle. CI can be invoked as a means of strategic resistance to external and even internal challenges to the territory of chief officers.

It is evident that the principle of CI survives, either defensively or proactively, as a central instrument of professional closure and strategies of resistance to territorial competition for senior police officers in Britain. The constitutional framework of CI has provided a ready made tool for chief officers to interpret and present in their discourses on 'policing business'. It is a cultural artefact which has a legal, or at least neo-legal, prop and it is stronger as a result. As such it has remained largely unchallenged by the various audiences who listen to its message and, as Shearing and Ericson (1991) have argued, 'listeners' are crucial to the survival of cultural forms, not just the actors who employ them. The point about CI is that, as we have argued, its very assertion can serve to silence its audience.

It is at this point that we must introduce a qualification. In our research we found some clear distinctions in the level of enthusiasm with which CI was invoked between chief officers who were retired or close to retirement and more recent appointments to ACPO positions. Those newer members were far less likely to interpret their roles and their relationships with other bodies through the spectrum of CI. They are more comfortable with the idea of 'sacrificing' a degree of autonomy (or 'sovereignty') for the 'greater good' of more coherence and consistency in policing policy nation-wide — in that sense they were more 'ACPO-Philes' than 'ACPO-Phobes' (see chapter 5). As one younger member stated:

local independence has been given up for pragmatic reasons (M02).

Another saw no compromise in independence in falling in line with ACPO:

[ACPO] is a legitimate part of the national structure which maintains a uniform police service against a backdrop of independent forces (M35).

The picture which has emerged in this respect is that newer members of ACPO would appear to be more pragmatic in their strategies of coping with their policing environments. For such members CI is less readily available as a legitimate articulation of professional autonomy and may even be identified very much with a 'dying breed' of chief officer:

Chief constables now do not demand their independence in a way they did three or four years ago, because I think they recognise that it is very much a case of standing together united and showing a united front for the benefit of the service (M02).

If some sectors of ACPO are prepared to take a less 'absolutist' approach to CI, this may involve issues wider than ACPO itself. It may be a reflection of the changing *environment* for the British police service within which CI will be more difficult to invoke as a defence mechanism for senior police officers. In turn this may lead others, outside of the police service, to view CI more critically and less reverentially. We would argue that, at the time of writing, there are indeed a range of environmental factors which are rendering CI less and less 'sellable'.

Constabulary Independence Against the Odds

If policing cultures are forms of articulation of the perceived working environment, significant changes to that environment will present new challenges to cultural production. Such changes and developments are indeed evident in the working environment of senior police managers in Britain. Contained within those changes are shifts in the propensity of policing 'audiences', as 'listeners' to the stories professed by chief officers, to accept without challenge the doctrine of CI.

The first environmental development is the *continuing rise of regulatory* governance and the regulatory state within the policing public sector, discussed in chapter 1. This development will continue to bite into the organisational autonomy of chief police officers through the operation of *inspection* via HMIC and *audit* via the Audit Commission. This rise of regulatory governance, if anything, has accelerated under the Labour Government in the form of the *best value* agenda (DETR, 1998). 'Best value' has created a range of new forms of challenges to the police service; one potential outcome of best value is the opening up of service provision to non-public or non-state sectors, including the private sector. The slogan of 'what matters is what works' is beginning to make inroads into former public sector monopolies by (further) undermining the sanctity of 'public' services (ibid). The best value doctrine is permeating governance and is increasingly enforced through the regulatory agencies. One expression of this is a growing emphasis on *competition* in public service provision. In the policing context this could be reflected in a widening of the scope for *private policing* (Johnston, 1992). Whatever else private policing holds in store for the future of British policing (ibid), in an environment in which competition between *alternative* providers, including private sector providers, becomes the order of the day, it will become more and more difficult for chief officers to insist that they and only they are entitled to dictate on policing matters. CI can only be invoked convincingly up to a point. As other forms of policing provision emerge this will serve to unsettle the 'monopoly' of the public police and in turn disrupt the doctrine of CI. At the very least, CI will have to be re-cast in the light of these developments. Indeed, we may find that one outcome of the best value agenda, as it is enforced through the regulatory agencies, is that local government will seek providers uncomplicated by the 'baggage' associated with CI; they can be found in the private sector. In this context chief officers may attempt to be more flexible and less absolutist in their approach to policing policies and decisions and find that CI is an *obstacle*, rather than an aid, to their effective management.

The second environmental development in question is the emergence of *regional governance*. Police governance is in the throes of *geo-*

graphical realignment (Savage, 1998). The Labour Government's commitment to *regionalisation*, through the establishment of 'regional assemblies', will eventually impact upon the structure and function of the 43 police services of England and Wales. Some form of reconfiguration of existing police services under umbrella, regionally-based, authorities is emerging. A number of ACPO members we interviewed were anticipating some move towards regionally-based 'super-forces' with a drastic reduction in the number of individual police services in the years ahead. Indeed, as long ago as the late 1980s, as a former member of HMIC informed us, there were draft plans, denied at the time, to amalgamate services into around twenty larger units. Since that time, of course, the Police and Magistrates' Courts Act 1994 has enabled Home Secretaries to take steps to alter the existing force structure (Loveday, 1995). However, the regionalisation agenda in terms of the formation of the regional assemblies may prove much more radical than service-by-service amalgamation. Furthermore, the regionalisation agenda presents a direct threat to the principle of CI. Not only would individual chiefs be forced to comply to some degree with policies formed at the regional level by chief officers working at that level, they would also have to embrace a degree of *power sharing* with *other chief executive officers* from the other public services which function at the regional level. Regionalisation would thus seem to present both *vertical* and *horizontal* challenges to the 'autonomy' of chief officers: 'vertical' in the sense of losing a degree of authority to police decision-making up to the regional level (for example, there might be a *regional* traffic policy); 'horizontal' in the sense of sharing policing-related decisions with *non*-police executives and agencies. In this environment CI would be increasingly difficult to invoke, at least convincingly. How receptive would members of such regional bodies be to the logic of 'not on my patch'?

Interestingly, what appears to be at work here is *a polarisation of police policy-making*. On the one hand policy will become more and more the province of bodies which exist over and above that of the individual chief officer, such as the regional assemblies. On the other, police decision-making will increasingly function in operational terms at the *basic command unit* level. For many years police services have been encouraged to concentrate police decision-making 'lower' down the organisation to the level of the 'basic command unit' — typically at the level of the police division under a chief inspector or superintendent.

This philosophy has been promulgated by the regulatory agencies and is now firmly established within policing management systems.

As a result we are witnessing a form of a 'pincer movement' between regionalisation and devolution which is having a significant effect on the role of chief officers. What is at stake in this respect is a loss of power over decision-making 'up' and 'down'; *up* to the regional assemblies and *down* to the basic command units. In this environment CI, as a doctrine invoked by *chief officers*, seems strangely out of place.

This is also the case for the third environmental development: the growth of *partnerships and inter-agency governance*. Linked to the issue of regional governance is the rise and rise of the ethos of *partnership* under the 'community safety' agenda. The Crime and Disorder Act 1998 places statutory responsibilities on parties associated with community safety to work in partnership with one another in auditing and responding to crime and disorder (Charman and Savage, 1999). The Act has many implications for the future of policing but in the context of this discussion it is CI which is in question. In the developing climate of partnership and the power-sharing with which partnership is, or should, be associated, it will become increasingly difficult for one party, the police, to withhold compliance and stand their ground on the basis of the principle of CI. Perhaps more importantly, as the 'culture' of partnership takes hold chief officers will be less and less *inclined* to frame their policy-making in terms of the *exclusive* philosophy of CI. Power-sharing and CI are not principles which sit easily side-by-side. Within the ranks of ACPO itself the emerging agenda of partnership and the realisation of its potential will, we would argue, serve further to disrupt the axiomatic status of CI as a tool within chief officers' discourse. In this changing environment, CI will become increasingly difficult to legitimise and less readily available as a defence mechanism when the authority of the police is challenged or compromised.

The fourth development which challenges the traditional discourse on CI lies with the formation of the new *national policing agencies*. The development of *supra-force* police organisations in Britain is not new. In 1965, the non-statutory Regional Crime Squads were established as collaborative bodies operating in the field of serious crime and criminal intelligence (Uglow and Telford, 1997:38–39). The Regional Crime Squads operated both to coordinate criminal intelligence and to undertake criminal investigations on a regional basis. However, during the 1990s more formalised, *national* statutory agencies emerged which have in a sense transformed the British policing system. The first to be formed was National Police Training (NPT), the body which has assumed national responsibility for core police training and, increasingly, the setting of the curriculum and standards for training which is still delivered at the level of individual police services. Soon to follow was the National Criminal Intelligence Service (NCIS), formed in 1992 as a non-statutory body and since founded on a statutory basis in the Police Act 1997. NCIS has been formed to gather and analyse information in order to provide criminal intelligence to police forces and other law enforcement agencies. Also established by the Police Act 1997 was the National Crime Squad (NCS), the 'investigative' arm of the national police agencies concerned with the prevention and detection of serious crime (Uglow and Telford, 1997). Both NCIS and NCS (and eventually NPT) are to be overseen by, or made 'accountable' to, a 'Service Authority'. The Service Authorities are made up of representatives of the Home Office, chief constables, the local police authorities, 'independent members' appointed by the Home Secretary and a range of other members (ibid).

Whatever else the issues surrounding the national police agencies and their Service Authorities (ibid), they introduce important qualifications to the chief constable's 'autonomy' over police decision- and policy-making. Whilst such agencies have been introduced with a great deal of caution and sensitivity to chief officers' protestations on CI, they are inevitably calling into question the old foundations on which the case for CI has been constructed. NPT, for example, despite opposition from some individual chief constables (see HMSO, 1999a), has managed to succeed in creating a national framework for police training, something which those chief officers had opposed as an interference with their 'operational independence'. The existence of *supra-force* machineries such as NCIS and NCS, whilst formally established without compromise of the doctrine of CI, inevitably places constraints and inhibitions on what were previously essentially *local* decision- and policy-making processes. It is difficult to envisage them functioning at all effectively without that being the case.

Alongside all of these developments, as we have argued in chapter 5, is what might be called the 're-emergence' of local government. If the history of British policing this century is, as some have argued (Lustgarten, 1986; Wall, 1998), a history of the demise of the power of local police authorities at the expense of the Home Office on the one hand and chief constables on the other, then that history may need some readjustment in the present context. As we have argued, it is possible that we are witnessing a form of rekindling of local government in the (unlikely) form of the new police authorities. The research by Jones and Newburn (1997) gives an indication that the new police authorities at least hold out the *potential* for a more assertive role for local authorities on policing plans and policing policy; indeed, as we have seen, a number of chief officers in our research commented on the more challenging and questioning stance adopted by some of the members of the new police authorities. Added to this is the establishment of the unified body representing the local police authorities, the Association of Police Authorities (APA). There is evidence that the Association is being encouraged by the Home Office to take a more vociferous role in the 'tripartite' relationship and become less of the 'Cinderella' in that arrangement (APA, 1998b — see chapter 1); certainly APA seems determined to become a more interventionist and assertive component of the tripartite relationship than its predecessor bodies, under the Association of Metropolitan Authorities and the Association of County Councils, ever managed to become. If this is the case then an area of territory open to further dispute will be the former hallowed ground of CI and chief officers' freedoms over policy-making. Taken together, these changes within the environment of British policing, driven by new political configurations, will place CI under increasing pressure. In this context there will, we would argue, be a continuing decline in the propensity of chief officers to invoke the doctrine — something which may further assist ACPO in its pursuit of corporacy — but more radically, the whole foundation on which CI has been built and survived may be called into question. An early sign that this might be the case was to be found in the report of the Patten Commission on policing in Northern Ireland (HMSO, 1999b). Whatever else the Patten Commission achieved within the particular confines of the policing agenda for Northern Ireland, its determination to 'un-pick' the concept of CI and to challenge its veracity has provided evidence that CI need not be treated as an absolute. The Patten Report was quite blunt in its stance of CI or 'operational independence'; it referred to concerns expressed by the Police Authority for Northern Ireland over the issue:

The Authority told us that under the present arrangements if a chief constable decided that a matter was operational, and therefore within the scope of police independence, there was nothing that they could do to pursue it.... The term 'operational independence' is neither to be found in nor is it defined in any legislation. It is an extrapolation from the phrase 'direction and control' included in statutory descriptions of the functions of chief constables. But, however it is defined, *it is not acceptable that scrutiny of the police should be impeded by the assertion, valid or otherwise, that the current legislation empowering such scrutiny is limited to matters outside the scope of operational independence.* Long consideration has led us to the view that the term 'operational independence' is part of the problem. In a democratic society, all public officials must be fully accountable to the institutions of that society for the due performance of their functions, and *a chief of police cannot be an exception.* No public official, including a chief of police, can be said to be 'independent' (HMSO 1999b:32, emphases added).

Significantly, the Report proposes that the term 'operational responsibility' replace that of 'operational independence' in defining the role of the chief police officer (ibid) in order that chief officers' actions and decisions can be fully open for inquiry and review and not 'exempted' by the invocation of operational independence 'by a recalcitrant chief constable' (ibid:33). These sentiments are not specific to the situation in Northern Ireland; it is quite clear that they (could) apply to British policing as a whole. The Patten Report has made it clear that the 'sanctity' of operational or constabulary independence, both as a doctrine and as part of the armoury of chief officers' discourse, should be challenged.

With all of these points in mind it could be argued that CI is a doctrine which is sailing against the wind. It is now very much exposed to questioning and scrutiny. If this is the case then one of the major 'limits' to the corporateness of ACPO, the assertion of CI by chief officers, might be less absolute than was thought to be the case. As we have seen, sectors within ACPO have been concerned that the invocation of CI has served to inhibit the extent to which the organisation can act collectively and cohesively. Should the doctrine be challenged further in the way the Patten Commission has done, that may not be as much of an obstacle to the development of a corporate culture within ACPO as it has been. That would serve to enable ACPO to operate more freely as a body acting on behalf of chief officers without constant recourse to the sacredness of individual chief officer's 'independence'. That, however, would present problems of a different, but related nature: the problem of *accountability*.

ACPO: A QUESTION OF ACCOUNTABILITY

As we have already argued, in one sense ACPO *suffers* as a result of the doctrine of constabulary or operational independence. As we have seen, it can be invoked by chief officers as a reason why *not* to follow ACPO's line on this or that area of policy. This means that the organisation has to tread a very careful path so as not to upset the delicate balance between collectivism and individualism, between operating corporately and allowing individual chief officers their own authority over how to police their particular forces or services. That balance may have been moved, as a result of the processes we have been examining in this study, to one more in favour of collectivism than individualism, but it is a balance nevertheless. In that sense constabulary, or operational, independence serves to *inhibit* ACPO as a corporate organisation. However, in another sense constabulary, or operational, independence serves to *protect* ACPO as an organisation. It serves as a *protective shield* to provide ACPO with a defence when challenged, particularly on the grounds of *accountability-deficit*. The problematic status of ACPO as an accountable body has been raised by many commentators (Kinsey *et al.*, 1986; Lustgarten 1986; Robertson 1989; Scraton 1985; see also chapter 2). The fact that ACPO does not have a clear statutory footing yet apparently wields great power has led inevitably to concerns about the absence of adequate accountability arrangements surrounding the role and activities of the organisation. Furthermore, as ACPO's influence has grown these concerns have become ever more acute. So how does ACPO stand in terms of accountability?

The central issue as regards the accountability of ACPO is its lack of *statutory* footing. It is not strictly the case that ACPO has *no* statutory basis. It always did have a formal role as a *negotiating* body in the forum for the determination of senior police pay and conditions — a role since passed over to CPOSA. Furthermore, ACPO itself now has a 'quasi-statutory' existence as a result of the Police and Magistrates' Courts Act 1994. Section 28 of the Act requires the Home Secretary, when determining national policing objectives, to consult 'persons whom he considers to represent the interests of chief constables', effectively

ACPO. Furthermore, the Police Act 1997, in establishing the Service Authorities for NCIS and NCS, stipulates that two members of each of these Authorities should be 'appointed' by chief officers of police, again, presumably ACPO (see Uglow and Telford, 1997:9 and 41). At best, this is an indirect form of statutory existence, with little relevance to the question of accountability. It also should be noted that a formal element of 'accountability' is attached to ACPO as an organisation in relation to the Home Office grant which funds the work of the Central Secretariat. In relation to this grant ACPO is required to present an Annual Report to the Home Secretary on the year's expenditure. The Report has in recent years also been used as a vehicle for broad statements about ACPO's strategies, policies and objectives for the future. This again, however, is a very limited form of accountability. To begin with, as was made clear in chapter 3, much of ACPO's activities, in effect, are financed indirectly by local forces and local police authorities, who partially fund ACPO by allowing their ACPO members to undertake national and regional ACPO work and allocate research tasks on behalf of ACPO to force personnel. More importantly, the deliberations which generate ACPO policy are not themselves the subject of public scrutiny. In the broad sense, ACPO is not required to account for its actions. It has many forms of *relationships* with bodies attached to policing and policing policies — including the Home Office and the local police authorities through the Association of Police Authorities — but these are not based on *accountability relationships*. In that sense the other parties in the 'tripartite' framework are distinct from ACPO in that they are directly accountable as institutions to a specific (external) constituency: the Home Secretary is accountable to Parliament and ultimately the electorate, the Association of Police Authorities are accountable to the police authorities and through them the local electorate. In this respect ACPO occupies a unique role.

In our research we were interested to pursue the question of the accountability of ACPO with the membership. How did they judge ACPO's standing in this area? Many found this a difficult question to answer, some indication of the arbitrariness surrounding ACPO's status. Some did not see accountability to be an issue to begin with, as one member put it:

Is ACPO accountable? Well first of all I don't accept that ACPO should be accountable (M09).

Most however did see the question of accountability as a challenging one, but differed in their interpretation of how it functioned in relation to ACPO. One type of response was to view the issue in terms of ACPO's *internal* mechanisms:

> I'm not aware that ACPO is accountable to anybody as an organisation other than the President in effect being accountable to his [sic] fellow chief constables ... (M10).

This thesis implies that ACPO is first and foremost a professional association whose business is essentially an internal affair. In this respect reference was frequently made to the ways in which ACPO was becoming an increasingly democratic organisation. For example, as we have seen in chapter 3, the Presidential role is now an elected one, based on a ballot involving the whole membership, whereas in the past the appointment was made by a small cabal of senior members. More generally, although chief constables still maintain the upper hand in decision-making through the Chief Constables' Council, which must ratify all ACPO policies, assistant chief constables have become more involved in ACPO business over time. As one member put it:

> I've been a member now for twelve years. I think it's more democratic now than it was.... It is less at the whim of long established or eccentric individuals (M40).

This approach to the issue of accountability, however, relates only to the accountability relationship between ACPO the organisation and its membership. That fails to address the area of most concern to those outside of ACPO: the *external* accountability of the organisation. On this front an interesting case is made by many which locates ACPO's accountability within its *individual members*. This entails what might be called 'aggregated accountability': ACPO is accountable because it inherits the aggregated accountability of its individual members. This logic has it that ACPO is little more than *the sum of its parts* which 'draws' its accountability from the accountabilities of its chief officers. As one member expressed it:

> As long as those rafts of accountability for the individuals within it [ACPO] are sound, then as an Association I think we've got nothing to fear ... (M19).

In other words, ACPO's accountability comes from the accountabilities of its component parts, the chief officers and their individual accountability relationships. The rationale is that the accountability of ACPO members to their individual police authorities constitutes an effective mechanism by which the organisation as a whole can be called to account. In other words *accountable people make up an accountable organisation*; the accountability of ACPO is constituted on the sum of the accountability of its parts. This can be used to justify the case that *as an organisation* ACPO need not have any special arrangements for accountability, as the member cited above went on to explain:

> The chief constables are accountable to the local police committees, they are accountable to the Home Secretary, they're accountable to the courts, they're accountable to the PCs [police constables] ... chief constables are more accountable than anybody I know but in terms of what the professional association does, they are directly accountable to no one.... They [chiefs] have a whole raft of accountability which makes them extremely responsible but to say that [ACPO are] accountable to the Home Office or to a Minister or to a police authority would actually skew what we're trying to achieve ... we are beholden to no-one (M19).

Notwithstanding the question of whether individual chief officers are themselves adequately accountable (McLaughlin, 1994), this thesis, which was expressed in some form or other by a significant number of the members, rests on a certain logic about ACPO being no more than the sum of its parts. The test of this case is whether ACPO is indeed *no more* than the sum of its parts. We would fundamentally disagree. As has been made clear at various points in this study, ACPO is now very much more than an amalgam of its constituent parts: it has become a *corporate* institution which seeks or serves to *drive* policing policy and *direct* criminal justice policy. It may be seriously inhibited in doing so, for the reasons examined in the previous chapters, but that does not invalidate the claim that ACPO is a *body corporate*. It is now extremely difficult to argue that ACPO is little more than what one member referred to as a 'friendly society' (M37), one which simply 'pools' the views of its members. That would imply that ACPO has no organisational energy of its own, a view which would not be supported by the evidence gathered in this study, much of it from the members

212 Conclusion: ACPO — Getting Their Act Together?

themselves. For this reason the 'aggregated accountability' thesis seems extremely difficult to sustain. There is still the question of how ACPO as an *organisation* is accountable. Apart from its accountability to its own members, to whom or what is ACPO required to account for its decisions and actions? The answer is no-one and nothing.

The crux of the matter, again part of what we have called the '*ACPO dilemma*', is that the *more* ACPO becomes a corporate, strategic and effective body the *more* the question of accountability presents itself. This issue is not lost on sectors of the membership. In the previous chapter we discussed the concern within ACPO that the more powerful and effective ACPO becomes on the policy and political front, the less easy it was to maintain the claim of 'independence'. For this reason some were of the view that ACPO should 'turn down the steam' and not seek to appear 'too professional, too effective'. The same rationale applies to the related question of accountability. The legitimacy of the case for 'aggregated accountability' is weakened by evidence that ACPO is an increasingly corporate and active body. One response to this, as outlined in the previous chapter, is to advocate caution and a lower profile in order that the 'accountability question' is not pressed further and the 'independence' case can be maintained. This implies that ACPO is sailing close to the wind and might be in danger of entering into uncharted waters where all sorts of questions and challenges may lurk.

Another response is to begin to address the problem of accountability itself. One member in particular raised concerns in this regard, in a way that summarises our point extremely well:

... ACPO would say they are accountable to their members. I think there is a difficulty there; I'm not sure ACPO as a body is truly accountable. I think each of the individual ACPO members would go back to their own home base and put forward arguments as to their accountability there ... ACPO it seems to me at the moment has a downward accountability, internally to its own members. I am not so sure whether there is an appropriate mechanism to which ACPO is accountable for the policy it introduces and when we bear in mind the fact that the whole trend seems to be that it is a policy that is more and more closely being followed on a national basis, then there undoubtedly should be some mechanism for accountability ... I don't think as a body that it is sufficiently accountable at the moment and bearing in mind the other dangers that if it's being listened to, as having more authority by Government, it has an increasing agenda to actually shape legislation, then all these things, which I think are very good and positive, bring about, I think, the need for some counter-vailing mechanisms of accountability (M13).

What those 'mechanisms' might be is a moot point. *Within* the confines of the existing structure and constitution of the British police service it would not be easy to arrive at mechanisms for new forms of accountability which relate to ACPO *as a body*. However, it is possible that the concept of the 'service authority' might offer some basis for any such development. The service authorities have been established, in effect, as forms of nationally-based 'police authorities' for the national policing agencies, NCIS and NCS (Uglow and Telford, 1997) and, in the not too distant future, NPT. They broadly parallel the role of the local police authorities in the tripartite framework for local policing with a responsibility for the 'maintenance' of the service in question. Although there is not as yet any evidence of their effectiveness in calling the national agencies to account, the service authorities do offer some constitutional framework within which the key parties associated with the police service, including central government and the local authori-ties, participate in debate over strategy and direction of their respective bodies. We might ponder whether some equivalent organisation could be established in relation to ACPO. Of course ACPO already has an established relationships with both central and local government through its regular, but essentially informal, contacts with the Home Office and the Home Secretary on the one hand and the Association of Police Authorities on the other. However, a model of relationship along the lines of a service authority would formalise and clarify the status of ACPO's relationships with central and local governments and indeed other bodies with legitimate interests in the direction and policies of the police service. A 'service authority for ACPO' could involve represen-tation from the Home Office, the local police authorities, ethnic minority associations, youth associations, the police staff associations, and, through working parties and subcommittees, representatives from a wide range of other constituencies affected by policing and policing policies. Such an authority might not have the duty of 'maintenance' in the form of the existing authorities, but it might have an established right to be consulted over and to comment on the direction of policing and even specific policing policies; it could have some form of 'ownership' in that respect. The creation of a 'service authority for ACPO' might be one way in which ACPO, as with the other parties in the national tripartite relationship, the Home Secretary and the Association of Police Authorities, has a constituency to answer to, one which is more than its own membership.

ACPO and the British System of Policing

To a great extent ACPO is a dependent variable. It has been shaped by the structure of the British police service and formed on the constitutional basis on which the British policing system has been constructed. Accordingly, it has inherited both the strengths and weaknesses of that system and is forced to operate within the parameters established by that system. In that capacity ACPO serves to *support and reinforce* the British policing system yet is also *constrained* by it.

ACPO *reinforces* the British system of policing above all by providing a machinery within which a *localised and decentralised* system of policing can nevertheless operate within some form of *standardised* national framework. Arguably, were it not for ACPO's role in harmonising and standardising policing policies across the 43 police services the calls for a *national* policing system may have been louder. Effectively, ACPO's position has been one of : 'leave the decentralised system of policing in place and we will deliver a level of standardisation and harmonisation on a national basis'. It is for this reason why, we would argue, it is misleading to view ACPO's growing activities as a measure of 'increasing *centralisation*'. To a great extent ACPO's role is one of protector and reinforcer of the *decentralised* system of British policing. It has sought, and largely achieved, a balance between localism and standardisation. Indeed, ACPO might not have been necessary in its present form were it not for the decentralised system of policing which characterises British policing. It is interesting to note that the European country with an organisation which parallels ACPO at all closely in structure and purpose is the Netherlands, which operates under a local/regional policing structure, unlike virtually all other European countries which have a national, or part-national, policing system. In the absence of a 'national head of policing' of the form to be found in national policing systems, ACPO manages to provide a 'multi-headed' policing service which is nevertheless broadly cohesive.

Linked with ACPO's role in reinforcing localism is the protection it provides for the doctrine of CI. It strives to deliver a standardised system of policing in terms of policing policy service-by-service without encroaching on the independence of each chief officer. Chiefs are never *compelled* to conform to a national policy imposed from without, they *comply* (more or less) to a national policy *which is of their own making*. Furthermore, even when a policy has been created and agreed upon by the chiefs who constitute ACPO, individuals can choose at any time, with the effective support of ACPO, not to fall in line. It is an arrangement which pushes and pulls chiefs in the direction of standardisation but which leaves CI intact. *Non*-compliance is always allowed if not respected.

However, if ACPO serves to *reinforce* localism and CI it is also *constrained* by them. As we have seen, traditionally ACPO had suffered as an organisation by the reluctance of many individual chiefs to accept any form of corporate stance on policing policies or to allow ACPO to speak with 'one voice'. ACPO as a consequence had totally failed to 'get its act together' — indeed, it failed to *have* an 'act' as such. If that situation has now changed in the ways examined in this study, it is nevertheless the case that the ultimate barrier to ACPO doing much more by way of making progress as a corporate body is the combination of localism in the delivery of policing services and the independence of chiefs responsible for that delivery. ACPO is limited to and by the structure and constitution of the British police service within which it functions. However, that structure and constitution is itself not immutable. As we have seen, British policing is now presented with a range of challenges created by new forms of governance and new forms of organisational relationships. Regionalisation, 'best value' and the 'crime and disorder' agenda alone all raise in differing ways questions about the future role of the police and ACPO within it. How will ACPO, as a body built upon and around the 43 police services of England and Wales, function within a framework of regional governance? How will ACPO stand in relation to the potential reconfigurations of policing which may follow the unfolding logic of best value, possibly including 'two-tier' policing and further privatisation or at least redistribution of policing tasks? How will ACPO respond to the power sharing and re-positioning of the police role which is attached to the 'crime and disorder' agenda? These are questions which face ACPO as the organisation heads into the twenty first century, an organisation which has had to live within the confines of a policing system still steeped in the nineteenth.

Appendix 1

COMMITTEE STRUCTURE OF ACPO

1. Operational Policing

Crime
General Policing
Terrorism and Allied Matters
Traffic

2. Support

Finance and Resources
Personnel and Training
Performance Management
Research
Information Technology
Constitution Committee

EXECUTIVE COMMITTEE OF ACPO

Membership:

President
1st Vice President
2nd Vice President
Immediate past President
Commissioner of the Metropolis
Honorary Treasurer

Representative of deputy chief constable/deputy assistant commissioner rank
Two representatives of Assistant Chief Constable rank
Representative of Commander rank
Representative of senior civilians

NON HOME OFFICE FORCES

British Transport Police
Gibraltar Police
Guernsey Police
Isle of Man Police
Ministry of Defence Police
Royal Cayman Islands Police
States of Jersey Police
UK Atomic Energy Authority Constabulary

Appendix 2

FUNDING OF ACPO

ACPO's income and expenses:
(all figures in £'s and as quoted by Companies House)

	1997–98	1998–99
INCOME		
Police Authority contributions	911,049	709,610
Home Office grant	458,000	458,000
Subscriptions	20,018	19,027
Surplus on conferences:		
Seminars	0	1,003
Other conferences	0	28,492
Spring	1,112	503
Summer	26,640	77,987
Autumn	2,417	6,271
Sundry income	16,985	36,211
Exceptional item (net book value of assets transferred from old ACPO)	118,951	
TOTAL	**1,555,172**	**1,337,098**

	1997-98	1998-99
ADMINISTRATIVE EXPENSES		
Secretariat & ACPO expenses	336,661	342,509
Staff costs	269,786	431,964
Establishment	288,971	296,767
Administration	63,135	90,723
Legal and professional	60,880	64,005
TOTAL	**1,073,370**	**1,248,914**

Also ACPO had £123,060 given in 1997–98 by the Metropolitan Police
Service in terms of seconded administrative staff.

	1997-98	1998-99
Operating surplus	**481,802**	**88,184**
Investment Income	**23,121**	**27,909**
Surplus on ordinary activities before tax	**504,923**	**116,093**
Tax on ordinary activities	**4,761**	**5,282**
SURPLUS	**500,162**	**110,811**
FIXED ASSETS		
Tangible	348,984	303,271
CURRENT ASSETS		
Investments	37,365	42,684
Stocks (past Presidents' medallions)	69	52
Debtors	137,811	115,221
Cash at bank and in hand	182,838	276,040
TOTAL	**358,838**	**433,997**
Creditors	**206,905**	**126,295**
Net current assets	**151,178**	**307,702**

Accumulated surplus in 1998–99 = 610,973

Average number of employees in 1997-98 was 11, increased to 17 by
1998–99.
Cost of lease was £178,688 per annum in 1997–98, increased to
£201,373 per annum in 1998–99.
ACPO invoiced CPOSA 3,360 (1997–98) and 5,289 (1998–99) in
respect of provision of employees' time.

Bibliography

ACPO, *Your Police: A Service to Value* (Fact Sheet No. 1) (London: Association of Chief Police Officers, 1994).

ACPO, *In Search of Criminal Justice* (London: Association of Chief Police Officers, 1995).

ACPO, *In Search of Criminal Justice: Three Years On* (London: Association of Chief Police Officers, 1998).

ACPO, *Fifty Years of Leadership in Policing* (West Mercia: Association of Chief Police Officers, 1998).

Alderson, J., *A New Cromwell: The Centralisation of the Police* (London: Charter 88 Enterprises, 1994).

Alderson, J., 'A Fair Cop', *Red Pepper* 24, 1996.

Association of Police Authorities, *Annual Report 1998*.

Association of Police Authorities, *Can You Manage It? A Review of the Approaches Police Authorities Take to Managing Performance* (London: Association of Police Authorities, 1998a).

Association of Police Authorities, *Objectives, Indicators, Targets: a Study of Policing Plans and Reports* (London: Association of Police Authorities, 1998b).

Association of Police Authorities, *Guide to Youth Initiatives* (London: Association of Police Authorities, 1999).

Audit Commission, *Annual Report and Accounts 1995* (London: HMSO, 1995).

Audit Commission, *Local Authority Performance Indicators 1995/96: Police Services* (London: Audit Commission, 1997).

Baker, K., *The Turbulent Years: My Life in Politics* (London: Faber and Faber, 1993)

Baldwin, R. and Kinsey, R., *Police Powers and Politics* (London: Quartet, 1982).

Baldwin, T. and Ford, R. ' "Ofcop" Launched in War on Crime', *The Times*, 14 February 2000.

Barnes, B., Hood, J. and Mead, G., 'Developing Tomorrow's Police Managers', *Public Money and Management*, Spring, 1990.

Barton, M., 'Double Vision', *Policing Today*, vol. 2. no. 1, April 1996.

Baxter, J., 'Policing and the Rule of Law', in J. Baxter and L. Koffman (eds) *Police: The Constitution and the Community* (Abingdon: Professional Books, 1985).

Benson, J. K., 'A Framework for Policy Analysis', in D. L. Rogers and D. A. Whetten (eds) *Interorganizational Coordination* (Ames: Iowa State University Press, 1982).

Benyon, J., 'Policing the European Union: the Changing Basis of Cooperation on Law Enforcement', *International Affairs* 70(3), 1994.

Bogason, P. and Toonen, T. A. J. (eds), 'Comparing Networks', *Public Administration* 76(2), 1998.

Börzel, T.A., 'Organizing Babylon — on the Different Conceptions of Policy Networks', *Public Administration* 76(2), 1998.

Bourdieu, P., *Outline of a Theory of Practice* (Cambridge: Cambridge University Press, 1977).

Boyne, G. A. (ed.) 'Special Issue on Managing Local Services: from CCT to Best Value', *Local Government Studies* 25(2), 1999.

Bradley, D., Walker, N. and Wilkie, R., *Managing the Police* (Brighton: Wheatsheaver Books, 1986).

Bramshill Police Staff College, *Strategic Leadership Development Programme — ACPO Selection and Development Project* (Bramshill: Bramshill Police Staff College, 1994).

Brogden, M., *The Police: Autonomy and Consent* (London: Academic Press, 1982).

Brogden, M., Jefferson, T. and Walklate, S., *Introducing Policework* (London: Unwin Hyman, 1988).

Butler, A. J. P.., 'Police and the Citizens' Charter', *Policing* 8, Spring 1992, p. 1.

Campbell, D., 'Policing: a Power in the Land', *New Statesman and Society*, 113, 8 May 1987.

Cashmore, E. and McLaughlin, E., *Out of Order? Policing Black People* (London: Routledge, 1991).

Cawson, A., *Corporatism and Political Theory* (Oxford: Basil Blackwell, 1986).

Cerny, P.G., 'Plurilateralism: Structural Differentiation and Functional Conflict in the Post-Cold War World Order', *Millennium* 22(1), 1993.

Chan, J., 'Changing Police Culture', *British Journal of Criminology* 36(1), 1996.

Chan, J., *Changing Police Culture* (Cambridge: Cambridge University Press, 1997).

Charman, S., Savage, S. and Cope, S., 'Singing From the Same Hymn Sheet: The Professionalisation of the Association of Chief Police Officers', *International Journal of Police Science and Management*, vol. 1, no. 1, March 1998.

Charman, S. and Savage, S., 'The New Politics of Law and Order: Labour, Crime and Justice', in M. Powell (ed.) *New Labour, New Welfare State* (Bristol: Policy Press, 1999).

Chibnall, S., *Law-and-Order News* (London: Tavistock Publications Ltd, 1977).

Clark, C., 'The Need for a National Policy', *Policing* 2, Summer 1991.

Cope, S., 'Globalisation, Europeanisation and Management of the British State' in S. Horton and D. Farnham (eds), *Public Management in Britain* (Basingstoke: Macmillan, 1999).

Cope, S., Leishman, F. and Starie, P., 'Globalization, New Public Management and the Enabling State: Futures of Police Management', *The International Journal of Public Sector Management* 10(6), 1997.

Cope, S., Starie, P. and Leishman, F., 'The Politics of Police Reform', *Politics Review* 5(4), 1996.

Critchley, T., *A History of the Police in England and Wales* (London: Constable, 1978).

Dahrendorf, R., 'Preserving Prosperity', *New Statesman and Society* 15, 29, December 1995.

Daugbjerg, C. and Marsh, D., 'Explaining Policy Outcomes: Integrating the Policy Network Approach with Macro-level and Micro-level Analysis', in D. Marsh (ed), *Comparing Policy Networks* (Buckingham: Open University Press, 1998).

Day, P. and Klein, R., *Accountabilities* (London: Tavistock, 1987).

de Bruijn, J. A. and ten Heuvelhof, E. F., 'Policy Networks and Governance', in D. L. Weimer (ed.), *Institutional Design* (Boston: Kluwer, 1995).

DETR, *Modernising Local Government: Improving Local Services Through Best Value* (London: Department of the Environment, Transport and the Regions, 1998).

Donovan, P., 'Tough on Liberty: Has Labour Changed Sides on Law and Order?', *The Independent*, 26 February 1997.

Dowding, K., 'Model or Metaphor? A Critical Review of the Policy Network Approach', *Political Studies* 43(1), 1995.

Downes, D. and Morgan, R., 'Dumping the "Hostages to Fortune?" The Politics of Law and Order in Post-War Britain', in M. Maguire, R. Morgan and R. Reiner (eds), *The Oxford Handbook of Criminology* (Oxford: Oxford University Press, 1997).

Dunleavy, P. and Hood, C., 'From Old Public Administration to New Public Management', *Public Money and Management* 14(3), 1994.

Dunleavy, P. and Rhodes, R. A. W., 'Core Executive Studies in Britain', *Public Administration* 68, 1990.

Dye, T. R., *Understanding Public Policy* (Englewood Cliffs: Prentice Hall, 1992).

Edelman, M., *The Symbolic Uses of Politics* (Urbana: University of Illinois Press, 1985).

Emsley, C., *The English Police* (London: Longman, 1991).

Evans, R., 'Feedback From Extended Interviews and Career Counselling for Senior Police Officers', *Home Office Report No. 6* (London: Home Office, 1990).

Farnham, D. and Horton, S. (eds), *Managing the New Public Services* (Basingstoke: Macmillan, 1993).

Farnham, D. and Horton, S., *Managing the New Public Services* (2nd edn) (London: Macmillan, 1996).

Fielding, N., *The Police and Social Conflict* (London: Athlone, 1991).

Fine, B. and Millar, R., 'Introduction: The Law of the Market and the Rule of Law', in B. Fine and R. Millar (eds), *Policing the Miners' Strike* (London: Lawrence and Wishart, 1985).

Fischer, F., *Politics, Values and Public Policy* (Boulder: Westview Press, 1980).

Foster, C. D. and Plowden, F. J., *The State under Stress* (Buckingham: Open University Press, 1996).

Gamble, A., *The Free Economy and the Strong State* (Basingstoke: Macmillan, 1994).

Gamble, A. 'Economic Governance', in J. Pierre (ed.), *Debating Governance: Authority, Steering, and Democracy* (Oxford: Oxford University Press, 2000).

Giddens, A., *Sociology* (Cambridge: Polity Press, 1993).

Grant, W., 'The Role and Power of Pressure Groups', in R. Borthwick and J. Spence (eds), *British Politics in Perspective* (Leicester: Leicester University Press, 1984).

Grant, W., *Pressure Groups, Politics and Democracy in Britain* (London: Philip Allan, 1989).

Green, P., *The Enemy Without: Policing and Class Consciousness in the Miners' Strike* (Buckingham: Open University Press, 1990).

Guyomarch, A., 'Problems and Prospects for European Police Cooperation after Maastricht', *Policing and Society* 5(3), 1995.

Hall, S., *Drifting into a Law and Order Society* (London: The Cobden Trust, 1979).

Halsey, A., Heath, A. and Ridge, J., *Origins and Destinations: Family, Class and Education in Modern Britain* (Oxford: Oxford University Press, 1980).

Hansard, *Lords Hansard text for 11 May*, 980511w02, 1998.

Hay, C., 'The Tangled Webs we Weave: the Discourse, Strategy and Practice of Networking', in D. Marsh (ed), *Comparing Policy Networks* (Buckingham: Open University Press, 1998).

Hay, C. and Richards, D., 'The Tangled Webs of Westminster and Whitehall: the Discourse, Strategy and Practice of Networking within the British Core Executive', *Public Administration* 78(1), 2000.

Hebenton, B. and Thomas, T., *Policing Europe: Cooperation, Conflict and Control* (Basingstoke: Macmillan Press, 1995).

Held, D. and McGrew, A., 'Globalization and the Liberal Democratic State', *Government and Opposition* 28(2), 1993.

Hennessy, P., *Whitehall* (London: Secker and Warburg, 1989).

Hewitt, P., *The Abuse of Power: Civil Liberties in the United Kingdom* (Oxford: Martin Robertson, 1982).

Hill, S. and Smithers, A., 'Enough of a Good Thing; Is there Still a Real Need for the Graduate Entry Scheme?', *Policing*, 7, Winter 1991 at p. 4.

Hills, A., 'Militant Tendencies: Paramilitarism in the British Police', *British Journal of Criminology*, 35(3), 1995.

HMSO, *Police Training and Recruitment* (Fourth Report of the Home Affairs Select Committee) (London: HMSO, 1999a).

HMSO, *The Report of the Independent Commission on Policing for Northern Ireland: A New Beginning* (London: HMSO, 1999b).

Horton, S. and Farnham, D. (eds), *Public Management in Britain* (Basingstoke: Macmillan, 1999).

Hoggett, P., 'A New Management in the Public Sector?', *Policy and Politics* 19(4), 1991.

Holliday, I., 'Organised Interests After Thatcher', in P. Dunleavy, A. Gamble, I. Holliday and G. Peele (eds), *Developments in British Politics 4* (Basingstoke: Macmillan, 1993).

Home Affairs Select Committee, *Home Office Expenditure: Common Police Services; ACPO Secretariat; Police Recruitment; Prisons Expenditure; Trial Delays and Custodial Remand,* Fourth Report, HCP 314 (London: HMSO, 1989).

Home Office, *Higher Police Training and the Police Staff College: Home Affairs Committee Third Report* (London: HMSO, 1989).

Home Office, *Inquiry into Police Responsibilities and Rewards* (London: HMSO, 1993a).

Home Office, *Police Reform: A Police Service for the Twenty-First Century* (Cm. 2281) (London: HMSO, 1993b).

Home Office, *Review of Police Core and Ancillary Tasks* (London: HMSO, 1995a).

Home Office, *Chief Officer Appointments in the Police Service: Guidelines on Selection Procedures* (London: HMSO, 1995b).

Hood, C., *Explaining Economic Policy Reversals* (Buckingham: Open University Press, 1994).

Hood Phillips, O. and Jackson, P., *O. Hood Phillips' Constitutional and Administrative Law* (London: Sweet and Maxwell, 1987).

Horton, S. and Jones, J., 'Who are the new public managers? An initial analysis of "Next Steps" Chief Executives and their managerial role', *Public Policy and Administration*, vol. 11, no. 4, 1996.

Hughes, G., Mears, R. and Winch, C., 'An Inspector Calls? Regulation and Accountability in Three Public Services', *Policy and Politics* 25(3), 1997.

Jefferson, T., *The Case Against Paramilitary Policing* (Buckingham: Open University Press, 1990).

Jefferson, T. and Grimshaw, R., *Controlling the Constable* (London: Frederic Muller, 1984).

Jenkins, S., *Accountable to None* (London: Hamish Hamilton, 1995).

Jessop, B., 'Towards a Schumpeterian Workfare State? Preliminary Remarks on Post-Fordist Political Economy' *Studies in Political Economy* 40, 1993.

Johnson, B., 'The Story of ACPO', *The Police Journal*, July 1992).

Johnson, T., *Professions and Power* (London: Macmillan, 1972).

Johnston, L., *The Rebirth of Private Policing* (London: Routledge, 1992).

Johnston, L., 'Policing Diversity: the Impact of the Public-Private Complex in Policing' in F. Leishman, B. Loveday and S. P. Savage (eds), *Core Issues in Policing* (Harlow: Longman, 1996).

Johnston, L., *Policing Britain* (Harlow: Pearson Education, 2000).

Jones, T. and Newburn, T., 'Local Government and Policing: Arresting the Decline of Local Influence', *Local Government Studies* 21(3), 1995.

Jones, T. and Newburn, T., *Policing after the Act* (London: Policy Studies Institute, 1997).

Jones, T., Newburn, T. and Smith, D., *Democracy and Policing* (London: Policy Studies Institute, 1994).

Jordan, A. G. and Schubert, K. (eds), 'Special Issue: Policy Networks', *European Journal of Political Science* 21(1/2), 1992.

Jordan, A. and Richardson, J., *British Politics and the Policy Process* (Hemel Hempstead: Unwin Hyman, 1987).

Judge, T., *The Forces of Persuasion* (Surbiton: Police Federation, 1994).

Kassim, H., 'Policy Networks, Networks and European Union Policy Making: a Sceptical View', *West European Politics* 17(4), 1994.

Kettle, M., (1980) 'The Politics of Policing and the Policing of Politics', in P. Hain (ed.), *Policing the Police Vol. 2* (London: John Calder, 1980).

Kettle, M., 'The National Reporting Centre and the 1984 Miners' Strike', in B. Fine and R. Millar (eds), *Policing the Miners' Strike* (London: Lawrence and Wishart, 1985).

Kickert, W., 'Autopoiesis and the Science of (Public) Administration: Essence, Sense and Nonsense', *Organization Studies* 14, 1993.

Kickert, W. J. M., Klijn, E-H. and Koppenjan, J. F. M. (eds), *Managing Complex Networks: Strategies for the Public Sector* (London: Sage, 1997a).

Kickert, W. J. M., Klijn, E-H. and Koppenjan, J. F. M., 'Introduction: a Management Perspective on Policy Networks', in W. J. M. Kickert, E-H. Klijn and J. F. M. Koppenjan (eds), *Managing Complex Networks: Strategies for the Public Sector* (London: Sage, 1997b).

Kinsey, R., Lea, J. and Young, J., *Losing the Fight Against Crime* (Oxford: Blackwell, 1986).

Klijn, E. H., 'Analyzing and Managing Policy Processes in Complex Networks: a Theoretical Examination of the Concept of Policy Network and its Problems', *Administration and Society* 28(1), 1996.

Kooiman, J., 'Governance and Governability: Using Complexity, Dynamics and Diversity', in J. Kooiman (ed.), *Modern Governance: New Government — Society Interactions* (London: Sage, 1993).

Leishman, F. and Savage, S., 'Officers or Managers?: Direct Entry into British Police Management', *The International Journal of Public Sector Management*, vol. 6, no. 5, 1993a).

Leishman, F. and Savage, S., 'The Police Service', in D. Farnham and S. Horton (eds), *Managing the New Public Services* (London: Macmillan, 1993b).

Leishman, F., Cope, S. and Starie, P., 'Reforming the Police in Britain: New Public Management, Policy Networks and a Tough "Old Bill"', *The International Journal of Public Sector Management* 8(4), 1995.

Leishman, F., Cope, S. and Starie, P., 'Reinventing and Restructuring: Towards a "New Policing Order"', in F. Leishman, B. Loveday and S. Savage (eds), *Core Issues in Policing* (London: Longman, 1996).

Loveday, B., 'The Police and Magistrates' Courts Act', *Policing* 10(4), 1994.

Loveday, B., 'Reforming the Police: From Local Service to State Police?', *Political Quarterly* 66(2), 1995.

Loveday, B., 'Business as Usual? The New Police Authorities and the Police and Magistrates' Courts Act', *Local Government Studies* 22(2), 1996a.

Loveday, B., 'Police Reform: Problems of Accountability and the Police and Magistrates' Courts Act 1994', in S. Leach, H. Davis and associates (eds), *Enabling or Disabling Local Government* (Buckingham: Open University Press, 1996b).

Loveday, B., 'Challenge and Change: Police Authorities and Chief Officer Responsibilities under the Police and Magistrates' Courts Act 1994', *Local Government Studies* 23(1), 1997a.

Loveday, B., 'Management and Accountability in Public Services: a Police Case Study', in K. Isaac-Henry, C. Painter and C. Barnes (eds), *Management in the Public Sector* (London: International Thomson Business Press, 1997b).

Loveday, B., '"Waving not Drowning" Chief Constables and the New Configuration of Accountability in the Provinces', *International Journal of Police Science and Management*, vol. 1, no. 2, 1998.

Lustgarten, L., 'Democratic Constitutionalism and Police Governance', in P. McAuslan and J. McEldowney (eds), *Law, Legitimacy and the Constitution* (London: Sweet and Maxwell, 1985).

Lustgarten, L., *The Governance of Police* (London: Sweet and Maxwell, 1986).

Lynn-Meek, V., 'Organisational Culture: Origins and Weaknesses', in D. McKevitt and A. Lawton (eds), *Public Sector Management* (London: Sage Publications, 1994).

Maloney, W., Jordan, G. and McLaughlin, A., 'Interest Groups and Public Policy: the Insider/Outsider Model Revisited', *Journal of Public Policy*, 14, 1, 1994.

Mann, M., 'The Autonomous Power of the State: its Origins, Mechanisms and Results', *Archives Européennes de Sociologie* 25(2), 1984.

Manning. P., (1978) 'The Police Mandate, Strategies and Appearances', in P. Manning and J. Van Maanen (eds), *Policing: A View for the Street* (Santa Monica: Goodyear, 1978).

Manning, P., 'Towards a Theory of Police Organisation: Polarities and Change' Paper to the International Conference on 'Social Change in Policing', Taipei, August 1993.

Marin, B. and Mayntz, R. (eds), *Policy Networks: Empirical Evidence and Theoretical Considerations* (Boulder: Westview Press, 1991).

Mark, R., *In the Office of Constable* (London: Collins, 1978).

Marsh, D. (ed.), *Comparing Policy Networks* (Buckingham: Open University Press, 1988a).

Marsh, D., 'The Development of the Policy Network Approach', in D. Marsh (ed.), *Comparing Policy Networks* (Buckingham: Open University Press, 1998b).

Marsh, D., 'The Utility and Future of Policy Network Analysis', in D. Marsh (ed.), *Comparing Policy Networks* (Buckingham: Open University Press, 1998c).

Marsh, D. and Rhodes, R. A. W. (eds), *Policy Networks in British Government* (Oxford: Clarendon Press, 1992a).

Marsh, D. and Rhodes, R. A. W., 'Policy Communities and Issue Networks: beyond Typology', in D. Marsh and R. A. W. Rhodes, (eds), *Policy Networks in British Government* (Oxford: Clarendon Press, 1992b).

Marsh, D., Richards, D. and Smith, M. J. 'Re-Assessing the Role of Departmental Cabinet Ministers', *Public Administration* 78(2), 2000.

Marsh, D. and Smith, M. 'Understanding Policy Networks: towards a Dialectical Approach', *Political Studies* 48(1), 2000.

Marshall, G., *Police and Government* (London: Methuen, 1965).

Marshall, G., 'Police Accountability Revisited', in D. Butler and A. H. Halsey (eds), *Policy and Politics* (London: Macmillan, 1978).

Marshall, G., *Constitutional Conventions* (Oxford: Oxford University Press, 1984).

Marshall, G. and Loveday, B., 'The Police: Independence and Accountability', in J. Jowell and S. Oliver (eds), *The Changing Constitution* (Oxford: Clarendon Press, 1994).

Martin, S., 'Implementing "Best Value": Local Public Services in Transition', *Public Administration* 78(1), 2000.

McCabe, S. and Wallington, P., *The Police, Public Order and Civil Liberties* (London: Routledge, 1988).

McLaughlin, E., *Community, Policing and Accountability* (Aldershot: Avebury, 1994).

McLaughlin, E. and Murji, K., 'The End of Public Policing? Police Reform and "the New Managerialism"', in L. Noaks, M. Maguire and M. Levi (eds), *Contemporary Issues in Criminology* (Cardiff: University of Wales Press, 1995).

McLaughlin, E. and Murji, K., 'Resistance Through Representation: "Story Lines", Advertising and Police Federation Campaigns', *Policing and Society*, 8(4), 1998.

McLeay, E., 'Defining Policing Policies and the Political Agenda', *Political Studies* 38, 1990.

McLeay, E., 'Policing Policy and Policy Networks in Britain and New Zealand', in D. Marsh (ed.), *Comparing Policy Networks* (Buckingham: Open University Press, 1998).

McRobbie, A., 'Folk Devils Fight Back', *New Left Review* 203, January/February 1994.

Morgan, R. and Newburn, T., *The Future of Policing* (Oxford: Oxford University Press, 1997).

Morris, T., 'The Case for the Riot Squad', *New Society*, 29 November 1985.

Newburn, T., *Crime and Criminal Justice Policy* (Harlow: Longman, 1995).

Newburn, T. and Jones, T., 'Police Accountability', in W. Saulsbury, J. Mott and T. Newburn (eds), *Themes in Contemporary Policing* (London: Policy Studies Institute, 1997).

Norman, P., 'European Union Police Policy Making and Co-operation', in F. Carr and A. Massey (eds), *Public Policy in the New Europe: Eurogovernance in Theory and Practice* (Cheltenham: Edward Elgar, 1999).

Norton, P., *The British Polity* (White Plains: Longman, 1991).

Olson, M., *The Logic of Collective Action* (Cambridge, Mass.: Harvard University Press, 1971).

Osborne, D. and Gaebler, T., *Reinventing Government* (Reading: Addison-Wesley, 1992).

Peters, G., 'Policy Networks: Myth, Metaphor and Reality', in D. Marsh (ed.), *Comparing Policy Networks* (Buckingham: Open University Press, 1998).

Peterson, J., 'Decision-Making in the European Union: towards a Framework for Analysis', *Journal of European Public Policy* 2(1), 1995.

Pierre, J. 'Introduction: Understanding Governance', in J. Pierre (ed.), *Debating Governance: Authority, Steering, and Democracy* (Oxford: Oxford University Press, 2000).

Pierre, J. and Stoker, G. 'Towards Multi-Level Governance', in P. Dunleavy, A. Gamble, I. Holliday and G. Peele (eds), *Developments in British Politics* 6 (Basingstoke: Macmillan, 2000).

Police, *Editorial*, May 1996.

Policing Today, *News*, 5(3) September 1999.

Pollitt, C., *Managerialism and the Public Services* (Oxford: Blackwell, 1993).

Popham, G., 'The Management of Law and Order', in I. Taylor and G. Popham (eds), *An Introduction to Public Sector Management* (London: Allen and Unwin, 1989).

Punch, M., (ed.), *Control in the Police Organisation* (London: MIT Press, 1983).

Raine, J. and Willson, M., *Managing Criminal Justice* (Hemel Hempstead: Harvester Wheatsheaf, 1993).

RCCJ, *The Royal Commission on Criminal Justice* (London: HMSO, 1993).

Reiner, R., 'The Politicization of the Police in Britain', in M. Punch (ed.), *Control in the Police Organisation* (Cambridge, Mass.: The Massachusetts Institute of Technology, 1983).

Reiner, R., *The Politics of the Police* (1st edn) (Brighton: Wheatsheaf, 1985).

Reiner, R., 'Where the Buck Stops: Chief Constables' View on Police Accountability', in R. Morgan and D. Smith (eds) *Coming to Terms with Policing* (London: Routledge, 1989).

Reiner, R., *Chief Constables* (Oxford: Oxford University Press, 1991).

Reiner, R., *The Politics of the Police* (2nd edn) (Hemel Hempstead: Harvester Wheatsheaf, 1992).

Reiner, R., 'The Dialectics of Dixon: the Changing Image of the TV Cop', in M. Stephens and S. Becker (eds), *Police Force, Police Service: Care and Control in Britain* (Basingstoke: Macmillan, 1994).

Reiner, R., 'Policing and the Police', in M. Maguire, R. Morgan and R. Reiner (eds), *The Oxford Handbook of Criminology* (Oxford: Oxford University Press, 1997).

Reuss-Ianni, E. and Ianni, F., 'Street Cops and Management Cops: The Two Cultures of Policing ', in M. Punch (ed.), *Control in the Police Organisation* (London: MIT Press, 1983).

Rhodes, R. A. W., *Control and Power in Central – Local Government Relations* (Aldershot: Gower, 1981).

Rhodes, R. A. W., *Beyond Westminster and Whitehall: The Sub-Central Governments of Britain* (London: Unwin Hyman, 1988).

Rhodes, R. A. W., 'Policy Networks: a British Perspective', *Journal of Theoretical Politics* 2(3), 1990.

Rhodes, R. A. W., 'The Hollowing out of the State: the Changing Nature of the State in Britain', *The Political Quarterly* 65(2), 1994.

Rhodes, R. A. W., *Understanding Governance: Policy Networks, Governance, Reflexivity and Accountability* (Buckingham: Open University Press, 1997).

Rhodes, R. A. W. 'Governance and Public Administration', in J. Pierre (ed.), *Debating Governance: Authority, Steering, and Democracy* (Oxford: Oxford University Press, 2000).

Rhodes, R. A. W. and Marsh, D., 'New Directions in the Study of Policy Networks', *European Journal of Political Research* 21(1/2), 1992.

Richardson, J. and Jordan, A., *Governing Under Pressure,* (Oxford: Martin Robertson, 1979).

Ritchie, E., 'Law and Order', in M. Harrop (ed.), *Power and Policy in Liberal Democracies* (Cambridge: Cambridge University Press, 1992).

Robertson, G., *Freedom, the Individual and the Law* (6th edn) (London: Penguin, 1989).

Rose, D., *In the Name of the Law: The Collapse of Criminal Justice* (London: Jonathan Cape, 1996).

Royal Commission on the Police, *Royal Commission on the Police: Final Report* (London: HMSO, 1962).

Rutherford, A., *Criminal Justice and the Pursuit of Decency* (Oxford: Oxford University Press, 1993).

Ryan, M., *The Acceptable Pressure Group* (Farnborough: Saxon House, 1978).

Saks, M., *Alternative Medicine* (Oxford: Clarendon Press, 1992).

Salisbury, R., 'Interest Representation: the Dominance of Institutions', *American Political Science Review* 78, 1, 1984.

Sanders, A., 'From Suspect to Trial', in M. Maguire, R. Morgan and R. Reiner (eds), *The Oxford Handbook of Criminology* (Oxford: Oxford University Press, 1997).

Savage, S., 'The Geography of Police Governance', *Criminal Justice Matters*, June 1998.

Savage, S. and Charman, S., 'In Favour of Compliance', *Policing Today* 2(1), (1996a).

Savage, S. and Charman, S., 'Managing Change', in F. Leishman, B. Loveday and S. Savage (eds), *Core Issues in Policing* (Harlow: Longman, 1996b).

Savage, S. and Charman, S., *ACPO: The Views of the Membership*, report submitted to the Association of Chief Police Officers, 1997.

Savage, S. and Charman, S., (forthcoming) 'The Bobby Lobby: Police Associations and the Policy Process', in M. Ryan, S. Savage and D. Wall (eds), *Policy Networks in Criminal Justice* (London: Macmillan).

Savage, S., Charman, S. and Cope, S., 'Police Governance: the Association of Chief Police Officers and Constitutional Change', *Public Policy and Administration* 11(2), 1996.

Savage, S., Charman, S. and Cope, S., 'ACPO: A Force to be Reckoned With?', *Criminal Lawyer*, April 1997.

Savage, S., Charman, S. and Cope, S., 'ACPO: Choosing the Way Ahead', *Policing Today*, vol. 4, No. 2, June, 1998.

Savage, S., Charman, S. and Cope, S., 'The State of Independence: The Discourse of Constabulary Independence', unpublished paper presented to the British Criminology Conference, Liverpool, July 1999.

Savage, S., Cope S. and Charman, S., 'Reform Through Regulation: Transformation of the Public Police in Britain', *Review of Policy Issues* 3(2), 1997.

Savage, S. and Leishman, F., 'The Police Service', in D. Farnhan and S. Horton (eds), *Managing the New Public Services* (London: Macmillan, 1996).

Savage, S. and Robins, L. (eds) *Public Policy Under Thatcher* (London: Macmillan, 1990).

Savage, S. and Nash, M., 'Law and Order Under Blair: New Labour or Old Conservatism?' in Savage, S. and Atkinson, R. (eds) *Public Policy under Blair* (Basingstoke: Palgrave, 2001).

Scarman, Lord, *The Scarman Report: The Brixton Disorders*, Cmnd 8427, London: HMSO, 1981.

Scheslinger, P. and Tumber, H., *Reporting Crime: The Media Politics of Criminal Justice,* (Oxford: Clarendon Press, 1994).

Scraton, P., *The State of the Police* (London: Pluto, 1985).

Scraton, P., 'ACPO Rules is Not OK', *New Statesman* 111, 23 May 1986.

Scraton, P., 'Unreasonable Force: Policing, Punishment and Marginalisation', in P. Scraton (ed.), *Law, Order and the Authoritarian State* (Buckingham: Open University Press, 1987).

Shearing, C. and Ericson, R., 'Culture as Figurative Action', *British Journal of Sociology*, 42, 1991.

Skolnick, J., *Justice Without Trial* (New York: John Wiley, 1966).

Smith, M., 'Pluralism, Reformed Pluralism and Neopluralism: the Role of Pressure Groups in Policy-Making', *Political Studies* 38, 1990.

Smith, M., *Pressure, Power and Policy* (Hemel Hempstead: Harvester Wheatsheaf, 1993).

Spencer, S., *Called to Account: The Case for Police Accountability in England and Wales* (London: NCCL, 1985a).

Spencer, S., *Police Authorities During the Miners' Strike* (Working Paper No. 1) (London: Cobden Trust, 1985b).

Straw, J., 'Crime and Old Labour's Punishment', *The Times*, 8 April 1998.

Sullivan, R., 'The Politics of British Policing in the Thatcher/Major State', *The Howard Journal* 37(3), 1998.

The Guardian, 28 February 1997.

The Guardian, 'Tougher Police Line on Speeding', 25 July 2000.

Thompson, E., 'Law and Order and the Police', *New Society*, 15 November 1979.

Thornton, P., *Decade of Decline: Civil Liberties in the Thatcher Years* (London: NCCL, 1989).

Tomkins, P. and Brunstrom, R., 'An Unprofessional Lottery?' *Policing Today*, April 1995.

Travis, A. 'Challenge to Speeding Buffer Zone', *The Guardian*, 26 May 2000.

Turner, B., *Medical Power and Social Knowledge* (London: Sage, 1987).

Turpin, C., *British Government and the Constitution* (3rd edn) (London: Butterworths, 1995).

Uçarer, E., 'Cooperation on Justice and Home Affairs Matters', in L. Cram, D. Dinan and N. Nugent (eds), *Developments in the European Union* (Basingstoke: Macmillan, 1999).

Uglow, S. and Telford, B., *The Police Act 1997* (Bristol: Jordans, 1997).

Waddington, P. A. J., 'Police (Canteen) Sub-Culture: An Appreciation', *British Journal of Criminology* 39(2), 1999.

Walker, N., 'The International Dimension', in R. Reiner and S. Spencer (eds) *Accountable Policing* (London: Institute for Public Policy Research, 1993).

Wall, D., *The Chief Constables of England and Wales* (Dartmouth: Ashgate, 1998).

Waters, I., 'Quality of Service: Politics or Paradigm Shift?', in F. Leishman, B. Loveday and S. P. Savage (eds), *Core Issues in Policing* (Harlow: Longman, 1996).

Watts-Pope, D., (1981) 'Preventative Policing in the Community', in D. Watts-Pope and N. Weiner (eds), *Modern Policing* (London: Croom Helm, 1981).

Weatheritt, M., *Policing Plans: The Role of Police Authority Members* (London: Committee of Local Police Authorities and Association of Metropolitan Authorities, 1995).

Weatheritt, D., *Innovations in Policing* (London: Croom Helm, 1986).

Weir, S. and Beetham, D., *Political Power and Democratic Control in Britain* (London: Routledge, 1999).

Wilson, J. Q., *Varieties of Police Behaviour* (Cambridge, Mass.: Harvard University Press, 1968).

Index